The Princeton Review®

Math Workout for the

GRE®

4th Edition

The Staff of The Princeton Review

PrincetonReview.com

Penguin
Random
House

The Princeton Review
555 W. 18th Street
New York, NY 10011
E-mail: editorialsupport@review.com

Published in the United States by Penguin Random House LLC, New York, and in Canada by Random House of Canada, a division of Penguin Random House Ltd., Toronto.

Terms of Service: The Princeton Review Online Companion Tools ("Student Tools") for retail books are available for only the two most recent editions of that book. Student Tools may be activated only twice per eligible book purchased for two consecutive 12-month periods, for a total of 24 months of access. Activation of Student Tools more than twice per book is in direct violation of these Terms of Service and may result in discontinuation of access to Student Tools Services.

ISBN: 978-0-451-48786-5
eBook ISBN: 978-1-5247-1033-0
ISSN: 1558-9692

GRE is a registered trademark of Educational Testing Service, which is not affiliated with The Princeton Review.

The Princeton Review is not affiliated with Princeton University.

Editor: Meave Shelton
Production Editors: Liz Rutzel, Kathy G. Carter, and Sara Kuperstein
Production Artist: Deborah A. Silvestrini

Printed in the United States of America on partially recycled paper.

10 9 8 7 6 5 4 3 2 1

Editorial
Rob Franek, Editor-in-Chief
Casey Cornelius, VP Content Development
Mary Beth Garrick, Director of Production
Selena Coppock, Managing Editor
Meave Shelton, Senior Editor
Colleen Day, Editor
Sarah Litt, Editor
Aaron Riccio, Editor
Orion McBean, Editorial Assistant

Penguin Random House Publishing Team
Tom Russell, VP, Publisher
Alison Stoltzfus, Publishing Director
Jake Eldred, Associate Managing Editor
Ellen Reed, Production Manager
Suzanne Lee, Designer

Acknowledgments

The Princeton Review would like to thank Doug French, author of the first edition, Kyle Fox and Kevin Kelly for their contributions to this edition, and John Fulmer, National Content Director for Graduate Programs, for his careful oversight.

Special thanks to Adam Robinson, who conceived of and perfected the Joe Bloggs approach to standardized tests, and many of the other successful techniques used by The Princeton Review.

Contents

Register Your

1 Go to **PrincetonReview.com/cracking**

2 You'll see a welcome page where you can register your book using the following ISBN: 9780451487865

3 After placing this free order, you'll either be asked to log in or to answer a few simple questions in order to set up a new Princeton Review account.

4 Finally, click on the "Student Tools" tab located at the top of the screen. It may take an hour or two for your registration to go through, but after that, you're good to go.

If you have noticed potential content errors, please e-mail EditorialSupport@review.com with the full title of the book, its ISBN number (located above), and the page number of the error.

Experiencing technical issues? Please e-mail TPRStudentTech@review.com with the following information:
- your full name
- e-mail address used to register the book
- full book title and ISBN
- your computer OS (Mac or PC) and Internet browser (Firefox, Safari, Chrome, etc.)
- description of technical issue

Book Online!

Once you've registered, you can...

- Download printable study plans for the content in this book, as well as a handy glossary of math terms

- Read important advice about the GRE and graduate school

- Access crucial information about the graduate school application process, including a timeline and checklist

- Check to see if there have been any corrections or updates to this edition

Look For These Icons Throughout The Book

 Online Articles

 Applied Strategies

 Proven Techniques

 More Great Books

The **Princeton Review**®

Chapter 1
Introduction

ADVICE FOR THE FAINT OF HEART

Welcome to The Princeton Review's *Math Workout for the GRE*, the one-stop shop for all of the mathematical knowledge and practice you'll need to effectively tackle the Math section of the GRE.

You've bought this book, which means you may be one of many grad school candidates who are approaching the math, or quantitative, portion of the GRE with a little bit of trepidation. This might be for any of several reasons, including the following:

- You come in contact with the word "variable" only when it's used to describe the weather.
- Your first thought about Pythagoras is that he might have been a character in *The Lord of the Rings*.
- You regard "standard deviation" as more of a psychological problem than a mathematical one.

If any of the above pertain to you, you're definitely not alone.

But don't worry, that's what this book is all about. Its two main objectives are (1) to give you an overview of all of the math concepts you could see on the GRE, and (2) to give you simple strategies for handling even the most complex math you could encounter on test day.

WHAT KIND OF MATH DOES THE GRE ROUTINELY TEST?

The good news is that the GRE's Math sections don't test anything that you learned after your sophomore year of high school, so the concepts aren't extremely advanced.

The bad news is that the GRE's Math sections don't test anything that you learned after your sophomore year of high school, so it may have been a long time since you studied them.

That's largely why this book was written: to help you build up an impressive canon of math knowledge that will help you score your best on the quantitative portion.

The GRE supposedly was written so that graduate schools might get a better sense of an applicant's ability to work in a postgraduate setting—a goal that is lofty and unrealistic at best. The test doesn't even measure how intelligent you are; if you take a test-prep course and your score improves, does that mean you're any smarter? Nope. Yet you can improve your score just by learning about what to expect on the GRE.

> All the GRE really tests is how well you take the GRE.

Succeeding on the quantitative portion of the GRE—or any standardized math test, for that matter—is as much about relearning math concepts as it is about modifying the way you think. There are several very important skills to cultivate when you're preparing to take the GRE, and each of them is attainable with the right guidance, a strong work ethic, and a healthy dose of optimism.

We'll discuss the math basics you'll need for the GRE, but if you need a quick reference, consult the glossary at the back of the book.

The Layout of the Test

Let's talk about the different sections of the GRE. The GRE contains five scored sections:

- one 60-minute Analytical Writing section, which contains two essay questions
- two 30-minute Verbal sections, which contain approximately 20 questions each
- two 30-minute Math sections, which contain approximately 20 questions each

The first section will always be the Analytical Writing section, followed by the Math and Verbal sections, which can appear in any order. You will get a 1-minute break—enough time to close your eyes and catch a breath—between each section. You will also get a full 10-minute break after the first multiple-choice section. Be sure to use it to visit the bathroom, take a drink of water, refresh your mind, and get ready for the rest of the exam.

Your Scores

You will be able to see your Verbal and Math scores immediately upon completion of the test, but you will have to wait about two weeks before your Analytical Writing section is scored.

Scores are given on a scale from 130 to 170, in 1-point increments. The questions within each section are always worth the same amount of points. So the easy questions in a section are just as important to get right as the hard questions in a section.

Once you've completed one scored Math or Verbal Section, the GRE will use your score on that section to determine the difficulty of the questions to give you in the next scored Math or Verbal section. This does not really affect how you will approach the test, so don't worry about it too much.

Experimental Section

In addition to the five scored sections listed above (one Analytical Writing, two Math, two Verbal), you may also have an unscored experimental section. This section is almost always a Math or Verbal section. It will look exactly like the other Math or Verbal sections, but it won't count at all toward your score. ETS administers the experimental section to gather data on questions before they appear on real GREs.

Thus, after your Analytical Writing section you will probably see five—not four—multiple-choice sections: either three Verbal and two Math, or two Verbal and three Math, depending on whether you get a Verbal or Math experimental section. These sections can come in any order. You will have no way of knowing which section is experimental, so you need to do your best on all of them. Don't waste time worrying about which sections count and which section does not.

Here is how a typical GRE might look:

Analytical Writing – 60 minutes
Verbal – 30 minutes
10-minute break
Math – 30 minutes
Math – 30 minutes
Verbal – 30 minutes
Math – 30 minutes

Remember, the Analytical Writing section will always be first, and it will never be experimental. In the above example, the two Verbal sections will be scored, but only two of the three Math sections will be scored. One of the three is an experimental section, but we don't know which one. Of course, on your GRE you might see three Verbal sections instead, meaning one of your Verbal sections is experimental, and they may come in any order. Be flexible, and you'll be ready for the test no matter the order of the sections. In fact, on occasion the test makers may not even include an experimental section! If so, count your lucky stars that you didn't have to waste your time on a meaningless section.

Research Section

At the end of the test, regardless of if you've seen an experimental section or not, you may also have an unscored Research section. At the beginning of this section, you will be told that the questions in the section are part of an unscored Research section, used only to help develop and test questions for the GRE. If you want to skip it, you have the option of skipping it. They normally offer some sort of financial incentive, such as entering your name into a drawing for a gift card, to induce people to take it, but by that point in the test you will probably be exhausted. Take it if you like, but also feel free to just go ahead and decline, get your scores, and go home.

A Quick Word About Answer Choices

On the real GRE, answers will be designated by a circle, square, or numeric entry box. For the purposes of explaining concepts and answers to questions in this book, we are going to label all answer choices with a corresponding letter (A, B, C, D, E, etc.). So, for example, when we say the correct answer is (C), you know that the correct answer is the third option. It is useful to think about your answer choices in terms of these letters, as it will help keep you organized and allow you to eliminate answers efficiently.

MATH OVERVIEW

There are three main skills that we emphasize throughout this book: *Don't do the math in your head, take the easy test first,* and *be prepared to walk away.* These are not necessarily what you would naturally do while taking a test, so you'll have to force yourself to apply these skills as you work through the problems in this book and as you take practice tests. If you do, you'll find that once you get to the real test your body and brain already know how to tackle each question, and you'll be able to breathe a bit easier.

Don't Do the Math in Your Head

Many students are guilty of trying to solve GRE math questions by doing some quick calculations in their heads, or phantom drawing information relevant to the question on the test screen. This is what the test makers want you to do. They know if you do this, you will likely make careless and avoidable mistakes.

Remember, your goal on the GRE is to get as many points as possible by answering questions correctly. There are no style points for getting the correct answer by doing all the calculations in your head.

On test day, you will be provided with six pieces of scratch paper. To avoid careless mistakes and to maximize your score on the Math section, it is important that you use that scratch paper. When you see an equation, rewrite it on the paper. When there is a geometry figure, draw the figure on the paper. When you are doing calculations, chart the steps on your paper.

Below is an example of a piece of scratch paper for two particular problems. This example is meant to provide an idea of how an organized piece of scratch paper may look. This student has written the question number and the answer choices on the left-hand side of the paper and left the remainder to show their work. If this example is a useful template for you, then we would suggest recreating it. But, if you have another method that you are more comfortable with, you should use that method. The method you use to track your problems is less important than making sure you always use the paper and avoid doing the math in your head.

Take the Easy Test First

All questions within a given section are worth the same amount. Many people rush through the easy questions so they can spend more time on the hard questions. However, if easy questions are worth just as much as hard questions, why not focus just as much on them?

There are a certain number of questions on the GRE that you can easily answer correctly. As soon as you read through them, you know what they're asking and how to get to the answer. Your job is to answer all of those questions first. Don't rush through them, because you can't afford to get these questions wrong. These are practically free points, as long as you're paying attention.

Save the hard questions for later. You can always return to them, even if it's just for a last-second guess. The goal with your first pass through any section is to get as many points as you can, without any mistakes. Once you've done that, you can use the time remaining to return to the other, harder questions. You'll find that after a second look, some of the hard questions are easier than you initially thought.

Go ahead and do those questions now. Some of the questions you thought were going to be hard are, in fact, hard questions. Leave those. You'll come back with any time remaining and either work through them or eliminate answers and guess.

> Easy questions are worth the same as hard questions.
> Work easy questions carefully, so you don't get any wrong.

Be Prepared to Walk Away

At the top of the screen are buttons labeled Mark, Review, and Next. Any question you're not sure about, click Mark; then click Next and move on. If you click on Review, you'll see a screen like this:

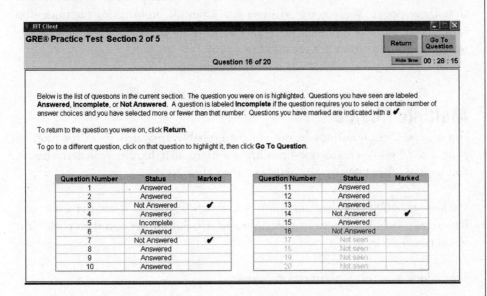

Here you can see every question you haven't answered, and every question you marked to come back to later. If you need to return to any question, you can click on that question on the review screen and you'll be brought right to it.

Why is all this so important? Because your time is limited, and on the GRE you can always come back to a question later. If you read a question and you don't immediately know what to do, move on. If a question seems particularly difficult, move on. If you start working through a question and realize you aren't getting any closer to the answer, move on. If you work through a question and the answer you get isn't among the answer choices, move on.

As we discussed before, you should take the easy test first. After you answer all the easy questions, you should work on the harder questions. Many times, you'll find the question you thought was difficult, you actually just misread. Once you've read a question one way, it's hard to get your brain to read that question any other way. So if you're not sure what the question is asking, if you realize you're doing a lot more math than you normally do for GRE questions, or if you get an answer that isn't one of the answer choices, then move on. Do a couple other questions, give your brain a chance to shift gears, and then come back to it. Sometimes, a new perspective is all you need to make a previously confusing question, more clear.

QUESTION TYPES

There are four types of math questions on the GRE. Once you know how these questions work, you'll save yourself the time of rereading the instructions each time they appear. We're going to show you a sample problem for each question type. Don't worry if you don't know how to solve these yet; these are here mostly for you to see the format for each question type.

Multiple Choice

You've seen these questions before. You've probably answered them for most of your life. Multiple-choice questions are questions that have five answer choices. You have to select one answer choice and then click Next.

The answer bubbles for these questions will always be round. Whenever a question has circular bubbles, you must select *one and only one answer* and then click Next to continue.

Take a look at an example question below:

If c is the greatest prime number less than 22, and d is the least prime number greater than 35, then $c + d =$

○ 33

○ 41

○ 50

○ 56

○ 58

Here's How to Crack It

Approach this question one step at a time. The questions asks for the value of $c + d$. The first part of the question states that *c is the greatest prime number less than 22.* List the prime numbers less than 22, which are 2, 3, 5, 7, 11, 13, 17, and 19. The greatest number is 19, so $c = 19$. The question then states that *d is the least prime number greater than 35.* The next greatest number, 36, is not prime so *d* does not equal 36. However, the following number, 37, is prime. Therefore, the least prime number greater than 35 is 37, so $d = 37$. The question asks for the value of $c + d$, which is 19 + 37 = 56. The correct answer is (D).

Quantitative Comparison

We'll refer to these questions as Quant Comp for short. These questions are variations of the basic multiple-choice question. You will sometimes be given a statement with information relevant to the problem. You will always be given two columns, labeled Quantity A and Quantity B, and each Quantity has a value underneath. You must select one of the following four answer choices:

○ Quantity A is greater.

○ Quantity B is greater.

○ The two quantities are equal.

○ The relationship cannot be determined from the information given.

These answer choices are the same for every single Quantitative Comparison question. Choice (A) means that Quantity A is always greater, (B) means that Quantity B is always greater, (C) means that the two quantities are always equal, and (D) means that the information provided is not enough to determine if one Quantity is always greater than the other.

Before we do a sample question, there's one important thing you should know about (D): It can never be the answer for questions that contain only numeric values that could be calculated. For instance, if Quantity A is 10^{12} and Quantity B is 5^{24}, then a calculator could solve that question, right? Whatever the answer is, it will always be one particular number for Quantity A, and one particular number for Quantity B. Sure, those numbers are super hard to find without the calculator, and we would have to use some clever tricks to actually find the answer, but the answer can't be (D). If there are no variables, and the problem is simply about doing calculations, the answer can't be (D) for a Quant Comp question, because the relationship *can* be determined, even if it may be a pain to determine it.

Point E lies in square $ABCD$ and the area of square $ABCD$ is 100.

Quantity A	Quantity B
The length of line DE	15

○ Quantity A is greater.

○ Quantity B is greater.

○ The two quantities are equal.

○ The relationship cannot be determined from the information given.

Here's How to Crack It

The question asks about a square but does not provide the figure, so draw the square and label the points and lengths as specified in the question. The question gives the area of the square, and the area of a square is defined as s^2, where s is the side of the square. Therefore, each side of the square is 10. Quantity A asks for the length of line DE. The question specifies that point E lies in the square but does not state where, so find the greatest possible length of line DE. The longest line in a square is the diagonal between two points, so draw a line from point D diagonally to the point opposite it, and assume that point E is just slightly inside that point. Therefore, the greatest length possible for DE is a length that is a little bit less than the diagonal of the square. Find the diagonal of the square. Because each corner in a square is 90°, and a diagonal line cuts the angles in half, the end result is a 45 : 45 : 90 right triangle. The side lengths of a 45 : 45 : 90 triangle are $x : x : x\sqrt{2}$. The value of x is 10, so the length of the diagonal is $10\sqrt{2}$. The value of $\sqrt{2}$ is approximately 1.4, so 10 × 1.4 = 14. Therefore, Quantity A is, at most, a little less than 14. The value of Quantity B is 15. Quantity B is always greater than Quantity A, so the correct answer is (B).

All That Apply

These are multiple-choice questions that have from three to eight answer choices, and you will have to select all the answers that correctly answer the question. The answer choices for these questions are always represented by squares. The question will typically state to select *all* values or statements that apply.

Note that there's no partial credit for these questions. You must choose every single answer that works, or you get no credit for that question. There will always be at least one answer for these questions, but there may be only one answer that works.

Keep track of your work and check each answer choice individually. Make sure you have selected all the appropriate answer choices before moving on to the next question.

If $\dfrac{12^{13}}{x}$ is an integer, which of the following could be the value of x ?

Indicate <u>all</u> such values.

☐ 8

☐ 10

☐ 36

☐ 64

☐ 112

☐ 432

Here's How to Crack It

This is an All that Apply question, so x could be equal to more than one number. The problem states that 12^{13} is an integer when divided by x, so x divides into 12^{13} evenly. The best way to tackle questions with great exponential values is to break the base numbers down into their prime factors. 12 is equal to $2 \times 2 \times 3$, so its prime factors are 2, 2, and 3. So, the prime factorization of 12^{13} is $(2^2 \times 3)^{13}$. Apply the Power-Multiply rule of exponents to find that the prime factorization of 12^{13} is $2^{26} \times 3^{13}$. (Don't worry if you don't know what the Power-Multiply rule is—we'll go over that later. For now, just take our word for it.)

Because the problem states that 12^{13} divided by x is an integer, the prime factorization of 12^{13} must cancel the prime factorization of x entirely when divided by each other. Evaluate the answer choices, looking for values of x that divide evenly into the prime factorization of 12^{13}. Try (A). The prime factorization of 8 is 2^3, which cancels out completely when dividing $2^{26} \times 3^{13}$, so keep (A). Try (B). If $x = 10$, the prime factorization of x is 2×5. This is not divisible by 12^{13} because the prime factors of 12^{13} do not include 5. Eliminate (B). Now look at (C). The prime factorization of 36 is $2^2 \times 3^2$, which divides evenly into $2^{26} \times 3^{13}$. Keep (C). Evaluate (D). The prime factorization of 64 is 2^6, which divides evenly into $2^{26} \times 3^{13}$. Keep (D). The prime factorization of 112 is $2^4 \times 7$, which does not divide evenly into $2^{26} \times 3^{13}$, so eliminate (E). Finally, for (F), the prime factorization of 432 is $2^4 \times 3^3$ which divides evenly into $2^{26} \times 3^{13}$, so keep (F).

The correct answer is (A), (C), (D), and (F).

Numeric Entry

These questions don't give you any answer choices at all. Instead, you'll be given a question and an empty box to type a number in. Your answer could be an integer, a decimal, positive, or negative. Never round your answer unless the question asks you to, or it's a question that cannot have decimal answers (the number of children on a school bus, for instance).

The GRE will give you the correct units—they'll be right there next to the box. So before you submit your answer, be sure that it uses the proper units. Be extra careful if problems involve dollars and cents, ounces and pounds, feet and inches, percents, and other common increments that have sub-increments.

If Jamal is charged $236.30 to rent a car and that charge consists of a flat fee of $95 and a charge of $0.075 for every tenth of a mile driven, how many miles did Jamal drive the rental car?

☐☐☐☐☐ miles

Click on the answer box; then type in a number.
Backspace to erase.

Here's How to Crack It

If Jamal paid a total of $236.30 and $95 of that was the flat fee, then the cost of the mileage must have been $236.30 – $95.00, or $141.30. If the rental company charged $0.075 per tenth of a mile, then each mile cost $0.075 × 10, or $0.75. Divide $141.30 by $0.75 to find that the answer is 188.4 miles.

If the correct answer should be given as a fraction, the space to fill in the answer will be represented by two boxes, one on top of the other, like this:

☐☐☐☐☐
☐☐☐☐☐

Each of these boxes can hold a maximum of five characters, so your fraction can get pretty complex. For example, if you solve a problem and the answer is $\dfrac{123}{347}$, you should enter the numerator and denominator separately, like this:

Also, note that when entering numbers into the fraction in this fashion, the fraction does not need to be reduced to the simplest form. So, where applicable, if you have the correct answer you can save yourself some time by not reducing the fraction to its simplest form, unless otherwise noted by the directions of the question.

HOW TO USE THIS BOOK

In *Math Workout for the GRE*, we focus solely on the math portions of the GRE. This book includes more than two hundred sample questions (including two sample GRE quantitative sections, complete with answers and explanations) on which to practice all of the new techniques you learn. This book is called a "workout" because if you resolve to "feel the burn" of diligent mental exertion, you won't just memorize a bunch of new techniques. Instead, you'll absorb them into your subconscious so completely that you will use them automatically.

Trust the Techniques

As we'll discuss in Chapter 2, you're about to do a lot of work toward *changing the way you think about taking this test*. To do that, you should be prepared to let go of a number of presumptions and give yourself over to the techniques, which we've designed to conserve your thinking power and greatly reduce the chance that you'll make careless errors come test day. Some of the techniques might seem a little strange or counterintuitive at first, but trust us: Part of the secret to a better score on a standardized test is to think in a non-standardized way.

When we encounter stress, we are hard-wired to fall back on our instincts to protect ourselves. If you start to feel anxious as you take the GRE, you might be tempted to abandon the new techniques in favor of whatever methods you used in order to get through high school and college—methods that won't be as useful.

So when you work with practice questions, be sure to practice using our techniques over and over again. Once you see them working, you'll build enough faith in them to let them *replace* your old habits. Soon you'll summon them without thinking.

Check out our downloadable study plans for the content in this book! Register your book online for access.

Set Up a Schedule—and Stick to It

When you've registered to take the GRE, it's important to keep preparing for the test almost every day. Cramming for eight hours on a Sunday and then leaving the book alone for a week won't be very useful because, like anything else, your new skills will atrophy with disuse. It will be far more effective if you set aside one hour per day to study.

When you set up your work regimen, keep these things in mind.

- As you work, look for patterns in the types of questions that you frequently answer correctly and patterns in the types you keep getting wrong. This will help you pinpoint your strengths and weaknesses and guide you to the areas in which you need more practice.
- Again, be sure to use the new techniques. If you read up about all these cool new methods for subverting the GRE and then just go back to your same old ways when it's time to try practice problems, you won't learn anything. All you'll do is further the same old bad habits.
- Practice under conditions that are as close to the real-life test situation as possible. This means that you should work only when you feel mentally fresh enough to absorb the benefits of what you're doing. If you come home late, don't stay up until the wee hours reading and fighting off yawns. If you can't absorb anything from the process, you're just doing homework for the sake of getting it done.

Other Resources

Keep in mind that there are many other tools available to you so that you can practice all the new techniques you're about to learn.

POWERPREP II Software

The GRE website (www.ets.org/gre) has a link to the *POWERPREP II* software. This free program contains two GRE tests, which you can take on your own computer. It's a great way to get used to the computerized format of the test and try various questions and essay prompts. However, the number of questions it has is limited, so you should probably save at least one of the tests until you've worked through most of this book.

Books

The most important book (besides this one, of course!) to check out is *The Official Guide to the GRE® revised General Test*. This book, which is published by ETS, contains questions for every single question type, Math and Verbal, and practice essay prompts. It also contains a CD with a copy of *POWERPREP II* software.

We at The Princeton Review have other helpful GRE titles to offer you, too, including the *Verbal Workout for the GRE,* (the sister to this book) and the larger and more comprehensive *Cracking the GRE*. If you're really pressed for time, the short *Crash Course for the GRE* will give you a quick overview of what you need to know for the test.

On the Web

Books are great learning resources, but they can't replicate the process of working with a computer interface. That's why The Princeton Review has developed several online test-prep resources. Go to the GRE section at **PrincetonReview.com** where you will find a free practice GRE exam, along with lots of helpful articles and information.

To find out more, surf over to **PrincetonReview.com** or call 1-800-2Review.

Above all: Keep practicing and stay focused. Good luck!

If you want to brush up on your basic math skills, you can also get *Math Smart*, which takes the time to explain, in step-by-step detail, mathematical concepts from the most basic to the most complex.

Chapter 2
Strategic Thinking
for the GRE

WHY ARE YOU HERE?

Some people describe themselves as "bad at math." These people believe that math is beyond their abilities and have a high level of anxiety about the Math section of the GRE. Maybe you picked up this book because you're one of these people and the very idea of engaging in a test of your math skills makes you nervous.

Other people are comfortable with math. They feel at home inside the numbers and are confident in their ability to execute on any kind of math problem.

Either way, both kinds of people often have the same misconceptions about the GRE. And both people tend to approach a math question on the GRE the same way. What's worse is that ETS knows both things, and actively uses them to their advantage on test day.

What Do Most People Think about the GRE?

Most people have a few perceptions about the GRE:

- The GRE is constructed to be fair.
- Knowing the content is enough to get most questions right.
- ETS wants you to get the questions right if you have the knowledge needed.

Unfortunately, none of these is true.

The Truth about the GRE

- The GRE is constructed to make you miss questions you *should* get right.
- You can completely understand the content behind the question and still get it wrong. In fact, almost all GRE test takers miss some questions this way.
- ETS wants to trick you into getting the question wrong, even if you understand the concepts.

The Anatomy of an Average Test Taker

Those misconceptions are ones of the average test taker. Imagine this scenario. It's test day. You've done all the important things you need to do to succeed—you've studied, gotten a good night's sleep, eaten a good breakfast—and you are ready to go.

Shortly into the test, a math question appears. You read the question, look at the answer choices, think you know the answer, do some quick calculations in your head, select your answer, and move on to the next question.

If this sounds like you, then you have done exactly what ETS wants you to do.

Don't Be Average

One of the single best lessons you can learn to succeed on the GRE is to not do what ETS wants you to do. ETS writes questions and answer choices designed to trip up the average test taker. The more you know about how ETS constructs questions and answer choices, and about how the average student responds to those questions and answer choices, the greater your chances of having a successful test day. So, what are the types of things that you can do to not be an average test taker?

THINK LIKE A TEST WRITER

Putting yourself inside the mind of an ETS question writer is a great first step to being able to succeed on the GRE. Let's imagine a test writer sits down to create a new math question for the GRE and they come up with the following question and correct answer.

> A store has a clearance on six-packs of gum for $2.70. If this price is 10% less per pack than purchasing individual packs at the original price, then what is the original price of a single pack of gum?

> Correct Answer: $0.50

The question writer has produced a question with a difficulty level of easy to medium. But, now the test writer must create 4 incorrect answer choices. The test writer could pick values at random, but that is not what test writers do. Instead, test writers try to predict how a student might make a mistake on the problem and use those mistakes to make their correct answer choices.

For instance, a student may have quickly read this problem and not realized that the store is having a clearance on six-packs of gum for $2.70 and assumed that the clearance price was for a single pack of gum. This student will immediately realize that if a clearance price of $2.70 is a discount of 10%, then the original price must be $3.00. So, the test writer will make $3.00 an answer choice.

What if a student misses that the question is asking for the *original price of a single pack of gum*? Well, that student will divide the clearance price of $2.70 by the six packs of gum, and get an answer of $0.45. So, the test writer will make $0.45 an answer choice.

And for the student who is rushing and therefore sees only the phrase *six-packs, $2.70, 10% less per pack,* and *price of a single pack?* Well that student will divide $2.70 by 6 and then subtract 10%, which yields $0.405. The test writer will round up and write $0.41 as an answer choice.

And what about the student who doesn't quite fully understand how to calculate a savings of 10%? Well, that student may multiply the clearance price of $2.70 by 10% to find $0.27. They may then add $0.27 to $2.70 to yield $2.97.

The completed question, with all five answer choices, looks like this:

> A store has a clearance on six-packs of gum for $2.70. If this price is 10% less per pack than purchasing individual packs at the original price, then what is the original price of a single pack of gum?
>
> ○ $0.41
>
> ○ $0.45
>
> ○ $0.50
>
> ○ $2.97
>
> ○ $3.00

The test writer has now created a GRE question that includes trap answers for common mistakes that a student might make. The good news for you is that now that you know a little bit about how a test writer constructs wrong answer choices, you can use this knowledge to help you eliminate incorrect answer choices.

Process of Elimination (POE)

When test writers create the question, they already know the correct answer. They must create the incorrect answer choices for multiple-choice questions. Because, for multiple-choice questions, there is only one correct answer choice, you know that most of the answer choices are going to be incorrect. So, sometimes, it is easier to work to find and eliminate bad answer choices than it is to find the correct answer choice. This is a strategy that not-average test takers will often employ.

We'll use this icon throughout the book to highlight proven techniques like POE.

Consider the following question.

> In a building with 100 occupants, the number of marketing firms that are occupants is $\frac{2}{3}$ the number of law firms that are occupants. If the building is occupied by only marketing firms and law firms, how many law firms are occupants in the building?
>
> ○ 75
>
> ○ 66
>
> ○ 60
>
> ○ 40
>
> ○ 33

Stop! Before you do any calculations, see if you can use what you know now about how test writers create wrong answers to do some Process of Elimination for incorrect answer choices.

You'll see this icon next to examples of the strategies in action.

The problem states that the number of marketing firms is $\frac{2}{3}$ the number of law firms, so the number of marketing firms is less than the number of law firms. There are 100 total occupants, and because there are more law firms than marketing firms, it is impossible for there to be 50 or fewer law firms in the building, so eliminate (D) and (E) because they are less than 50. Now, look at the remaining choices. Do any of them seem like potential trap answer choices? Choice (B) is close to $\frac{2}{3}$ of 100, and the question does use both of those numbers. However, the question states that *the number of marketing firms that are occupants is $\frac{2}{3}$ the number of law firms that are occupants,* not that the number of law firms is $\frac{2}{3}$ the total number of occupants. This is a trap answer for a student who is rushing. Eliminate (B).

Without doing a single piece of math on this question, you have now successfully narrowed the potential answer choices down to two. Even if you did not know how to solve this problem, you have a fifty-fifty chance of getting the question correct, just because you thought like a test writer.

Well done.

Turn Algebra into Arithmetic

Later in this book, we will discuss Plugging In, a strategy for turning algebra into arithmetic. The basics of the strategy are that when a problem contains a variable and could be solved using algebra, you should plug in actual numbers for the variables and then solve. A lot of times, this will turn an algebra question into an arithmetic question. We are generally much better at arithmetic than we are at algebra, which works in your favor.

While we'll discuss this strategy in much more detail later in this book, we felt the need to provide a preamble to it here. Why? Because Plugging In, and all its variations, is one of the most powerful tools in your belt to turn questions that may otherwise be difficult or time-consuming into questions that you can answer with relative ease. You should take extra effort to be very comfortable with this strategy, as it is one of the best ways to ensure that you are not being an average test taker and not doing what ETS wants you to do.

In short, Plugging In is an essential tool to the test taker seeking to not be average.

Be Aware of All Types of Numbers

Part of successfully navigating Plugging In and not being an average student is to show awareness of all kinds of different numbers. What do we mean by that? Consider the following.

If a GRE question gave the variable x and there were no restrictions on what x could be, what number would you plug in for x? Many test takers will plug in 2, 3, 5, 10, or some other common number. But x could also be -2, -3, 0, $\frac{1}{2}$, $10\frac{1}{3}$, or any other number you could imagine. Test writers will often rely on test takers to not consider all possible types of numbers when creating a question that contains variables. The more aware you are of the types of numbers available to you on any given question, the better chance you have of avoiding choosing one of ETS's trap answers.

This is not to say that you should ignore the common numbers. You shouldn't. You should always work with the common numbers first to eliminate as many answer choices as possible. But, after you've plugged in a common number, if you still have a couple of answer choices remaining, plugging in a less common number is a good strategy to try to eliminate more answer choices.

Bite-Sized Pieces

Many of the math questions on the GRE read like verbal questions. These word problems are often long and contain a lot of information to process. The average test taker approaches this type of problem by trying to do all the steps at once, finding a shortcut, or trying to keep track of everything in their head. These are bad strategies. Avoid them.

Instead, approach these problems by breaking them into bite-sized pieces. By breaking the question into smaller parts that you can handle individually, you will stay more organized and run less risk of making a careless mistake.

Look at the following example.

> Point B is 18 miles east of point A, and point C is 6 miles west of point B. If point D is halfway between points B and C, and point E is halfway between points D and B, how far, in miles, is point E from point D?

At first glance, there is a lot of information in this question. Don't try to answer the question all at once. Instead, break the question down into bite-sized pieces.

The question begins by stating that point B is 18 miles east of point A, so draw a line with points A and B on the ends and the length labeled 18. Point C is 6 miles west of point B, so draw another line from point B to point C and label the length 6. Point D is halfway between points B and C, so put a point between points B and C and label it D. Because point D is halfway between B and C and the length of BC is 6, the lengths of BD and DC are 3. Point E is halfway between D and B, so put a point between D and B and label it E. The distance between D and B is 3, and E is halfway between them, so the distance from point D to point E is 1.5 miles.

By breaking this question down into bite-sized pieces, it was easy to keep organized and to work your way to the correct answer.

Ballparking

Occasionally, the GRE will present to you a problem that contains strange numbers, such as long decimals or numbers that don't appear to divide evenly. Many times, those questions will ask for a nonspecific value. When confronted with a question like those, the writers at ETS are hoping that you spend a considerable amount of time working with difficult numbers.

At these times, a good strategy to remember is to use Ballparking. With this technique, a number is designed to make difficult numbers easier to work with by rounding or approximating them to a more favorable number. After ballparking the numbers in a question, the correct answer will be the one that is closest to the value that you determined from your ballparked numbers. At various points throughout this book, we present examples of how to use the technique of ballparking.

PRACTICE

You should take the time to sharpen your GRE math skills if you want to succeed. If you don't spend much time working with numbers, or if all your numerical calculations are done by calculator or spreadsheet, it is worth your time to go out of your way to become comfortable with numbers again. Here are a couple ways that you can reintroduce numbers into your daily life that are relevant to the GRE.

- Figure out a 15% tip by calculating 10% and adding half again (because 10% plus 5% equals 15%).
- Take a few measurements and find out exactly how much storage space that old armoire has.
- Calculate the exact miles per gallon your car got on that last trip to your sister's house.
- Figure out what fraction of your monthly budget is taken up by housing expenses, food, utilities, or loan payments.

It also should go without saying that probably the best action you can take is to use the strategies in this book and do the practice problems correctly. While it is true that speed is important when taking the GRE, so is accuracy. You will get faster at employing the techniques we outline here the more familiar you become with them. But you will become faster and more accurate only if you employ the techniques with precision. So, do not feel rushed to work through a practice set in this book. Work consistently and work accurately and you will eventually begin to work at a faster pace.

THE CALCULATOR

As we mentioned before, on the GRE you'll be given an on-screen calculator. The calculator program on the GRE is a rudimentary one that gives you the five basic operations: addition, subtraction, multiplication, division, and square root, plus a decimal function and a positive/negative feature. It follows the order of operations, or PEMDAS (more on this topic in Chapter 3). The calculator also has the ability to transfer the answer you've calculated directly into the answer box for certain questions. The on-screen calculator can be a huge advantage—if it's used correctly!

As you might have realized by this point, ETS is not exactly looking out for your best interests. Giving you a calculator might seem like an altruistic act, but rest assured that ETS knows that there are certain ways in which calculator use can be exploited. Keep in mind the following:

1. **Calculators Can't Think.** Calculators are good for one thing and one thing only: calculation. You still have to figure out how to set up the problem correctly. If you're not sure what to calculate, then a calculator isn't helpful. For example, if you do a percent calculation on your calculator and then hit "Transfer Display," you must remember to move the decimal point accordingly, depending on whether the question asks for a percent or a decimal.

2. **The Calculator Can Be a Liability.** ETS will give you questions that you can solve with a calculator, but the calculator can actually be a liability. You will be tempted to use it. For example, students who are uncomfortable adding, subtracting, multiplying, or dividing fractions may be tempted to convert all fractions to decimals using the calculator. Don't do it. You are better off mastering fractions than avoiding them. Working with exponents and square roots is another way in which the calculator will be tempting but may yield really big and awkward numbers or long decimals. You are much better off learning the rules of manipulating exponents and square roots. Most of these problems will be faster and cleaner to solve with rules than with a calculator. The questions may also use numbers that are too big for the calculator. Time spent trying to get an answer out of a calculator for problems involving really big numbers will be time wasted. Find another way around.

3. **A Calculator Won't Make You Faster.** Having a calculator should make you more accurate, but not necessarily faster. You still need to take time to read each problem carefully and set it up. Don't expect to blast through problems just because you have a calculator.

4. **The Calculator Is No Excuse for Not Using Scratch Paper.** Scratch paper is where good technique happens. Working problems by hand on scratch paper will help to avoid careless errors or skipped steps. Just because you can do multiple functions in a row on your calculator does not mean that you should be solving problems on your calculator. Use the calculator to do simple calculations that would otherwise take you time to solve. Make sure you are still writing steps out on your scratch paper, labeling results, and using set-ups (we'll go into this in more depth later). Accuracy is more important than speed!

Of course, you should not fear the calculator; by all means, use it and be grateful for it. Having a calculator should help you eliminate all those careless math mistakes.

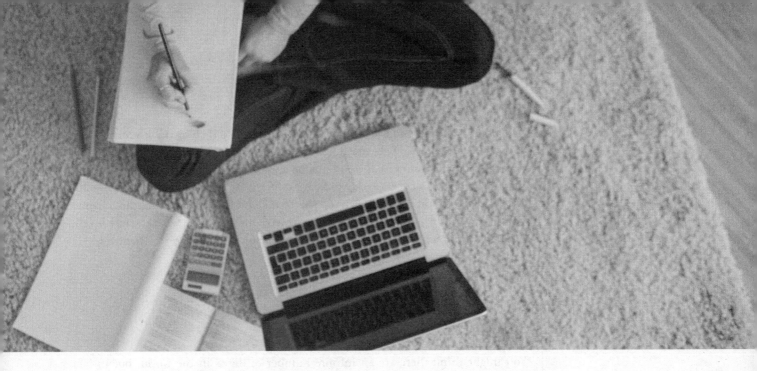

Chapter 3
Math Fundamentals

DEALING WITH NUMBERS

Whenever you decide to learn a new language, what do they start with on the very first day? Vocabulary. Well, math has as much of its own lexicon as any country's mother tongue, so now is as good a time as any to familiarize yourself with the terminology. These vocabulary words are rather simple to learn—or relearn—but they're also very important. Any of the terms you'll read about in this chapter could show up in a GRE math question, so you should know what the test is talking about. (For a more lengthy list, you can consult the glossary in Chapter 14.)

We'll start our review with the backbone of all Arabic numerals: the digit.

Digits

You might think there are an infinite number of digits in the world, but in fact there are only ten: 0, 1, 2, 3, 4, 5, 6, 7, 8, and 9. This is the mathematical "alphabet" that serves as the building block from which all numbers are constructed.

Modern math uses digits in a decile system, meaning that every digit in a number represents a multiple of ten. For example, $1{,}423.795 = (1 \times 1{,}000) + (4 \times 100) + (2 \times 10) + (3 \times 1) + (7 \times 0.1) + (9 \times 0.01) + (5 \times 0.001)$.

You can refer to each place as follows:

- 1 occupies the **thousands** place.

- 4 occupies the **hundreds** place.

- 2 occupies the **tens** place.

- 3 occupies the **ones**, or **units**, place.

- 7 occupies the **tenths** place, so it's equivalent to seven tenths, or $\dfrac{7}{10}$.

- 9 occupies the **hundredths** place, so it's equivalent to nine hundredths, or $\dfrac{9}{100}$.

- 5 occupies the **thousandths** place, so it's equivalent to five thousandths, or $\dfrac{5}{1{,}000}$.

When all the digits are situated to the left of the decimal place, you've got yourself an integer.

Integers

When we first learn about addition and subtraction, we start with *integers*, which are the numbers you see on a number line.

Integers and digits are not the same thing; for example, 39 is an integer that contains two digits, 3 and 9. Also, integers are not the same as **whole numbers,** because whole numbers are non-negative, which include zero. Conversely, integers include negative numbers. Any integer is considered greater than all of the integers to its left on the number line. So just as 5 is greater than 3 (which can be written as 5 > 3), 0 is greater than –4, and –4 is greater than –10. (For more about greater than, less than, and solving for inequalities, see Chapter 4.)

Consecutive Integers and Sequences

Integers can be listed consecutively (such as 3, 4, 5, 6…) or in patterned sequences such as odds (1, 3, 5, 7…), evens (2, 4, 6, 8…), and multiples of 6 (6, 12, 18, 24…). The numbers in these progressions always get larger, except when explicitly noted otherwise. Note also that, because zero is an integer, a list of consecutive integers that progresses from negative to positive numbers must include it (–2, –1, 0, 1…).

Zero

Zero is a special little number that deserves your attention. It isn't positive or negative, but it is even. (So a list of consecutive even integers might look like –4, –2, 0, 2, 4….) Zero might also seem insignificant because it's what's called the *additive identity*, which basically means that adding zero to any other number doesn't change anything. (This will be an important consideration when you start plugging numbers into problems in Chapter 5.)

Positives and Negatives

On either side of zero, you'll find positive and negative numbers. For the GRE, the best thing to know about positives and negatives is what happens when you multiply them together.

- A positive times a positive yields a positive ($3 \times 5 = 15$).
- A positive times a negative yields a negative ($3 \times -5 = -15$).
- A negative times a negative yields a positive ($-3 \times -5 = 15$).

Even and Odd

As you might have guessed from our talk of integers above, even numbers (which include zero) are multiples of 2, and odd numbers are not multiples of 2. If you were to experiment with the properties of these numbers, you would find that

- any number times an even number yields an even number
- the product of two or more odd numbers is always odd
- the sum of two or more even numbers is always even
- the sum of two odd numbers is always even
- the sum of an even number and an odd number is always odd

Obviously, there's no need to memorize stuff like this. If you're ever in a bind, try working with real numbers. After all, if you want to know what you get when you multiply two odd numbers, you can just pick two odd numbers—like 3 and 7, for example—and multiply them. You'll see that the product is 21, which is also odd.

Digits Quick Quiz

Question 1 of 3

If x, y, and z are consecutive even integers and $x < 0$ and $z > 0$, then $xyz =$

```
┌─────────────┐
│             │
└─────────────┘
```

The hundreds digit and ones digit of a three-digit number are interchanged so that the new number is 396 less than the old number. Which of the following could be the number?

○ 293

○ 327

○ 548

○ 713

○ 801

a, b, and c are consecutive digits, and $a > b > c$

Quantity A	**Quantity B**
abc	$a + b + c$

○ Quantity A is greater.

○ Quantity B is greater.

○ The two quantities are equal.

○ The relationship cannot be determined from the information given.

Explanations for Digits Quick Quiz

1. If x, y, and z are consecutive even integers and $x < 0$ and $z > 0$, then x must be -2, y must be 0, and z must be 2. Therefore, their product is 0, and you would enter this number into the box.

2. Take the answer choices and switch the hundreds digit and ones digit. When the result is 396 less than the old number, you have a winner. Choices (A), (B), and (C) are out, because their ones digits are greater than their hundreds digits; therefore, the result will be greater (for example, 293 becomes 392). If you rearrange 713, the result is 317, which is 396 less than 713. The answer is (D).

3. Pick three consecutive digits for a, b, and c, such as 2, 3, and 4. Quantity A becomes $2 \times 3 \times 4$, or 24, and Quantity B becomes $2 + 3 + 4$, or 9. Quantity A is greater so eliminate (B) and (C). But if a, b, and c are -1, 0, and 1, respectively, then both quantities become 0 so eliminate (A). Therefore, the answer is (D).

MORE ABOUT NUMBERS

Prime Numbers

Prime numbers are special numbers that are divisible by only two distinct factors: themselves and 1. Since neither 0 nor 1 is prime, the least prime number is 2. The rest, as you might guess, are odd, because all even numbers are divisible by two. The first ten prime numbers are 2, 3, 5, 7, 11, 13, 17, 19, 23, and 29.

Note that not all odd numbers are prime; 15, for example, is not prime because it is divisible by 3 and 5. Said another way, 3 and 5 are *factors* of 15, because 3 and 5 divide evenly into 15. Let's talk more about factors.

Factors

As we said, a prime number has only two distinct factors: itself and 1. But a number that isn't prime—like 120, for example—has several factors. If you're ever asked to list all the factors of a number, the best idea is to pair them up and work through the factors systematically, starting with 1 and itself. So, for 120, the factors are

- 1 and 120
- 2 and 60
- 3 and 40
- 4 and 30
- 5 and 24
- 6 and 20
- 8 and 15
- 10 and 12

Notice how the two numbers start out far apart (1 and 120) and gradually get closer together? When the factors can't get any closer, you know you're finished. The number 120 has 16 factors: 1, 2, 3, 4, 5, 6, 8, 10, 12, 15, 20, 24, 30, 40, 60, and 120. Of these factors, three are prime (2, 3, and 5).

That's also an important point: Every number has a *finite* number of factors.

Prime Factorization

Sometimes the best way to analyze a number is to break it down to its most fundamental parts—its prime factors. To do this, we'll break down a number into factors, and then continue breaking down those factors until we're stuck with a prime number. For instance, to find the prime factors of 120, we could start with the most obvious factors of 120: 12 and 10. (Although 1 and 120 are also factors of 120, because 1 isn't prime, and no two prime numbers can be multiplied to make 1, we'll ignore it when we find prime factors.) Now that we have 12 and 10, we can break down each of those. What two numbers can we multiply to make 12? 3 and 4 work, and since 3 is prime, we can break down 4 to 2 and 2. 10 can be broken into 2 and 5, both of which are prime. Notice how we kept breaking down each factor into smaller and smaller pieces until we were stuck with prime numbers? It doesn't matter which factors we used, because we'll always end up with the same prime factors: $12 = 6 \times 2 = 3 \times 2 \times 2$, or $12 = 3 \times 4 = 3 \times 2 \times 2$. So the prime factor tree for 120 could look something like this:

The prime factorization of 120 is $2 \times 2 \times 2 \times 3 \times 5$, or $2^3 \times 3 \times 5$. Note that these prime factors (2, 3, and 5) are the same ones we listed earlier.

Multiples

Since 12 is a factor of 120, it's also true that 120 is a *multiple* of 12. It's impossible to list all the multiples of a number, because multiples trail off into infinity. For example, the multiples of 12 are 12 (12×1), 24 (12×2), 36 (12×3), 48 (12×4), 60 (12×5), 72 (12×6), 84 (12×7), and so forth.

If you ever have trouble distinguishing factors from multiples, remember this:

Factors are Few; Multiples are Many.

Divisibility

If *a* is a multiple of *b*, then *a* is divisible by *b*. This means that when you divide *a* by *b*, you get an integer. For example, 65 is divisible by 13 because 65 ÷ 13 = 5.

Divisibility Rules The most reliable way to test for divisibility is to use the calculator that they give you. If a problem requires a lot of work with divisibility, however, there are several cool rules you can learn that can make the problem a lot easier to deal with. As you'll see later in this chapter, these rules will also make the job of reducing fractions much easier.

1. All numbers are divisible by one. (Remember that if a number is prime, it is divisible by only itself and 1.)
2. A number is divisible by 2 if the last digit is even.
3. A number is divisible by 3 if the sum of the digits is a multiple of 3. For example, 13,248 is divisible by 3 because 1 + 3 + 2 + 4 + 8 = 18, and 18 is divisible by 3.
4. A number is divisible by 4 if the two digits at the end form a number that is divisible by 4. For example, 13,248 is divisible by 4 because 48 is divisible by 4.
5. A number is divisible by 5 if it ends in 5 or 0.
6. A number is divisible by 6 if it is divisible by both 2 and 3. Because 13,248 is even and divisible by 3, it must therefore be divisible by 6.
7. There is no easy rule for divisibility by 7. It's easier to just try dividing by 7!
8. A number is divisible by 8 if the three digits at the end form a number that is divisible by 8. For example, 13,248 is divisible by 8 because 248 is divisible by 8.
9. A number is divisible by 9 if the sum of the digits is a multiple of 9. For example, 13,248 is divisible by 9 because 1 + 3 + 2 + 4 + 8 = 18, and 18 is divisible by 9.
10. A number is divisible by 10 if it ends in 0.

Remainders If an integer is not evenly divisible by another integer, whatever integer is left over after division is called the *remainder*. You can find the remainder by finding the greatest multiple of the number you are dividing by that is still less than the number you are dividing into. The difference between that multiple and the number you are dividing into is the remainder. For example, when 19 is divided by 5, 15 is the greatest multiple of 5 that is still less than 19. The difference between 19 and 15 is 4, so the remainder when 19 is divided by 5 is 4.

Working with Numbers

A lot of your math calculation on the GRE will require you to know the rules for manipulating numbers using the usual mathematical operations: addition, subtraction, multiplication, and division.

PEMDAS (Order of Operations)

When simplifying an expression, you need to perform mathematical operations in a specific order. This order is easily identified by the mnemonic device that most of us come in contact with sooner or later at school—PEMDAS, which stands for Parentheses, Exponents, Multiplication and Division, and Addition and Subtraction. (You might have remembered this as a kid by saying "Please Excuse My Dear Aunt Sally," which is a perfect mnemonic because it's just weird enough not to forget. What the heck did Aunt Sally do, anyway?)

In order to simplify a mathematical term using several operations, perform the following steps:

1. Perform all operations that are in parentheses.
2. Simplify all terms that use exponents.
3. Perform all multiplication and division from left to right. Do not assume that all multiplication comes before all division, as the acronym suggests, because you could get a wrong answer.
    WRONG: $24 \div 4 \times 6 = 24 \div (4 \times 6) = 24 \div 24 = 1$.
    RIGHT: $24 \div 4 \times 6 = (24 \div 4) \times 6 = 6 \times 6 = 36$.
4. Fourth, perform all addition and subtraction, also from left to right.

It's important to remember this order, because if you don't follow it, your results will very likely turn out wrong.

Try it out in a GRE example.

$$(2 + 1)^3 + 7 \times 2 + 7 - 3 \times 4^2 =$$

- ○ −16
- ○ 0
- ○ 288
- ○ 576
- ○ 1,152

Here's How to Crack It

Simplify $(2 + 1)^3 + 7 \times 2 + 7 - 3 \times 4^2$ like this:

Parentheses:	$(3)^3 + 7 \times 2 + 7 - 3 \times 4^2$
Exponents:	$27 + 7 \times 2 + 7 - 3 \times 16$
Multiply and Divide:	$27 + 14 + 7 - 48$
Add and Subtract:	$41 + 7 - 48$
	$48 - 48 = 0$

The answer is (B).

Working with Numbers Quick Quiz

Question 1 of 7

Quantity A	Quantity B
The number of even multiples of 11 between 1 and 100	The number of odd multiples of 22 between 1 and 100

- ○ Quantity A is greater.
- ○ Quantity B is greater.
- ○ The two quantities are equal.
- ○ The relationship cannot be determined from the information given.

Which of the following numbers has the same distinct prime factors as 42 ?

- ○ 63
- ○ 98
- ○ 210
- ○ 252
- ○ 296

p and r are factors of 100

Quantity A	Quantity B
pr	100

- ○ Quantity A is greater.
- ○ Quantity B is greater.
- ○ The two quantities are equal.
- ○ The relationship cannot be determined from the information given.

Quantity A	Quantity B
The remainder when 33 is divided by 12	The remainder when 200 is divided by 7

- ○ Quantity A is greater.
- ○ Quantity B is greater.
- ○ The two quantities are equal.
- ○ The relationship cannot be determined from the information given.

$6(3 - 1)^3 + 12 \div 2 + 3^2 =$

- ○ 24
- ○ 39
- ○ 63
- ○ 69
- ○ 105

If *r*, *s*, *t*, and *u* are distinct, consecutive prime integers less than 31, then which of the following could be the average (arithmetic mean) of *r*, *s*, *t*, and *u* ?

Indicate all such numbers.

☐ 4

☐ 4.25

☐ 6

☐ 9

☐ 14

☐ 22

☐ 24

Question 7 of 7

The greatest prime number that is less than 36 is represented by *x*. *y* represents the least even number greater than 19 that is divisible by 3. What is the sum of 2 and the value of *x* divided by *y* ?

$$\frac{\boxed{}}{\boxed{}}$$

Explanations for Working with Numbers Quick Quiz

1. The only even multiples of 11 between 1 and 100 are 22, 44, 66, and 88, so Quantity A equals 4. Quantity B is tricky, because if 22 is even, all multiples of 22 are also even. There are no odd multiples of 22, so Quantity B equals 0. The answer is (A).

2. The prime factorization of 42 is $2 \times 3 \times 7$ so those are the distinct prime factors. Choice (A) can be eliminated, because 63 is odd. The prime factorization of 252 is $2 \times 2 \times 3 \times 3 \times 7$, so its distinct prime factors are the same. The answer is (D).

3. If *p* and *r* are factors of 100, then each must be one of these numbers: 1, 2, 4, 5, 10, 20, 25, 50, or 100. If you plug in *p* = 1 and *r* = 2, for example, then *pr* = 2 and Quantity B is greater so eliminate (A) and (C). If *p* = 50 and *r* = 100, however, then *pr* = 5,000, which is much greater than 100 so eliminate (B). Therefore, the answer is (D).

4. 12 goes into 33 two times. The remainder is 9. Since 9 is greater than 7, there is no need to calculate the remainder for Quantity B because it can't possibly be greater than 6. Remember that the remainder is always less than the number you are dividing by. The answer is (A).

5. Follow PEMDAS and calculate the parentheses and exponents first: $6 \times (3 - 1)^3 + 12 \div 2 + 3^2 = 6 \times 8 + 12 \div 2 + 9$. Second, perform all multiplication and division: $6 \times 8 + 12 \div 2 + 9 = 48 + 6 + 9$. Now, it's just a matter of addition: $48 + 6 + 9 = 63$. The answer is (C).

6. This one can be tricky because of the math vocabulary; the question is really asking for the average of four prime numbers in a row. Start by making a list of all the consecutive prime numbers less than 31. Remember that 1 is not prime, and that 2 is the least prime number. Your list is 2, 3, 5, 7, 11, 13, 17, 19, 23, 29. Starting with 2, 3, 5, 7, use the on-screen calculator to work out the different possible averages for four consecutive primes. Choices (B), (D), and (F) are the answers.

7. Work this question in bite-sized pieces. The greatest prime number less than 36 is 31, so $x = 31$. The least even number greater than 19 that is divisible by 3 is 24, so $y = 24$. The problem states that x is divided by y, so $\frac{31}{24}$. The question asks for the sum of 2 plus the value of x divided by y, so $2 + \frac{31}{24}$. When adding a whole number to a fraction, set the denominators equal, so $2 + \frac{31}{24} = \frac{48}{24} + \frac{31}{24} = \frac{79}{24}$.

PARTS OF THE WHOLE (FRACTIONS AND DECIMALS)

It's still necessary to be knowledgeable when it comes to fractions, decimals, and percents. Each of these types of numbers has an equivalent in the form of the other two, and fluency among the three of them can save you precious time on test day.

For example, say you had to figure out 25% of 280. You could take a moment to realize that the fractional equivalent of 25% is $\frac{1}{4}$. At this point, you might see that $\frac{1}{4}$ of 280 is 70, and your work would be done.

If nothing else, memorizing the following table will increase your math IQ and give you a head start on your calculations.

The Conversion Table

Fraction	Decimal	Percent	Fraction	Decimal	Percent
$\frac{1}{2}$	0.5	50%	$\frac{3}{5}$	0.6	60%
$\frac{1}{3}$	$0.33\bar{3}$	$33\frac{1}{3}\%$	$\frac{4}{5}$	0.8	80%
$\frac{2}{3}$	0.666	$66\frac{2}{3}\%$	$\frac{1}{6}$	0.166	$16\frac{2}{3}\%$
$\frac{1}{4}$	0.25	25%	$\frac{1}{8}$	0.125	12.5%
$\frac{3}{4}$	0.75	75%	$\frac{3}{8}$	0.375	37.5%
$\frac{1}{5}$	0.2	20%	$\frac{5}{8}$	0.625	62.5%
$\frac{2}{5}$	0.4	40%			

Fractions

Each fraction is made up of a *numerator* (the number on top) divided by a *denominator* (the number down below). In other words, the numerator is the *part*, and the denominator is the *whole*. By most accounts, the part is less than the whole, and that's the way a fraction is "properly" written.

Improper Fractions

For a fraction, when the part is greater than the whole, the fraction is considered *improper*. The GRE won't quiz you on the terminology, but it usually writes its multiple-choice answer choices in proper form. A proper fraction takes this form:

$$Integer \: \frac{remainder}{divisor}$$

Converting from Improper to Proper

To convert the improper fraction $\frac{16}{3}$ into proper form, find the remainder when 16 is divided by 3. Because 3 goes into 16 five times with 1 left over, rewrite the fraction by setting aside the 5 as an integer and putting the remainder over the number you divided by (in this case, 3). Therefore, $\frac{16}{3}$ is equivalent to $5\frac{1}{3}$, because 5 is the integer, 1 is the remainder, and 3 is the divisor.

The expression $5\frac{1}{3}$ is also referred to as a *mixed number*, because the number contains both an integer and a fraction.

Converting from Proper to Improper

Sometimes you'll want to convert a mixed number into its improper format. Converting to an improper fraction from a mixed number is a little easier, because all you do is multiply the divisor (the denominator) by the integer and then add the remainder.

$$4\frac{2}{7} = \frac{(4 \times 7) + 2}{7} = \frac{28 + 2}{7} = \frac{30}{7}$$

Improper formats are much easier to work with when you have to add, subtract, multiply, divide, or compare fractions. The important thing to stress here is flexibility; you should be able to work with any fraction the GRE gives you, regardless of what form it's in.

Adding and Subtracting Fractions

There's one basic rule for adding or subtracting fractions: You can't do anything until all of the fractions have the same denominator. If that's already the case, all you have to do is add or subtract the numerators, like this:

$$\frac{3}{13} + \frac{5}{13} = \frac{3 + 5}{13} = \frac{8}{13}$$

$$\frac{7}{19} - \frac{5}{19} = \frac{7 - 5}{19} = \frac{2}{19}$$

When the fractions have different denominators, you must convert one or both of them first in order to find their common denominator.

When you were a kid, you may have been trained to follow a bunch of complicated steps in order to find the "lowest common denominator." It might be a convenient thing to learn in order to impress your math teacher, but on the GRE it's way too much work.

The Bowtie

The Bowtie method has been a staple of The Princeton Review's materials since the company began in a living room in New York City in 1981. It's been around so long because it works so simply.

To add $\dfrac{3}{5}$ and $\dfrac{4}{7}$, for example, follow these three steps:

Step One: Multiply the denominators together to form the new denominator.

$$\frac{3}{5} + \frac{4}{7} = \frac{}{5 \times 7} = \frac{}{35}$$

Step Two: Multiply the first denominator by the second numerator (5 × 4 = 20) and the second denominator by the first numerator (7 × 3 = 21) and place these numbers above the fractions, as shown below.

See? A bowtie!

Step Three: Add the products to form the new numerator.

$$\frac{3}{5} + \frac{4}{7} = \frac{21 + 20}{5 \times 7} = \frac{41}{35}$$

Subtraction works the same way.

Note that with subtraction, the order of the numerators is important. The new numerator is 21 − 20, or 1. If you somehow get your numbers reversed and use 20 − 21, your answer will be $-\dfrac{1}{35}$, which is incorrect. One way to keep your subtraction straight is to always multiply **up** from denominator to numerator when you use the Bowtie so the product will end up in the right place.

———————○———————

Quantity A	Quantity B
$\dfrac{5}{13}$	$\dfrac{3}{8}$

○ Quantity A is greater.

○ Quantity B is greater.

○ The two quantities are equal.

○ The relationship cannot be determined from the information given.

Here's How to Crack It

First, eliminate (D) because both Quantity A and Quantity B contain numbers. Next, the Bowtie can also be used to compare fractions. Multiply the denominator of the fraction in Quantity B by the numerator of the fraction in Quantity A and write the product (40) over the fraction in Quantity A. Next, multiply the denominator of the fraction in Quantity A by the numerator of the fraction in Quantity B and write the product (39) over the fraction in Quantity B. Since 40 is greater than 39, the answer is (A).

———————○———————

Multiplying Fractions

Multiplying fractions isn't nearly as complicated as adding or subtracting, because any two fractions can be multiplied by each other *exactly as they are*. In other words, the denominators don't have to be the same. All you have to do is multiply all the numerators to find the new numerator, and multiply all the denominators to find the new denominator, like this:

$$\frac{3}{5} \times \frac{4}{7} = \frac{3 \times 4}{5 \times 7} = \frac{12}{35}$$

The great thing is that it doesn't matter how many fractions you have; all you have to do is multiply across.

$$\frac{2}{5} \times \frac{3}{8} \times \frac{9}{2} \times \frac{7}{3} = \frac{2 \times 3 \times 9 \times 7}{5 \times 8 \times 2 \times 3} = \frac{378}{240}$$

Dividing Fractions

Dividing fractions is almost exactly like multiplying them, except that you need to perform one extra step:

> When dividing fractions, don't ask why; just flip the second fraction and multiply.

Dividing takes two forms. When you're given a division sign, flip the *second* fraction and multiply them, like this:

$$\frac{2}{5} \div \frac{3}{8} = \frac{2}{5} \times \frac{8}{3} = \frac{2 \times 8}{5 \times 3} = \frac{16}{15}$$

Sometimes, you'll be given a compound fraction, in which one fraction sits on top of another, like this:

$$\frac{\frac{4}{7}}{\frac{5}{8}} =$$

The fraction bar might look a little intimidating, but remember that a fraction bar is just another way of saying "divide." In this case, flip the *bottom* and multiply.

$$\frac{\frac{4}{7}}{\frac{5}{8}} = \frac{4}{7} \div \frac{5}{8} = \frac{4}{7} \times \frac{8}{5} = \frac{32}{35}$$

Reciprocals of Fractions

When a fraction is multiplied by its *reciprocal,* the result is always 1. You can think of the reciprocal as being the value you get when the numerator and denominator of the fraction are "flipped." The reciprocal of $\frac{5}{7}$, for example, is $\frac{7}{5}$.

$$\frac{5}{7} \times \frac{7}{5} = \frac{5 \times 7}{7 \times 5} = \frac{35}{35} = 1$$

Knowing this will help you devise a nice shortcut for working with problems such as the following.

Which of the following is the reciprocal of $\dfrac{2\sqrt{3}}{5}$?

○ $\dfrac{10}{\sqrt{3}}$

○ $\dfrac{6}{5\sqrt{3}}$

○ $\dfrac{5\sqrt{3}}{6}$

○ $\dfrac{5}{\sqrt{6}}$

○ $\dfrac{2\sqrt{12}}{10}$

Here's How to Crack It

To solve this problem, multiply each answer choice by the original expression, $\dfrac{2\sqrt{3}}{5}$.

If the product is 1, you know you have a match. In this case, the only expression that works is $\dfrac{5\sqrt{3}}{6}$, so the answer is (C).

Reducing Fractions

Are you scared of reducing, or canceling, fractions because you're not sure what the rules are? If so, there's only one rule to remember:

> You can do anything to a fraction as long as you do exactly the same thing to both the numerator and the denominator.

When you reduce a fraction, you divide both the top and bottom by the same number. If you have the fraction $\frac{6}{15}$, for example, you can divide both the numerator and denominator by a common factor, 3, like this:

$$\frac{6 \div 3}{15 \div 3} = \frac{2}{5}$$

Be Careful If you are worried about when you can cancel terms in a fraction, here's an important rule to remember. If you have more than one term in the numerator of a fraction but only a single term in the denominator, you can't divide into one of the terms and not the other.

$$\text{WRONG:} \quad \frac{15 + 8}{4} = \frac{15 + \overset{2}{\cancel{8}}}{\cancel{4}} = \frac{15 + 2}{1} = 17$$

The only way you can cancel something out is if you can factor out the same number from both terms in the numerator and then divide.

$$\frac{15 + 3b}{9} = \frac{3 \times (5 + b)}{3 \times 3} = \frac{5 + b}{3}$$

Decimals

Decimals are just fractions with a hidden denominator: Each place to the right of the decimal point represents a fraction.

$$0.146 = \frac{1}{10} + \frac{4}{100} + \frac{6}{1,000} = \frac{146}{1,000}$$

Comparing Decimals

To compare decimals, you have to look at the decimals place by place, from left to right. As soon as the digit in a specific place of one number is greater than its counterpart in the other number, you know which is bigger.

For example, 15.345 and 15.3045 are very close in value because they have the same digits in their tens, units, and tenths places. But the hundredths digit of 15.345 is 4 and the hundredths digit of 15.304 is 0, so 15.345 is greater.

Rounding Decimals

In order to round a decimal, you have to know how many decimal places the final answer is supposed to have (which the GRE will usually specify) and then base your work on the decimal place immediately to the right. If that digit is 5 or higher, round up; if it's 4 or lower, round down.

For example, if you had to round 56.729 to the tenths place, you'd look at the 2 in the hundredths place, see that it was less than 5, and round *down* to 56.7. If you rounded to the hundredths place, however, you'd consider the 9 in the thousandths place and round *up* to 56.73.

Fractions and Decimals Quick Quiz

Question 1 of 8

The fraction $\frac{21}{56}$ is equivalent to what percent?

○ 30%

○ $33\frac{1}{3}\%$

○ 35%

○ 37.5%

○ 62.5%

Question 2 of 8

What is the sum of $\frac{7}{12}$ and $\frac{2}{5}$?

○ $\frac{11}{60}$

○ $\frac{11}{17}$

○ $\frac{14}{17}$

○ $\frac{59}{60}$

○ $\frac{59}{17}$

$$\left(\frac{1}{27}\right)^{-1}\left(\frac{1}{9}\right)^{-2}\left(\frac{1}{3}\right)^{-3} =$$

Indicate <u>all</u> such values.

☐ 59,049

☐ 3^{10}

☐ $\left(\frac{1}{3}\right)^{-10}$

If x is the 32nd digit to the right of the decimal point when $\frac{3}{11}$ is expressed as a decimal, and y is the 19th digit to the right of the decimal point when $\frac{7}{11}$ is expressed as a decimal, what is the value of xy ?

☐

If two-thirds of 42 equals four-fifths of x, what is the value of x ?

○ 28

○ 35

○ 42

○ 63

○ 84

Quantity A	**Quantity B**
$\dfrac{8}{11}$	$\dfrac{5}{7}$

○ Quantity A is greater.

○ Quantity B is greater.

○ The two quantities are equal.

○ The relationship cannot be determined
   from the information given.

Question 7 of 8

How many digits are there between the decimal

point and the first even digit after the decimal point

in the decimal equivalent of $\dfrac{1}{2^8 5^3}$?

Question 8 of 8

A set of digits under a bar indicates that those
digits repeat infinitely. What is the value of
$(0.0000\overline{23})(10^6 - 10^4)$?

○ 0.023

○ $0.\overline{23}$

○ 22.77

○ 23

○ $23.\overline{23}$

Explanations for Fractions and Decimals Quick Quiz

1. Reduce $\frac{21}{56}$ to $\frac{3}{8}$ and remember the common conversion table to convert the fraction to 37.5%. The answer is (D).

2. Use the Bowtie method. First, multiply the denominators:

    $5 \times 12 = 60$. When you multiply diagonally, as in the diagram given in the text, the numerator becomes $35 + 24$, or 59. The new fraction is $\frac{59}{60}$, and the answer is (D).

3. Simplify the negative exponents by taking the reciprocal of the corresponding positive exponent, which gives you

    $$\left(\frac{1}{\frac{1}{27}}\right)\left(\frac{1}{\left(\frac{1}{9}\right)^2}\right)\left(\frac{1}{\left(\frac{1}{3}\right)^3}\right) = \left(\frac{1}{\frac{1}{27}}\right)\left(\frac{1}{\frac{1}{81}}\right)\left(\frac{1}{\frac{1}{27}}\right).$$ Now you have

    three reciprocals, so flip them over and calculate:

    $\left(\frac{27}{1}\right)\left(\frac{81}{1}\right)\left(\frac{27}{1}\right) = 59{,}049$. You can also express each number as a power of 3, which gives you $(3^3)(3^4)(3^3) = 3^{10}$, which makes (B) correct. 3^{10} can also be expressed as $\left(\frac{1}{3}\right)^{-10}$. Thus, the correct answer is (A), (B), and (C).

4. Divide to convert the fractions into decimals. First, $\frac{3}{11} = 0.27\overline{27}$. This is really a pattern question: The odd numbered terms are 2 and the even numbered terms are 7. The 32nd digit to the right of the decimal is an even term, so $x = 7$. Next, $\frac{7}{11} = 0.63\overline{63}$. This time, the odd numbered terms are 6 and the even numbered terms are 3. The 19th digit on the right side of the decimal place is an odd term, so $y = 6$. Lastly, $xy = 7 \times 6 = 42$.

5. One-third of 42 is 14, so two-thirds is 28. 28 equals $\frac{4}{5}$ of x translates to $28 = \left(\frac{4}{5}\right)x$. Multiply both sides by the reciprocal, $\frac{5}{4}$, to eliminate the fraction and isolate the x. The fractions on the right cancel out and on the left you have $(28)\left(\frac{5}{4}\right) = 35$, so $35 = x$. The answer is (B).

6. To compare two fractions, just cross-multiply and compare the products. $7 \times 8 = 56$ and $11 \times 5 = 55$, so Quantity A is greater.

7. The answer is 0. First, divide to convert $\frac{1}{2^8 5^3}$ into a decimal. The on-screen calculator doesn't do exponents, so you may want to factor the denominator: $\frac{1}{2^4 2^4 5^3} = \frac{1}{16 \times 16 \times 125} = \frac{1}{32{,}000} = 0.00003125$. Since 0 is even, there are no digits between the decimal point and the first even digit after the decimal point, and the correct answer is 0. In fact, if you noticed that any decimal starting with a 0 would have the same answer, you only needed to make sure the denominator was larger than 10.

8. Before you break out the calculator, distribute the $(0.000\overline{23})$. This gives you $(0.000\overline{23})(10^6) - (0.000\overline{23})(10^4)$. Now move the decimal point 6 places to the right for the first term and 4 places to the right for the second term, which gives you $23.\overline{23} - .\overline{23} = 23$. The correct answer is (D).

PARTS OF A WHOLE (PERCENTS)

As you may have noted from the conversion chart, decimals and percents look an awful lot alike. In fact, all you have to do to convert a decimal to a percent is to move the decimal point two places to the right and add the percent sign: 0.25 becomes 25%, 0.01 becomes 1%, and so forth. This is because they're both based on multiples of 10. Percents also represent division with a denominator that is always 100.

Calculating Percents

Now, let's review four different ways to calculate percents: translating, conversion, proportions, and tip calculations. Some people find that one way makes more sense than others. There is no best way to find percents. Try out all four, and figure out which one seems most natural to you. You will probably find that some methods work best for some problems, and other methods work best for others.

Translating

Translating is one of the more straightforward and versatile methods of calculating percents. Each word in a percent problem is directly translated into a mathematical term, according to the following chart:

Term	Math equivalent
what	x (variable)
is	=
of	× (multiply)
percent	÷ 100

This table can be a great help. For example, take a look at this Quant Comp problem.

Quantity A	**Quantity B**
24% of 15% of 400	52% of 5% of 600

○ Quantity A is greater.

○ Quantity B is greater.

○ The two quantities are equal.

○ The relationship cannot be determined from the information given.

Here's How to Crack It

Since it's not immediately obvious which quantity is larger, you're going to have to do some actual calculation. Start with Quantity A. 24% of 15% of 400 can be translated, piece by piece, into math. Remember that % means to divide by 100 and *of* means to multiply. As always, write down everything on your scratch paper. After translation, we get $\frac{24}{100} \times \frac{15}{100} \times \frac{400}{1}$. Cancel out one of the 100s in the denominator with the 400 in the numerator of the last fraction to get $\frac{24}{100} \times \frac{15}{1} \times \frac{4}{1}$. Now feel free to use the calculator. Multiply the top of the fractions first and then the bottom, resulting in $\frac{1,440}{100} = 14.4$. Now do the same with Quantity B. 52% of 5% of 600 becomes $\frac{52}{100} \times \frac{5}{100} \times \frac{600}{1}$. Cancel out the first 100 with the 600 and you'll have $\frac{52}{1} \times \frac{5}{100} \times \frac{6}{1} = \frac{1,560}{100} = 15.6$. Quantity B is therefore bigger, and the answer is (B).

Word Problems and Percents

Word problems are also far less onerous when you apply the math translation table.

> Thirty percent of the graduate students at Hardcastle State University are from outside the state, and 75% of out-of-state students receive some sort of financial aid. If there are 3,120 graduate students at Hardcastle State, how many out-of-state students do NOT receive financial aid?
>
> ○   234
>
> ○   468
>
> ○   702
>
> ○   936
>
> ○   1,638

Here's How to Crack It

Note the range in answer choices. This is another problem that is ripe for Ballparking. Estimate that there are 3,000 graduate students. 10% of 3,000 is 300, so 30% is 900. 25% do not receive financial aid, which is what you're looking for, so $\frac{1}{4}$ of 900 is 225. Since there are a few more than 3,000 graduate students, the answer must be a few more than 225. Only (A) is even close. Note that (C) represents the 75% who do receive financial aid. Make sure you read slowly and carefully and take all word problems in bite-sized pieces.

Conversion

The second way to deal with percentage questions is to use the chart on page 40. This will allow you to quickly change each percentage into a fraction or a decimal. This method works well in tandem with Translating, as reduced fractions are often easier to work with when you are setting up a calculation.

Proportions

You can also set up a percent question as a proportion by matching up the part and whole. Look at a couple quick examples:

1)   60 is what percent of 200?
Because 60 is some part of 200, you can set up the following proportion:

$$\frac{60}{200} = \frac{x}{100}$$

Notice that each fraction is simply the part divided by the whole. On the left side, 60 is part of 200. You want to know what that part is in terms of a percent, so on the right side set up x (the percent you want to find), divided by 100 (the total percent).

2)   What is 30% of 200?
Now you don't know how much of 200 you're dealing with, but you know the percentage. So put the unknown, x, over the whole, 200, and the percentage on the right:

$$\frac{x}{200} = \frac{30}{100}$$

3)　　　60 is 30% of what number?
　　　You know the percentage, and you know the part, but
　　　you don't know the whole, so that's the unknown:

$$\frac{60}{x} = \frac{30}{100}$$

Notice that the setup for each problem (they're actually just variations of the same problem: 30% of 200 is 60) is essentially the same. You had one unknown, either the part, the whole, or the percentage, and you wrote down everything you knew.

Every proportion will therefore look like this:

$$\frac{part}{whole} = \frac{percentage}{100}$$

Once you've set up the proportion, cross-multiply to solve.

Ben purchased a computer and paid 45% of the price immediately. If he paid $810 immediately, what is the total price of the computer?

Here's How to Crack It

Find the parts of the proportion that you know. You know he paid 45%, so you know the percentage, and you know the part he paid: $810. You're missing the whole price. On your scratch paper, set up the proportion $\frac{810}{x} = \frac{45}{100}$. Cross-multiply to get $45x = 81{,}000$. Divide both sides by 45 (feel free to use the calculator here) to get $x = \$1{,}800$.

Tip Calculation

The last method for calculating percentages is a variation on a method many people use to calculate the tip for a meal.

To find 10% of any number, simply move the decimal one place to the left.

> 10% of 100 = 10.0
> 10% of 30 = 3.0
> 10% of 75 = 7.5
> 10% of 128 = 12.8
> 10% of 87.9 = 8.79

To find 1% of any number, move the decimal two places to the left.

> 1% of 100 = 1.00
> 1% of 70 = 0.70
> 1% of 5 = 0.05
> 1% of 2,145 = 21.45

You can then find the value of any percentage by breaking the percentage into 1%, 10%, and 100% pieces. Remember that 5% is half of 10%, and 50% is half of 100%.

> 5% of 60 = half of 10% = half of 6 = 3
> 20% of 35 = 10% + 10% = 3.5 + 3.5 = 7
> 52% of 210 = 50% + 1% + 1% = 105 + 2.1 + 2.1 = 109.2
> 40% of 70 = 10% + 10% + 10% + 10% = 7 + 7 + 7 + 7 = 28

Generally, we'll use this most often with Ballparking, especially on Charts and Graphs questions, which are covered in Chapter 6.

Last month Dave spent at least 20% but no more than 25% of his monthly income on groceries. If his monthly income was $2,080.67, which of the following could be the amount Dave spent on groceries?

Indicate <u>all</u> such values.

☐ $391.92

☐ $432.88

☐ $456.02

☐ $497.13

☐ $530.17

☐ $545.60

☐ $592.43

Here's How to Crack It

Ugh. Those are some ugly numbers. Ballpark a little bit, and use some quick tip calculations to simplify. First, write down A B C D E F G vertically on your scratch paper. Look for a number greater than 20% of $2,080.67. Ignore the 67 cents for now. If any answers are only a couple pennies away from the answer, then you can go back and use more exact numbers, but that's fairly unlikely. 10% of $2,080 is $208, which means that 20% is $208 + $208 = $416. Dave must have spent at least $416 on groceries, so cross off (A). You know he spent no more than 25% of his income. 5% of $2,080 is half of 10%, which means that 5% of $2,080 is $104, and 25% of $2,080 is 10% + 10% + 5% = $208 + $208 + $104 = $520. He couldn't have spent more than $520 on groceries, so cross off (E), (F), and (G). The answers are everything between $416 and $520: (B), (C), and (D).

Percent Change

Percent change is based on two quantities: the change and the original amount.

$$\% \ change = \frac{change}{original} \times 100$$

Quantity A	Quantity B
The percent change from 10 to 11	The percent change from 11 to 10

○ Quantity A is greater.

○ Quantity B is greater.

○ The two quantities are equal.

○ The relationship cannot be determined from the information given.

Here's How to Crack It

At first glance, you might assume that the answer is (C), because the numbers in each quantity look so similar. However, even though both quantities changed by a value of 1, the original amounts are different. When you follow the formula, you find that Quantity A equals $\frac{1}{10} \times 100$, or 10%, while Quantity B equals $\frac{1}{11} \times 100$, or 9%. The answer is (A).

Percentage change also factors into charts and graphs questions, so we'll talk about it more in Chapter 6. From here, we head to a powerful little device that helps us convey very big and very small numbers with very little effort: exponents. Before we get into exponents, though, practice those percents.

Percents Quick Quiz

Question 1 of 6

What is 26% of 3,750 ?

- ○ 753
- ○ 975
- ○ 1,005
- ○ 2,775
- ○ 9,750

Question 2 of 6

Quantity A	**Quantity B**
200% of 20% of 300	120% of 25% of 400

- ○ Quantity A is greater.
- ○ Quantity B is greater.
- ○ The two quantities are equal.
- ○ The relationship cannot be determined from the information given.

Question 3 of 6

A think tank projects that people over the age of 65 will comprise 25% of the U.S. population by 2010. If the current population of 300 million is expected to grow by 8% by 2010, how many people over age 65, in millions, will there be in 2010 ?

☐

Question 4 of 6

Marat sold his condo at a price that was 18% more than the price he paid for it. If he bought his condo at a price that was 42% less than the buyer's $175,000 asking price, which of the following must be true?

Indicate all such values.

- ☐ The person who sold Marat the condo lost money.
- ☐ Marat bought the condo for $101,500.
- ☐ 36 percent of the price at which Marat sold the condo is $43,117.20.

If 25% of p equals 65% of 80 and if q is 50% of p, which of the following must be true?

Indicate <u>all</u> such values.

☐ 65 is 62.5% of q

☐ q is 130% of 80

☐ p is 200% of q

☐ $\dfrac{q}{p} = 50\%$ of 1

When John withdraws x% of his \$13,900 balance from his checking account, his new balance is less than \$10,000.

Quantity A	**Quantity B**
x	25

○ Quantity A is greater.

○ Quantity B is greater.

○ The two quantities are equal.

○ The relationship cannot be determined from the information given.

Explanations for Percents Quick Quiz

1. Convert. 26% is close to 25%, so what is $\dfrac{1}{4}$ of 3,750? Only (B) is close.

2. In Quantity A, 20% or $\dfrac{1}{5}$ of 300 is 60. 100% of 60 is 60, so 200% must be 120. In Quantity B, 25% or $\dfrac{1}{4}$ of 400 is 100. 20% of 100 is 20, so 120% is 120. The two quantities are equal, and the answer is (C).

3. 1% of 300 million is 3 million, so 8% is 24 million. If the population grew by 8%, that means that it added another 24 million people, so the new total is 324 million. 25% or $\dfrac{1}{4}$ of 324 million is 81. So there will be 81 million people over 65 in the United States in 2010; enter 81 in the box.

4. Take bite-sized pieces. Marat bought his condo for 58% of $175,000 = $101,500. (Alternatively, you could take 42% of $175,000 and subtract that from $175,000 to get $101,500.) Choice (B) is correct. Marat later sold his condo for 18% more than he paid for it: $1.18 \times \$101,500 = \$119,770$. Calculate 36% of that selling price: $0.36 \times \$119,700 = \$43,117.20$. Choice (C) is correct. Because you know only the asking price of the person who sold Marat the condo, and not how much he or she paid for it, (A) may or may not be true. Eliminate it. The correct answers are (B) and (C).

5. Start by translating: $0.25p = 0.65(80)$, so $0.25p = 52$ and $p = 208$. That means $q = 0.50(208) = 104$. Now replace p and q in the answer choices with the appropriate values. For (A), you have $65 = \frac{62.5}{100} \times 104$, which is true. Choice (A) is correct. For (B), $104 = \frac{130}{100} \times 80$. This equation is also true, so keep (B). Choice (C) is also correct because $208 = \frac{200}{100} \times 104$. Finally, (D) is correct because $\frac{104}{208} = \frac{1}{2}$, which is 50% of 1. The correct answers are (A), (B), (C), and (D).

6. Whenever you see a variable in one column and an actual number in the other column, try plugging the number in for the variable. In this case, if John withdrew 25% of his savings, that would be $3,475, and his balance would still be $10,425. Therefore, he must withdraw more than 25% in order for his balance to dip below $10,000. The answer is (A).

EXPONENTS

The superscripted number to the upper right corner of an integer or other math term is called an exponent, and it tells you the number of times that number or variable is multiplied by itself. For example, $5^4 = 5 \times 5 \times 5 \times 5$. The exponent is 4, and the base is 5.

You can add or subtract two exponential terms as long as both the base and the exponents are the same.

$5x^5 + x^5 = 6x^5$

$6b^3 - 4b^3 = 2b^3$

$15ab^2c^3 - 9ab^2c^3 + 2ab^2c^3 = 8ab^2c^3$

Multiplying and Dividing Exponential Terms

Let's say we're multiplying $a^2 \times a^3$. If we expand out those terms, then we get $(a \times a)(a \times a \times a) = a^5 = a^{(2+3)}$. So when multiplying terms that have the same base, add the exponents.

Note that the terms have to have the same base. If we're presented with something like $a^2 \times b^3$, then we can't simplify it any further than that.

Now let's deal with division. Let's start by expanding out an exponent problem using division, to see what we can eliminate.

$$\frac{a^5}{a^3} = \frac{a \times a \times a \times a \times a}{a \times a \times a} = \frac{a \times a}{1} = a^2$$

Notice that the three a terms on the bottom canceled out with three a terms on top? We ended up with a^2, which is the same as $a^{(5-3)}$. So when dividing terms that have the same base, subtract the exponents.

Parentheses with exponents work exactly as they do with normal multiplication. $(ab)^3 = (ab)(ab)(ab) = a^3b^3$. When a term inside parentheses is raised to a power, the exponent is applied to each individual term within the parentheses.

What if a term inside the parentheses already has an exponent? For example, what if we have $(a^2)^3$? Well, that's $(a^2)(a^2)(a^2) = (a \times a)(a \times a)(a \times a) = a^6 = a^{2 \times 3}$. So when you raise a term with an exponent to another power, multiply the two exponents.

To review, the big rules with exponents are as follows:

- When **Multiplying** terms with the same base, **Add** the exponents.
- When **Dividing** terms with the same base, **Subtract** the exponents.
- When raising a term with an exponent to another **Power, Multiply** the exponents.

Most exponent questions use one or more of these rules. You can memorize them as **MADSPM**: Multiply, Add, Divide, Subtract, Power, Multiply.

When in Doubt, Expand It Out

If you ever have trouble remembering any of these rules, you can always fall back on a very valuable guideline: "When in doubt, expand it out." Here's an example of how this works:

Which of the following expressions is equivalent to $(2x)^3(5x^2)(x^4)^5$?

○ $10x^{15}$

○ $20x^{15}$

○ $20x^{25}$

○ $40x^{15}$

○ $40x^{25}$

Here's How to Crack It

When you expand everything out, the factors look like this:

$$(2x)^3(5x^2)(x^4)^5 = [(2x) \cdot (2x) \cdot (2x)] \cdot [5 \cdot x \cdot x] \cdot [(x^4) \cdot (x^4) \cdot (x^4) \cdot (x^4) \cdot (x^4)]$$

$$= 2 \cdot 2 \cdot 2 \cdot 5 \cdot x^1 \cdot x^1 \cdot x^1 \cdot x^1 \cdot x^1 \cdot x^4 \cdot x^4 \cdot x^4 \cdot x^4 \cdot x^4$$

$$= 40 \cdot x^{(1+1+1+1+1+4+4+4+4+4)} = 40x^{25}$$

The answer is (E).

Rules, Quirks, Anomalies, and Other Weirdness

There are several other general peculiarities about exponential terms that you should at least appreciate.

- Any number raised to the first power equals itself: $5^1 = 5$.
- Any nonzero number raised to the zero power equals one: $5^0 = 1$.
- Raising a negative number to an even power results in a positive number: $(-2)^4 = 16$.
- Raising a negative number to an odd power results in a negative number: $(-2)^5 = -32$.
- Raising a fraction between 0 and 1 to a power greater than one results in a smaller number: $\left(\dfrac{1}{2}\right)^2 = \dfrac{1}{2} \times \dfrac{1}{2} = \dfrac{1}{4}$.
- Finding a root of a fraction between 0 and 1 results in a greater number: $\sqrt{\dfrac{1}{4}} = \dfrac{\sqrt{1}}{\sqrt{4}} = \dfrac{1}{2}$.

Comparing Exponential Terms

Comparing two exponential terms is easy if all of the numbers are positive and the two terms have the same base. Just by looking, you can determine that 3^5 is greater than 3^4, because 5 is greater than 4. So what happens when the bases are different?

Quantity A	Quantity B
64^5	16^8

- ○ Quantity A is greater.
- ○ Quantity B is greater.
- ○ The two quantities are equal.
- ○ The relationship cannot be determined from the information given.

Here's How to Crack It

Holy smokes! Those two numbers sure look huge, don't they? And they are, but lucky for you their exact value isn't important. All you have to do is compare them. So resist the temptation to plug $64 \times 64 \times 64 \times 64 \times 64$ into your calculator. That's exactly what ETS wants you to do, because it's clumsy and time-consuming. The way to improve your math score is to recognize patterns that *save* time.

So which number is greater? Is it Quantity A, which has the greater base? Or is it Quantity B, which has the greater exponent? Find out by first looking for common bases.

Both 16 and 64 are multiples of 4. In fact, $16 = 4 \times 4$, or 4^2, and $64 = 4 \times 4 \times 4$, or 4^3. Therefore, you can rewrite each of the numbers above using 4 as the common base, and if you apply your newfound knowledge of exponential rules, the comparison becomes much more apparent:

$$64^5 = (4^3)^5 = 4^{3 \times 5} = 4^{15}$$

$$16^8 = (4^2)^8 = 4^{2 \times 8} = 4^{16}$$

Do you care how much either of those two quantities is? Absolutely not. Because all the numbers are positive, it must be true that 4 raised to the greater power is the greater number. Therefore, the answer is (B).

Negative Exponents

Any number raised to a negative exponent can be rewritten in reciprocal form with a positive exponent: $x^{-3} = \dfrac{1}{x^3}$, so $8^{-3} = \dfrac{1}{8^3} = \dfrac{1}{512}$. You can analyze a Quant Comp question that involves negative exponents in much the same way.

Quantity A	Quantity B
27^{-4}	9^{-8}

○ Quantity A is greater.

○ Quantity B is greater.

○ The two quantities are equal.

○ The relationship cannot be determined from the information given.

Here's How to Crack It

Because 27 and 9 are both multiples of 3, you can rewrite each quantity using 3 as the common base.

$$27^{-4} = (3^3)^{-4} = 3^{3 \times -4} = 3^{-12}$$

$$9^{-8} = (3^2)^{-8} = 3^{2 \times -8} = 3^{-16}$$

Again, you don't care about the actual values of these numbers, which are very, very small. All you need to do is compare the exponents: Because −12 is greater than −16, the answer is (A).

Scientific Notation

In real life, the chief purpose of exponents is to express humongous or teeny-tiny numbers conveniently. The sciences are chock full of these sorts of numbers—such as Avogadro's number (6.022×10^{23}), which helps chemistry students determine the molecular weight of each element in the periodic table. On the GRE, you probably won't see Avogadro's number, but you may well see a number expressed in scientific notation. Scientific notation is basically a number multiplied by 10 raised to a positive or negative power.

Scientific notation merely serves to make unwieldy numbers a little more manageable. If you see one on the GRE, just remember these rules:

- If the exponent is positive, then move the decimal point that many spaces to the right (6.022×10^{23} = 602,200,000,000,000,000,000,000); and
- If the exponent is negative, then move the decimal point that many spaces to the left (4.5×10^{-15} = 0.0000000000000045).

Fractional Exponents

Any number raised to a fractional exponent can be rewritten as a root: $x^{\frac{1}{3}} = \sqrt[3]{x}$ (or "the cube root of x"), so $8^{\frac{1}{3}} = \sqrt[3]{8} = 2$.

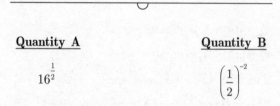

Quantity A	Quantity B
$16^{\frac{1}{2}}$	$\left(\dfrac{1}{2}\right)^{-2}$

○ Quantity A is greater.

○ Quantity B is greater.

○ The two quantities are equal.

○ The relationship cannot be determined from the information given.

Here's How to Crack It

Quantity A can be rewritten as $\sqrt{16}$, which equals 4. Quantity B is a little trickier, but you can figure it out if you follow a few of the rules we've discussed in this chapter.

$$\left(\frac{1}{2}\right)^{-2} = \frac{1}{\left(\frac{1}{2}\right)^2} = \frac{1}{\frac{1}{4}} = 1 \times \frac{4}{1} = 4$$

Both quantities are equal to 4, so the answer is (C).

What's that? Never heard of roots? Well, roots are covered in the next section, right after the quick quiz.

Exponents Quick Quiz

Question 1 of 4

What is the product of $2a^3$ and $5a^7$?

- ○ $7a^{10}$
- ○ $7a^{21}$
- ○ $10a^{10}$
- ○ $10a^{21}$
- ○ $14a^{15}$

Question 2 of 4

Quantity A	**Quantity B**
$200x^{295}$	$10x^{294}$

- ○ Quantity A is greater.
- ○ Quantity B is greater.
- ○ The two quantities are equal.
- ○ The relationship cannot be determined from the information given.

Quantity A	**Quantity B**
$3^{-2} + 4^{-2}$	$\left(\dfrac{5}{12}\right)^2$

○ Quantity A is greater.

○ Quantity B is greater.

○ The two quantities are equal.

○ The relationship cannot be determined from the information given.

Question 4 of 4

Which of the following is equivalent to $144^{\frac{1}{2}} \div 2^2$?

○ $27^{\frac{1}{3}}$

○ $2^3 \times 3^2$

○ $64^{\frac{1}{6}}$

○ $8^{\frac{1}{3}} + 4^{\frac{1}{2}}$

○ $4^{\frac{1}{2}} \times 16^{\frac{1}{2}}$

Explanations for Exponents Quick Quiz

1. Multiply the coefficients first: $2 \times 5 = 10$. When you multiply the exponential terms, add 3 and 7 to get 10. The combined term is $10a^{10}$, and the answer is (C).

2. This is a tricky one, because it looks like Quantity A will always be greater due to the greater exponent and greater coefficient. If x is negative, however, it's a different story. Because -1 to any odd power is negative and -1 to any even power is positive, Quantity B is greater when $x = -1$. The answer is (D).

3. Quantity A translates to $\dfrac{1}{3^2} + \dfrac{1}{4^2}$, or $\dfrac{1}{9} + \dfrac{1}{16}$. You can use the Bowtie to add these and get $\dfrac{25}{144}$, which happens to equal $\left(\dfrac{5}{12}\right)^2$. The answer is (C).

4. An exponent of $\frac{1}{2}$ is equivalent to a square root, so you can rewrite the term as $\sqrt{144} \div 4$, which equals $12 \div 4$, or 3. An exponent of $\frac{1}{3}$ is equivalent to a cube root, and because 3 is the cube root of 27, the answer is (A).

ROOTS

A square root is denoted by a *radical sign*, the funny little check mark with an adjoining roof: $\sqrt{}$. The number inside the house is called a *radicand*.

Square roots can cause a lot of confusion and despair because it can be hard to remember when you can combine them and when you can't. As a result, you see people adding square roots like this:

$$\text{WRONG: } \sqrt{4} + \sqrt{9} = \sqrt{13}$$

This is absolutely wrong, and it's easy to prove it: $\sqrt{4} = 2$ and $\sqrt{9} = 3$, so the left side of the equation can be rewritten as $2 + 3$, or 5, and 5 is equal to $\sqrt{25}$, not $\sqrt{13}$.

If you ever find yourself in a jam when it comes to remembering square-root rules, try fiddling around with some numbers as we did in that last example. You'll start to see which manipulations of square roots work and which don't, and that will help you understand the rules more easily.

Perfect Squares

If the square root of a number is an integer, then that number is known as a *perfect square*. Perfect squares will come up a lot in the rest of this chapter, and it pays to be able to recognize them on sight. The first ten perfect squares are 1, 4, 9, 16, 25, 36, 49, 64, 81, and 100 (and it couldn't hurt if you added the next five—121, 144, 169, 196, and 225—to your list).

Knowing your perfect squares is a great tool to use when estimating. Because 70 is between 64 and 81, for example, it must be true that $\sqrt{70}$ is between 8 and 9, because $\sqrt{64} = 8$ and $\sqrt{81} = 9$.

The on-screen calculator can find any square root you're unsure of, but get in the habit of being able to estimate square roots for numbers up to 200. It'll save you time, since you won't have to keep bringing up the calculator, and it'll help you realize when you've made a mistake entering something in your calculator. Feel free to go back to the calculator if you're not sure, but learn those perfect squares.

How many even integers are there between $\sqrt{50}$ and $\sqrt{150}$?

$\bigcirc$ 3

$\bigcirc$ 5

$\bigcirc$ 10

$\bigcirc$ 50

$\bigcirc$ 100

Here's How to Crack It

7^2 is 49, and 8^2 is 64. The $\sqrt{50}$, therefore, is a number just greater than 7 but much less than 8. As you know, 12^2 is 144, and 13^2 is 169. The $\sqrt{150}$, therefore, is a number just greater than 12 but a lot less than 13. Count the even integers between 7 and 12, including the 12: 8, 10, 12. The answer is (A).

Multiplying Roots

Multiplying two square roots is a rather straightforward process; just multiply the numbers and put the result under a new square root sign.

$$\sqrt{15} \times \sqrt{3} = \sqrt{15 \times 3} = \sqrt{45}$$

If there are numbers both outside and inside the square-root sign, multiply them separately and then put the pieces together.

$$6\sqrt{15} \times 2\sqrt{3} = (6 \times 2) \times \sqrt{15 \times 3} = 12\sqrt{45}$$

Dividing Roots

Dividing roots involves much the same process as multiplying roots, but in reverse. When you divide roots, it's often helpful to set the division up as a fraction, like this:

$$\sqrt{15} \div \sqrt{3} = \frac{\sqrt{15}}{\sqrt{3}} = \sqrt{\frac{15}{3}} = \sqrt{5}$$

Again, if you have numbers both outside and inside the square root sign, divide them separately, like this:

$$6\sqrt{15} \div 2\sqrt{3} = \frac{6\sqrt{15}}{2\sqrt{3}} = \frac{6}{2} \times \frac{\sqrt{15}}{\sqrt{3}} = 3 \times \sqrt{\frac{15}{3}} = 3\sqrt{5}$$

Simplifying Roots

If the radicand has a factor that is a perfect square, the term can be simplified. The GRE doesn't ask you to do this very often, but it pays to have the ability, just in case your answer is not in its simplest form but the answer choices are.

When the two expressions were multiplied in the above example, the answer included the term $\sqrt{45}$. Because $45 = 9 \times 5$, and 9 is a perfect square, you can simplify the expression using factoring and the rules of multiplication that you just learned. In fact, you just follow the directions in reverse order.

$$\sqrt{45} = \sqrt{9 \times 5} = \sqrt{9} \times \sqrt{5} = 3\sqrt{5}$$

If there's already a number sitting outside the square-root sign, you will need to combine it with the simplified term like this:

$$12\sqrt{45} = 12 \times \sqrt{9 \times 5} = 12 \times \sqrt{9} \times \sqrt{5} = 12 \times 3 \times \sqrt{5} = 36\sqrt{5}$$

Adding and Subtracting Roots

You can add and subtract square roots just like variables as long as they have the same radicands.

$$5\sqrt{13} + 3\sqrt{13} = 8\sqrt{13}$$

$$9\sqrt{6} - 2\sqrt{6} = 7\sqrt{6}$$

If the radicands are different, however, you can't do a thing with them; $\sqrt{6} + \sqrt{5}$, for example, cannot be combined or simplified. The only way you can hope to combine two square roots that have different radicands is if you factor them to find a common radicand. The key to factoring is to determine if the radicands have factors that are perfect squares.

For example, look at the expression $2\sqrt{12} + \sqrt{75}$:

$$2\sqrt{12} = 2 \times \sqrt{4 \times 3} = 2 \times \sqrt{4} \times \sqrt{3} = 2 \times 2 \times \sqrt{3} = 4\sqrt{3}$$

$$\sqrt{75} = \sqrt{25 \times 3} = \sqrt{25} \times \sqrt{3} = 5 \times \sqrt{3} = 5\sqrt{3}$$

Therefore, $2\sqrt{12} + \sqrt{75}$ can be rewritten as $4\sqrt{3} + 5\sqrt{3}$, which equals $9\sqrt{3}$.

Rationalizing Roots

There's a rule in lots of moldy old math textbooks that says you have to rationalize a square root in the denominator of a fraction. You should be able to recognize equivalent values of fractions with square roots in them, especially since answer choices on the GRE are most commonly in rationalized form. (This is especially important for geometry questions, as we'll discuss in Chapter 8.) In order to rationalize a fraction with a square root in its denominator, you need to multiply both the numerator and the denominator by the square root.

To rationalize $\dfrac{1}{\sqrt{2}}$, for example, watch what happens when you multiply the top and bottom by $\sqrt{2}$.

$$\frac{1 \times \sqrt{2}}{\sqrt{2} \times \sqrt{2}} = \frac{1 \times \sqrt{2}}{2} = \frac{\sqrt{2}}{2}$$

See? The denominator is now an integer, and everything's all nice and legal.

Roots Quick Quiz

Question 1 of 4

$5\sqrt{18} \times 2\sqrt{10} =$

○ $20\sqrt{7}$

○ $30\sqrt{2}$

○ $40\sqrt{3}$

○ $50\sqrt{6}$

○ $60\sqrt{5}$

Question 2 of 4

$12\sqrt{60} \div 2\sqrt{5} =$

○ $6\sqrt{55}$

○ $12\sqrt{3}$

○ $18\sqrt{2}$

○ $60\sqrt{5}$

○ $240\sqrt{3}$

Quantity A	**Quantity B**
The number of multiples of 3 between $\sqrt{100}$ and $\sqrt{1,000}$	21

○ Quantity A is greater.

○ Quantity B is greater.

○ The two quantities are equal.

○ The relationship cannot be determined from the information given.

Question 4 of 4

$3\sqrt{18} + 2\sqrt{50} =$

○ $10\sqrt{17}$

○ $12\sqrt{17}$

○ 15

○ $19\sqrt{2}$

○ 180

Explanations for Roots Quick Quiz

1. Multiply the numbers outside the square-root sign first:

   $5 \times 2 = 10$. Next, multiply the radicands: $18 \times 10 = 180$. The

   combined expression is $10\sqrt{180}$, but you're not done. The great-

   est perfect square that is a factor of 180 is 36, so factor it out:

   $\sqrt{180} = \sqrt{36 \times 5} = \sqrt{36} \times \sqrt{5} = 6\sqrt{5}$. The new expression is

   $10 \times 6\sqrt{5}$, which combines to $60\sqrt{5}$. The answer is (E).

2. Divide the coefficients first: $12 \div 2 = 6$. Now you can divide the radicands to get a new one: $\sqrt{60} \div \sqrt{5} = \sqrt{\dfrac{60}{5}} = \sqrt{12}$, which, when simplified, becomes $2\sqrt{3}$. The new expression is $6 \times 2\sqrt{3}$, which combines to $12\sqrt{3}$. The answer is (B).

3. The $\sqrt{100}$ is 10. Use a calculator to find that $\sqrt{1,000}$ is a number between 31 and 32. Now count the multiples of 3: 12, 15, 18, 21, 24, 27, and 30. There are seven. The answer is (B).

4. You can't do a thing until you convert the terms so that they have the same radicand. The first term, $3\sqrt{18}$, can be simplified to $3 \times 3\sqrt{2}$, or $9\sqrt{2}$. The second term, $2\sqrt{50}$, can be rewritten as $2 \times 5\sqrt{2}$, or $10\sqrt{2}$. Now, you can add the terms, which combine to $19\sqrt{2}$. The answer is (D).

This was a long chapter, chock full of mathematical goodness. To see how well you retained it, try these questions and review the answers that immediately follow. We'll see you over in the next chapter, which tells you how much you should know about algebra—and how little of it you should use.

Math Fundamentals Drill

Review and test your new skills on the nuts and bolts of GRE math in the following drill. Remember to work carefully!

What is the sum of the distinct prime factors of 36 ?

- ○ 2
- ○ 5
- ○ 6
- ○ 8
- ○ 10

If a certain fraction with a numerator of 12 has a value of 0.25, then the denominator is

- ○ 3
- ○ 12
- ○ 25
- ○ 48
- ○ 300

If 5 less than $\dfrac{40}{x}$ is –1, then $x =$

- ○ –10
- ○ –4
- ○ 4
- ○ 8
- ○ 10

The numbers that correspond to points A, B, and C on the number line are $-\dfrac{5}{3}$, $-\dfrac{2}{3}$, and, $\dfrac{2}{3}$, respectively. Which of the following values fall between the average (arithmetic mean) of A and B and the average of B and C ?

Indicate <u>all</u> such values.

- ☐ –1
- ☐ $-\dfrac{2}{3}$
- ☐ 0
- ☐ $\dfrac{1}{2}$
- ☐ 1

If $\dfrac{0.0017}{x} > 1$, then each of the following could be the value of x EXCEPT

- ○ 0.0011
- ○ 0.0013
- ○ 0.0015
- ○ 0.0017
- ○ 0.0091

$27^0 + 36^0 =$

○   0

○   2

○   9

○   15

○   63

How many positive integers that are multiples of 3 are also divisors of 42 ?

○ One

○ Two

○ Three

○ Four

○ Five

In a certain hardware store, 3 percent of the lawnmowers need new labels. If the price per label is \$4 and the total cost for new lawnmower labels is \$96, how many lawnmowers are in the hardware store?

○ 1,600

○   800

○   240

○   120

○   24

Quantity A	**Quantity B**
$15 - 18 \div (7 - 4)^2 \times 8 + 2$	1

○ Quantity A is greater.

○ Quantity B is greater.

○ The two quantities are equal.

○ The relationship cannot be determined from the information given.

What is the greatest possible value of integer n if $6^n < 36^{10}$?

○   6

○   9

○ 12

○ 15

○ 19

5×10^3 is what percent of $\frac{1}{5} \times 10^2$?

○   2,500%

○   4,900%

○ 20,000%

○ 24,900%

○ 25,000%

Quantity A	**Quantity B**
$\dfrac{9^{17} - 9^{15}}{12^2}$	$9^{14} \times 5$

○ Quantity A is greater.

○ Quantity B is greater.

○ The two quantities are equal.

○ The relationship cannot be determined from the information given.

A is a positive odd number less than 5. Which of the following could be the value of $\dfrac{(10 + A)}{2} + 3$?

○ 9

○ 9.5

○ 10

○ 10.5

○ 11

In the number 4,A34, A represents a digit. For which of the following values of A is 4,A34 a multiple of 3 ?

○ 2

○ 3

○ 4

○ 6

○ 9

At a certain animal shelter, the previous annual budget for cat food was $3,900 and the current cat food budget is 125 percent greater than the previous budget. What is the amount, in dollars, of the current annual cat food budget?

Which of the following are true statements?

I. $\quad 5^3 \times 5^{\frac{1}{3}} = 1$

II. $\quad 5 \times \sqrt{5^{-2}} = 1$

III. $\quad \sqrt{5} \times \dfrac{\sqrt{5}}{5} = 1$

○ I only

○ II only

○ III only

○ I and II only

○ II and III only

Quantity A	**Quantity B**
$\sqrt{16 + 121}$	15

○ Quantity A is greater.

○ Quantity B is greater.

○ The two quantities are equal.

○ The relationship cannot be determined from the information given.

If 15% of j is greater than 55% of k, and $325 < k < 375$, then which of the following are possible values for j ?

Indicate <u>all</u> such values.

☐   57

☐   332

☐   782

☐ 1,087

☐ 1,192

☐ 1,314

How many more integers between 552 and 652 are divisible by 3 than are divisible by 4 ?

○   1

○   6

○   8

○   9

○   12

EXPLANATIONS FOR MATH FUNDAMENTALS DRILL

1. **B**

   To solve this question, list out the prime factors of 36. The correct factorization is $(2 \times 2 \times 3 \times 3)$. The question asks for the sum of the distinct prime factors. Distinct means different, so the distinct prime factors of 36 are 2 and 3. The sum of these two numbers is 5. The correct answer is (B).

2. **D**

   The numerator is the number on the top of a fraction, so this question can be rewritten as $\frac{12}{x} = 0.25$. To solve for x, convert the decimal 0.25 into a fraction and rewrite the equation to reveal that $\frac{12}{x} = \frac{1}{4}$. Cross-multiply to find that $x = 48$. The correct answer is (D).

3. **E**

   Rewrite this question as an equation to find that $\frac{40}{x} - 5 = -1$. Now, solve for x. Add 5 to both sides of the equation to yield $\frac{40}{x} = 4$. Clear the variable from the denominator by multiplying both sides of the equation by x to find that $40 = 4x$ and divide both sides of the equation by 4 so that $x = 10$. The correct answer is (E).

4. **A and B**

   Find the average of A and B and the average of B and C. Because the average is found by adding together the relevant numbers and dividing by the number of items, the average of A and B is $\dfrac{\left(-\frac{5}{3}\right) + \left(-\frac{2}{3}\right)}{2}$. Solve to find the average of A and B is $-\frac{7}{6}$. Next, do the same for B and C to find an average of 0. Therefore, the correct answer choices will fall between $-\frac{7}{6}$ and 0. The correct answer is (A), -1, and (B), $-\frac{2}{3}$.

5. **E**

   If $\frac{0.0017}{x} > 1$, then the value of x must be less than 0.0017. Because this is an EXCEPT question, the correct answer will make the value of the fraction less than 1, so the value of x will be greater than 0.0017. To begin this problem, isolate the variable x by multiplying both sides by x to get $0.0017 > x$. Next, make the decimal 0.0017 easier to look at by moving the decimal point four places to the right to create a whole number and find that $17 > x$. Now compare the answer choices by also moving the decimal points in the answer choices four places to the right. Look for the answer choice that makes the inequality false because the value of x is greater than 17. Since 17 is not greater than 91, the correct answer is (E).

6. **B**

Any number raised to the power of zero is equal to one. Therefore, this question simply asks you to solve $1 + 1$. The correct answer is (B).

7. **D**

List out the divisors (also known as factors) of 42. These are the integers that can multiply to create 42, such as 42×1, 21×2, 14×3, and 7×6. Of these, only 3, 6, 21, and 42 are multiples of three. The correct answer is (D).

8. **B**

To find how many lawnmowers need new labels, divide $96 by $4 to get 24. These lawnmowers account for 3% of the total lawnmowers in the store. The question "24 is 3% of what total?" can be written as the equation $24 = \left(\dfrac{3}{100}\right)x$. Solve for x to find 800. The correct answer is (B).

9. **C**

This question is focused on order of operations, so it is important to keep PEMDAS in mind. Since $7 - 4$ is written in parentheses, it is the first part of Quantity A to solve. Next, square it to get 3^2, or 9. The next part of PEMDAS is multiplication and division, so moving from left to right, solve $18 \div 9 \times 8$ and get 16. Finally, do the addition and subtraction operations: $15 - 16 + 2$. This equals 1. Therefore, the quantities are equal and the correct answer is (C).

10. **E**

To best compare both sides of the inequality, find a common base. 6^2 is 36, so 6 makes a good common base. 6^2 raised to the 10th power is 6^{20}. The inequality can now read $6^n < 6^{20}$, making 19 the greatest possible value of n. The correct answer is (E).

11. **E**

The question can be rewritten as the mathematical equation $5 \times 10^3 = \dfrac{p}{100} \times \dfrac{1}{5} \times 10^2$.
This simplifies to $5{,}000 = \left(\dfrac{p}{100}\right)20$. Solve for p to find that $p = 25{,}000$. The correct answer is (E).

12. **C**

There are exponents with great numbers, so factor. Factor out 9^{15} in the numerator of Quantity A and rewrite the expression as $\dfrac{9^{15}(9^2 - 1)}{12^2} = \dfrac{9^{15}(80)}{12^2}$. Now work with the denominator of Quantity A, which can be rewritten as $3^2 \times 4^2$. Because $3^2 = 9$, cancel out one of the nines from the numerator and rewrite the equation as $\dfrac{9^{14}(80)}{4^2}$. Because $4^2 = 16$, and $\dfrac{80}{16} = 5$, rewrite Quantity A as $9^{14}(5)$. This is equal to Quantity B. The correct answer is (C).

13. **B**

Because A is a positive odd number less than 5, it can only be either 1 or 3. If $A = 1$, then $\dfrac{10+1}{2} + 3 = 8.5$, which is not an answer choice. If $A = 3$, then $\dfrac{10+3}{2} + 3 = 9.5$, which is (B). Therefore, the correct answer is (B).

14. **C**

A good technique to find a multiple of 3 is to ensure that all of the digits within a number add up to a multiple of 3. Add up the known digits in the number, so $4 + 3 + 4 = 11$. The only answer choice, when added to 11, that creates a multiple of 3 is (C). Therefore, the correct answer is (C).

15. **8,775**

To find 125% of \$3,900, set up the equation $x = \left(\dfrac{125}{100}\right) 3,900$. Solve for x to get 4,875. The question says that the new budget is 125% greater than the previous budget, so the correct answer is \$4,875 + \$3,900 = \$8,775.

16. **E**

Look at each of the statements separately and use Process of Elimination. For Roman numeral I, use the Multiply-Add rule of exponents to find that $5^3 \times 5^{\frac{1}{3}} = 5^{3+\frac{1}{3}} = 5^{\frac{10}{3}}$. This is greater than 1, so Roman numeral I is not true. Eliminate (A) and (D), as they contain Roman numeral I. For Roman numeral II, use the rules of exponents to find that $\sqrt{5^{-2}} = \sqrt{\dfrac{1}{5^2}} = \dfrac{\sqrt{1}}{\sqrt{5^2}} = \dfrac{1}{5}$. Therefore, Roman numeral II can be rewritten as $5 \times \dfrac{1}{5} = 1$, which is true. Eliminate (C) because it does not include Roman numeral II. Roman numeral III is true because $\sqrt{5} \times \dfrac{\sqrt{5}}{5} = \dfrac{\sqrt{5} \times \sqrt{5}}{5} = \dfrac{5}{5} = 1$. Therefore, the correct answer is (E).

17. **B**

Combine the values in Quantity A to establish that Quantity A is $\sqrt{137}$. Recognize that $\sqrt{137}$ is less than $\sqrt{144}$, which is equal to 12. Therefore, Quantity A is not greater than 12 and Quantity B is greater. The correct answer is (B).

18. **E and F**

Find the range of values for 55% of k. If $k = 325$, then 55% of k is $\dfrac{55}{100}(325) = 178.75$. If $k = 375$, then 55% of k is $\dfrac{55}{100}(375) = 206.25$. Therefore, $178.75 < 55\%$ of $k < 206.25$. The problem also states that 55% of k is also 15% of j, so 15% of j is between 178.75 and 206.25. To solve for the least value of j, set up the proportion $\dfrac{15}{100} = \dfrac{178.75}{j}$ and $j = 1,191.67$. To find the greatest value of j, set up the proportion

$\dfrac{15}{100} = \dfrac{206.25}{j}$ and $j = 1{,}375$. Therefore, $1{,}191.67 < j < 1{,}375$. The only answer choices that fall between those values are (E) and (F), so the correct answer is (E) and (F).

19. **D**

While it is possible to list out the consecutive multiples of 3 and then list out the multiples of 4, it is easier to just see that there is a difference of 100 between the two numbers in the problem. 100 divided by 3 is just over 33. Therefore, there are 33 multiples of 3 between 552 and 652. Therefore, there are 33 numbers divisible by three that fall between 552 and 652. Do the same thing with multiples of 4, and find that $100 \div 4 = 25$.

Since 652 is the hundredth number when counting up from 552, and it is divisible by 4, it also happens to be the 25th number in the list of numbers divisible by 4. However, the question asks about numbers between 552 and 652; therefore, 652 should not count as one of those numbers. Subtract 1 from the 25 multiples of 4 to get 24. The difference between 33 and 24 is 9. Choice (D) is the correct answer.

Chapter 4
The Basics of
Algebra

ALGEBRA

If you're planning to attend graduate school, you've probably had some sort of algebraic training in the dark reaches of your past. Algebra is the fine art of determining how variable quantities relate to each other within complex functions, and it dates back more than 3,000 years to ancient Babylon.

If it seems like it's been 3,000 years since you last studied algebra, or even if you flunked algebra last year, fear not. This chapter is devoted to reintroducing you to the basic algebraic operations that you will need to execute on test day.

In the next chapter, we will outline for you ways to subvert the rules and solve algebraic problems with strategies designed to reduce the amount of algebra you have to do. But, it is impossible, and not in your best interests, to ignore algebra altogether. And even on problems that algebra can be subverted, many times these problems can be made easier to work with after applying some basic algebra work.

Know the Lingo

Any letter in an algebraic term or equation is called a *variable*; you don't know what its numerical value is. It varies. Until you solve an equation, a variable is an unknown quantity. Any number that's directly in front of a variable is called a *coefficient*, and the coefficient is a constant multiplied by that variable. For example, $3x$ means "three times x," whatever x is.

Combining Like Terms

If two terms have the same variables or series of variables in them, they're referred to as *like terms*. You can combine them like this:

$$6a + 4a = 10a$$

$$13x - 7x = 6x$$

For example, if you have six apples in one hand and four in the other, you have a total of 10 apples (and a pair of humongous hands).

Solving an Equation

Whenever a variable appears in an equation and you have to find the value of the variable, you have to "isolate" it. To isolate a variable, you must use mathematical operations to put all the terms that contain the variable on one side of the equals sign and all terms that don't contain the variable on the other. Then you'll need to manipulate the side of the equation with the variable to find the value the question asks for.

In order to solve an equation, you must rely on the following paramount rule of algebraic manipulation:

> You can do anything you want to an equation as long as you do exactly the same thing to both sides.

If $4x - 5 = 19$, what is the value of x?

$$\boxed{}$$

Here's How to Crack It

In order to get all variable terms on one side of the equals sign and all constant terms on the other, add 5 to both sides. The new equation is

$$4x = 24$$

Now manipulate the new equation to isolate the variable by dividing both sides of the equation by 4.

$$\frac{4x}{4} = \frac{24}{4}$$
$$x = 6$$

Always Check

After manipulating an equation using algebra on the GRE, it always pays to check your work by replacing the variable with the value you found for the variable. Let's do it.

$$4(6) - 5 = 19$$

$$24 - 5 = 19$$

$$19 = 19. \text{ Check.}$$

Keep in mind that solutions to equations don't always have to be integers, so don't be concerned if your result is a fraction. As long as it works when you plug it back into the equation, you're fine.

If $4m + 7 = 16 - 2m$, then what is the value of m ?

Here's How to Crack It

Get all the variables onto the left side of the equation by adding $2m$ to both sides; then move all the constants to the right side by subtracting 7 from both sides.

$$4m + 7 \; (+ \, 2m) = 16 - 2m \; (+ \, 2m)$$

$$6m + 7 = 16$$

$$6m + 7 \; (- \, 7) = 16 \; (- \, 7)$$

$$6m = 9$$

Now isolate the variable by dividing both sides of the equation by 6.

$$\frac{6m}{6} = \frac{9}{6}$$

$$m = \frac{9}{6} = \frac{3}{2}$$

Check your work just to make sure.

$$4\left(\frac{3}{2}\right) + 7 = 16 - 2\left(\frac{3}{2}\right)$$

$$\frac{12}{2} + 7 = 16 - \frac{6}{2}$$

$$6 + 7 = 16 - 3$$

$$13 = 13$$

Solving an Equation Quick Quiz

Solve for x in each of the following equations:

1. $2x - 5 = 11$
2. $3 - 5x = 13$
3. $12x + 4 = 4x$
4. $8x - 9 = x - 2$
5. $\dfrac{x}{2} + 5 = -9$

Explanations for Solving an Equation Quick Quiz

1. Add 5 to both sides of the equation and then divide both sides of the equation by 2 to find that $x = 8$.

2. Subtract 3 from both sides and then divide both sides of the equation by –5 to find that $x = -2$.

3. Subtract 12x from both sides of the equation to find that $4 = -8x$. Divide both sides of the equation by –8 to find that $x = -\dfrac{1}{2}$.

4. Subtract x from both sides of the equation to find that $7x - 9 = -2$. Now add 9 to both sides of the equation to find that $7x = 7$. Divide both sides of the equation by 7 to find that $x = 1$.

5. Subtract 5 from both sides of the equation and then multiply both sides of the equation by 2 to find that $x = -28$.

Inequalities

Inequality symbols are used to convey that one number is greater than or less than another.

The symbols used in inequalities are as follows:

> means "is greater than"
< means "is less than"
≥ means "is greater than or equal to"
≤ means "is less than or equal to"

Even though the two sides of an inequality aren't equal, you can manipulate them in much the same way as you do the expressions in regular equations when you have to solve for a variable.

If $5b - 3 > 2b + 9$, then which of the following must be true?

- ○ $b > -4$
- ○ $b > 2$
- ○ $b < 2$
- ○ $b > 4$
- ○ $b < 4$

Here's How to Crack It

Adding and subtracting take place as usual, like this:

$$5b - 3 > 2b + 9$$

$$3b - 3 > 9$$

$$3b > 12$$

At this point, because the coefficient of b is positive, divide both sides by 3 and get the final range of values for b.

$$\frac{3b}{3} > \frac{12}{3}$$

$$b > 4$$

To check your solution for inequality problems, try a number that is greater than the value found for the variable. In this case $b > 4$, so replace the variable with a number such as 5 and check the solution.

$$5(5) - 3 > 2(5) + 9$$

$$25 - 3 > 10 + 9$$

$$22 > 19$$

Flip That Sign!

The only difference between solving equalities and inequalities is this one very important rule:

> Whenever you multiply or divide both sides of an inequality by a negative number, you must flip the inequality sign.

Try a problem.

If $5 - 11p \leq 9$, then which of the following could be the value of p ?

Indicate <u>all</u> such values.

- ☐ −15
- ☐ −10
- ☐ −2
- ☐ 0
- ☐ 1
- ☐ 8
- ☐ 24

Here's How to Crack It

Manipulate the problem as you would a regular equality by subtracting 5 from both sides of the equation to find that

$$5 - 11p \leq 9$$

$$-11p \leq 4$$

To isolate the variable, you must divide both sides of the inequality by −11. Because you are dividing by a negative number, make sure to flip the sign.

$$\frac{-11p}{-11} \leq \frac{4}{-11}$$

$$p \geq -\frac{4}{11}$$

Any value that is greater than $-\dfrac{4}{11}$ is a possible value of p, so you should check the box next to 0 and every other box with a number that's greater than zero. See how important that little rule is? If you didn't know about it, you might have picked all the numbers that were less than $-\dfrac{4}{11}$, which would be the exact opposite of the correct answers. And that would have been unfortunate.

———————◯———————

Range of Inequalities

Some GRE questions present two inequalities and ask for the range of possible values when the inequalities are combined through addition, subtraction, multiplication, or division. The range of possible values is the greatest distance between two possible values that satisfy the inequalities. So, answering a question that asks for the range of possible values for two separate inequalities is as easy as finding the least and the greatest possible values and placing those values as a part of an inequality.

To find the least and greatest possible values, you'll need to combine the end ranges of the individual inequalities. Combine the least number for each inequality, the least number of the first inequality with the greatest number of the second inequality, the greatest number of the first inequality with the least number of the second inequality, and the greatest number for each inequality. This will result in four numbers. The range of the combined inequalities will be the difference between the greatest and the least of those four numbers.

———————◯———————

If $-5 \leq a \leq 12$ and $-10 \leq b \leq 25$, which of the following represents all possible values of $a - b$?

◯ $-30 \leq a - b \leq 22$

◯ $-30 \leq a - b \leq 5$

◯ $-13 \leq a - b \leq 5$

◯ $5 \leq a - b \leq 22$

◯ $5 \leq a - b \leq 30$

Here's How to Crack It

For the range of a, there are two numbers: -5 and 12. Make sure that each of those numbers combines with each of the two numbers from the range of b.

$$a - b$$
$$(-5) - (-10) = 5$$
$$(-5) - (25) = -30$$
$$(12) - (-10) = 22$$
$$(12) - (25) = -13$$

Notice how each number from a was paired up with each number from b. The least result for $a - b$ is -30, and the greatest is 22. The full range is $-30 \leq a - b \leq 22$, and the correct answer is (A).

Inequalities Quick Quiz

For questions 1–3, find the range of values for x.

1. $3x + 7 > 22$

2. $8 - 3x < 13$

3. $-\dfrac{x}{2} + 2 \geq 5x - 9$

Question 4 of 6

If y is a positive integer and $6y + 9 > 5 + 8y$, then what is the value of y ?

Question 5 of 6

If $5f + 11 \geq 17 + f$ and $7 - 4f > -13$, then f could equal each of the following EXCEPT

○ 1.6

○ 2.4

○ 3.9

○ 4.1

○ 5.3

Question 6 of 6

If $-7 \leq x \leq 5$ and $-15 \leq y \leq 0$, then what is the greatest possible value of xy ?

Explanations for Inequalities Quick Quiz

1.   Subtract 7 from both sides of the inequality and divide both sides by 3 to find that $x > 5$.

2.   Subtract 8 from both sides to find that $-3x < 5$. Now divide both sides of the inequality by -3 and flip the sign to find that $x > -\dfrac{5}{3}$.

3.   Subtract 2 from both sides of the inequality and then multiply both sides by -2, remembering to flip the sign, to find that $x \leq -10x + 22$. Now add $10x$ to both sides to find that $11x \leq 22$. Divide both sides of the inequality by 11 to find that $x \leq 2$.

4.   Solve for the inequality to find that $y < 2$. The only positive integer less than 2 is 1, so y equals 1.

5.   Solve both inequalities. If $5f + 11 \geq 17 + f$, then $f \geq 1.5$, and if $7 - 4f > -13$, then $f < 5$. Therefore, the range is $1.5 \leq f < 5$. The only answer choice that is not in this range is (E).

6.   Solve this problem by determining the greatest value of xy. To do that, multiply the ends of the range for x and the ends of the range for y, looking for the greatest value of xy. The end values for the range of x are -7 and 5. The end values for the range of y are -15 and 0. Multiply these together, two at a time to find that

$(-7) \times (-15) = 105$
$(-7) \times (0) = 0$
$(5) \times (-15) = -75$
$(5) \times (0) = 0$

Therefore, the greatest value of xy is 105.

Quadratics

FOILing and factoring are two important algebraic functions on the GRE. Oftentimes, performing these operations can make a difficult-looking equation much more manageable.

FOIL

When FOILing you combine two binomials, which are algebraic elements that contain two terms, such as $2x + y$, by multiplying the First, Outside, Inside, and Last terms, and then simplify wherever possible. Give it a shot.

––––––––––––––––––––––––––––––

What is the product of $(x - 3)$ and $(2x + 7)$?

- $\bigcirc$ $2x^2 - 21$
- $\bigcirc$ $2x^2 + x - 21$
- $\bigcirc$ $2x^2 + 13x - 21$
- $\bigcirc$ $2x^2 + x + 21$
- $\bigcirc$ $2x^2 - 13x + 21$

Here's How to Crack It

If you're new to FOILing, it helps to line up your products so you can keep track of what you're doing:

Firsts: $x \cdot 2x = 2x^2$

Outsides: $x \cdot 7 = 7x$

Insides: $-3 \cdot 2x = -6x$

Lasts: $-3 \cdot 7 = -21.$

Now combine: $2x^2 + 7x - 6x - 21 = 2x^2 + x - 21.$

So, the correct answer is (B).

––––––––––––––––––––––––––––––

Solving Quadratic Equations

When quadratics and equals signs come together, the result is a quadratic equation. On the GRE, quadratics are usually set equal to zero, and you'll have find an equation's solutions, or roots, by factoring.

If $x > 0$ and $x^2 - 5x - 6 = 0$, then what is the value of x ?

Here's How to Crack It

To answer this question, its necessary to find the value of x. When dealing with a quadratic, this is called finding the roots of the equation. There is more than one possible root for a quadratic equation, so find them both by factoring the original equation. Factoring is basically the opposite of FOILing, and it usually requires a little trial and error. In this case, the challenge lies in finding two numbers whose sum is –5 (the middle coefficient) and whose product is –6 (the last term). When you find those numbers, place them inside parentheses with the variable x.

$$x^2 - 5x - 6 = 0$$

$$(x \quad)(x \quad) = 0$$

$$(x - 6)(x + 1) = 0$$

In order for the product of two numbers to be 0, one of them must be 0. So set both factors equal to 0 and solve for x.

$$x - 6 = 0 \qquad x + 1 = 0$$

$$x = 6 \qquad x = -1$$

Check your answers to make sure you didn't make any unfortunate slip-ups.

$$6^2 - 5(6) - 6 = 0 \qquad\qquad (-1)^2 - 5(-1) - 6 = 0$$

$$36 - 30 - 6 = 0 \qquad\qquad 1 + 5 - 6 = 0$$

$$0 = 0 \qquad\qquad 0 = 0$$

Now, 6 and –1 are the roots of the equation, but the question asks for only the positive root. So the answer is 6.

Common Quadratics

As basic as FOILing is, there are a few very common multiplications of binomials that come up so frequently that you're better off memorizing them. The writers of standardized tests like them a lot, because they're great for making easier problems seem a lot more difficult.

$$(x + y)^2 = x^2 + 2xy + y^2$$

$$(x - y)^2 = x^2 - 2xy + y^2$$

$$(x + y)(x - y) = x^2 - y^2$$

Knowledge of the last formula—which is commonly referred to as a "difference of squares"—is especially useful if you come across a question that looks like this:

If $\dfrac{x^2 - 9}{x - 3} = 7$, then what is the value of x?

Here's How to Crack It

Rather than resort to cross-multiplication here, recognize that the fraction on the left is in the form of $\dfrac{x^2 - y^2}{x - y}$; in this case, y is the constant. Use the difference of squares to simplify the numerator. Because $\dfrac{x^2 - 9}{x - 3} = \dfrac{(x + 3)(x - 3)}{(x - 3)}$. Cancel out $x - 3$ from both the numerator and denominator leaving only $x + 3$. Now, the original question asks for the value of x if $x + 3 = 7$, so $x = 4$.

Here's another one on which a little quadratic knowledge can save you some time.

Quantity A	**Quantity B**
$\dfrac{836^2 - 835^2}{836 + 835}$	1

○ Quantity A is greater.

○ Quantity B is greater.

○ The two quantities are equal.

○ The relationship cannot be determined from the information given.

Here's How to Crack It
The numerator of Quantity A is a difference of squares, so it can be rewritten as $(836 + 835)(836 - 835)$. Cancel out $836 + 835$ from both the numerator and denominator of Quantity A. Therefore, the value of Quantity A is $836 - 835 = 1$. The quantities are equal and the correct answer is (C).

Quadratics Quick Quiz

1. If $x^2 - 5x + 6 = 0$, then what are the possible values of x ?

2. If $x^2 + 7x - 18 = 0$, then what are the possible values of x ?

3. If $x^2 - 8x + 15 = 0$, then what are the possible values of x ?

4. $\dfrac{x^2 - 169}{x - 13} = 15$, then what is the value of x ?

5. If $a + b = 5$ and $a^2 + b^2 = 15$, then what is the value of ab ?

Explanations for Quadratics Quick Quiz

1. Because $x^2 - 5x + 6$ can be factored to $(x - 2)(x - 3)$, then the possible values of x are 2 and 3.

2. Because $x^2 + 7x - 18$ can be factored to $(x - 2)(x + 9)$, the two possible values of x are 2 and −9.

3. Since $x^2 - 8x + 15$ can be factored to $(x - 3)(x - 5)$, the two possible values of x are 3 and 5.

4. Because $\dfrac{x^2 - 169}{x - 13} = \dfrac{(x + 13)(x - 13)}{(x - 13)}$, the equation can be rewritten as $x + 13 = 15$. Therefore, $x = 2$.

5. This question makes you think you have to solve for a and b, but you don't. If $a + b = 5$, then $(a + b)^2 = 5^2$, or 25. When you expand the term on the left, $(a + b)^2$ becomes $a^2 + 2ab + b^2$. Rewrite the equation as $a^2 + b^2 + 2ab = 25$; because $a^2 + b^2 = 15$, you can substitute 15 in the equation like this: $15 + 2ab = 25$. Therefore, $2ab = 10$, and $ab = 5$.

Simultaneous Equations

If a single equation has two variables, you can't solve for either one. If $2x + y = 5$, for example, then $x = 2$ and $y = 1$ could be one solution; but $x = 1$ and $y = 3$ could be another. But if you have two distinct equations and two variables, then each variable has only one possible solution.

If a question asks you to find the value of one variable, you can usually add or subtract the equations and solve.

If $2x - 3y = 7$ and $x + 3y = 8$, then what is the value of x?

Here's How to Crack It

To solve a problem with two equations and two variables, stack the equations and look for a way to eliminate one of the variables. Stacking the equations in this problem reveals that adding the two equations together will eliminate y. So, add the two equations and solve for x.

$$
\begin{array}{r}
2x - 3y = 7 \\
+\ \underline{x + 3y = 8} \\
3x + 0y = 15
\end{array}
$$

From here, you can determine that $x = 5$.

When There's Less Work Than You Think

ETS likes to build its simultaneous equation questions to look a lot more daunting and time-consuming than they actually are. Take this problem for example.

If $a + 3b = 10$ and $a - b = 8$, then what is the value of $a + b$?

$$\boxed{}$$

At first glance, you might think you have to solve for a and b individually and then add them together to get your final answer. But that isn't the case.

Here's How to Crack It

Add the two equations together to find a new equation.

$$
\begin{array}{r}
a + 3b = 10 \\
+\ \underline{a - b = 8} \\
2a + 2b = 18
\end{array}
$$

Factor out the 2 from the left side of the equation and divide each side of the equation by 2.

$$2(a + b) = 18$$

$$\frac{2(a + b)}{2} = \frac{18}{2}$$

$$a + b = 9$$

The question asks for the value of $a + b$, so the correct answer is 9.

Simultaneous Equations Quick Quiz

1. If $2x - 3y = 2$ and $x - 5y = -6$, then what is the value of y ?

2. If $3a - b = 200$ and $5a + 2b = 40$, then what is the value of $a - b$?

3. If $4m - 3n = 12$ and $m - 2n = 3$, then $m - n =$

4. At a stationery store, three pens and five notebooks cost a total of $19.02 and two pens and three notebooks cost a total of $11.63. What is the price of one notebook?

Explanations for Simultaneous Equations Quick Quiz

1. Solve for y by stacking the equations and finding a way to eliminate the x's. After stacking, multiply the second equation by -2 so that it becomes $-2x + 10y = 12$. Now, add the equations to eliminate the x's and solve for y.

$$
\begin{array}{r}
2x - 3y = 2 \\
+\ \underline{-2x + 10y = 12} \\
7y = 14 \\
y = 2
\end{array}
$$

2. Solve for a first by stacking the equation and multiplying the first equation by 2 to yield $6a - 2b = 400$. Now add the equations for eliminate b and find the value of a.

$$
\begin{array}{r}
6a - 2b = 400 \\
+\ \underline{5a + 2b = \ \ 40} \\
11a \quad\ \ = 440 \\
a \quad\ \ = \ \ 40
\end{array}
$$

Find the value of b by replacing the variable a with 40 in either of the original equations to find that $3(40) - b = 200$, so $b = -80$. Therefore, $a - b = 40 - (-80) = 120$.

3. Stack and add the equations to find the value of $m - n$.

$$
\begin{array}{r}
4m - 3n = 12 \\
+\ \underline{m - 2n = \ \ 3} \\
5m - 5n = 15 \\
5(m - n) = 15 \\
m - n = \ \ 3
\end{array}
$$

4. This is a simultaneous equation problem masquerading as a word problem. If three pens and five notebooks cost a total of $19.02, then $3p + 5n = 19.02$. Similarly, the second equation can be rewritten as $2p + 3n = 11.63$. To find the value of n, stack the equations and find a way to eliminate the p's.

$$2(3p + 5n = 19.02)$$
$$-3(2p + 3n = 11.63)$$

$$
\begin{array}{r}
6p + 10n = 38.04 \\
+ \underline{-6p - 9n = -34.89} \\
n = 3.15
\end{array}
$$

Each notebook costs $3.15.

All right, that was a lot of algebra to learn. But, it's good to know how to perform basic algebraic operations. In the next chapter, we'll show you a way to replace algebra with arithmetic. Nonetheless, knowing these algebraic rules will make your life easier on test day.

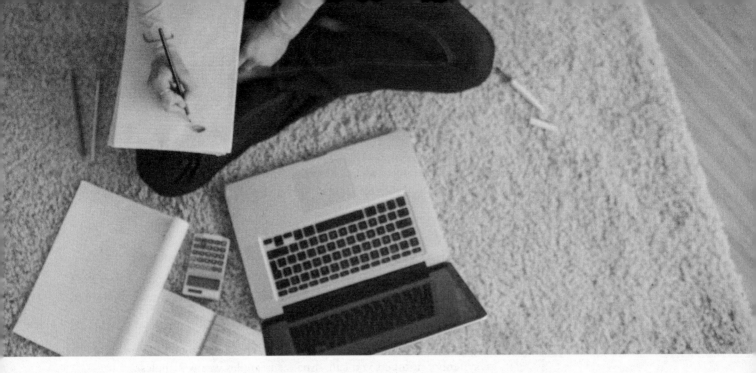

Chapter 5
Turning Algebra into Arithmetic

THE PROBLEM WITH ALGEBRA

Knowing algebraic manipulation is important for your success on the GRE. But, the truth is, unless you study and work with algebra regularly, you're probably much more comfortable with arithmetic. Using algebra when you are unfamiliar with it is likely to lead to errors that could have been avoided.

Let Us Count the Ways

A basic appreciation of algebra is crucial for a good quantitative score on the GRE. But whenever you have the option, you should use arithmetic instead of algebra, for a number of reasons.

- Algebra is based on abstract unknowns, while arithmetic is a concrete system of numbers you can visualize (x apples versus 2 apples).
- You started doing arithmetic long before you even knew what algebra was, so arithmetic is far more ingrained in your brain.
- You probably haven't done a lick of algebra in a very long time, but you perform some sort of arithmetic every day (whether you realize it or not), so arithmetic is far more familiar.
- Your calculator can help you with arithmetic calculations, but it's useless for algebraic manipulations.

Some of you out there might think your algebra skills are passable, and that you're not worried about making mistakes. That may well be, but the possibility of a mistake is greatly heightened by the manipulation of algebra and greatly diminished by the use of arithmetic.

The other bad thing about algebra is that often when you're performing it, you can mess something up and not even know it. GRE question writers are experts at predicting common mistakes that students will make using algebra. They'll use that prediction to create incorrect answer choices to trap those students who made that mistake.

PLUGGING IN

So, what should you do to try to avoid algebra as much as possible? You should plug in actual numbers! Plugging In is a lot like writing your own novel; rather than wonder how many candies Phil has in his hand, assume the power to write the narrative. Decide *for yourself* how many he has.

The Steps to Plugging In

There are two dead giveaways when you're identifying problems that you can solve using your own numbers.

- The problems often feature the phrase "in terms of."
- The answer choices have variables in them.

1. **Recognize the Opportunity to Plug In.** If you have variables in the answer choices, Plug In. If there is an unknown quantity in a problem that cannot be solved for, Plug In.

2. **Set Up Your Scratch Paper.** Write down letters for each answer choice and any important information from the problem.

3. **Plug In an Easy Number for the Variable.** Choose an easy number, such as 2, 3, 5, 10, or 100, for one of the variables. If the problem gives you certain limitations for the value of the variable, such as "odd integer larger than 30," be sure to choose a number that follows those limitations. If there are multiple variables in a problem, see if you can solve for the other variables once you've plugged in for the first one. If you can't, Plug In for those variables as well.

4. **Find Your Target Number.** Solve the question using your numbers. Whatever is asked at the end of the question is your target number. It's helpful to write this number down, as well as the numbers you used to Plug In, so you don't forget them.

5. **Check All of the Answer Choices.** Using the numbers that you plugged in for the variable or unknown in the question, try out every answer choice. You must check *every* answer. Most of the time, only one answer choice will work out, but if you end up with two or more answer choices that give you your target number, plug in a new set of numbers, find a new target number, and check the remaining answer choices.

Try an example:

George is twice as old as Mary, and Mary is three years older than Juan. If Juan is j years old, then, in terms of j, how old will George be in 10 years?

○ $2j - 4$

○ $2j - 14$

○ $2j + 13$

○ $2j + 16$

○ $2j + 26$

Here's How to Crack It

Look at the answer choices first. You should **recognize the opportunity to Plug In** as soon as you see answer choices like those. There are variables in all of our answer choices, which means this is a perfect Plug In problem. Since our variable is j, let's **plug in an easy number** for Juan's age. Let's say Juan is 5, so $j = 5$.

Now work through the problem. Take it apart piece by piece. The first part of the problem states that George is twice as old as Mary, which is nice for George and Mary, but you know only how old Juan is. Leave that part of the problem alone, and move on. The next part of the sentence states that Mary is three years older than Juan. Since Juan is 5, and Mary is three years older than Juan, Mary must be 8.

If George is twice as old as Mary, then George is 16 years old. Now you can answer the question: "If Juan is j years old, then, *in terms of j*, how old will George be in 10 years?" Ignore the phrase **in terms of**. Whenever you see that in a problem, it is just another sign to Plug In. If George is 16 now, how old will he be in 10 years? He'll be 26 years old, so that's **the target number**. Write down 26 and circle it.

Now check all of the answer choices.

Replace j with 5 in each of the answer choices; the one that gives you an answer of 26 is the correct answer.

(A) $2(5) - 4 = 6$ Nope.

(B) $2(5) - 14 = -4$ Nope.

(C) $2(5) + 13 = 23$ Nope.

(D) $2(5) + 16 = 26$ Correct!

(E) $2(5) + 26 = 36$ Nope.

Since (D) is the only answer that yielded the target number of 26, that's the correct answer.

If you had solved this algebraically, you might have added j and 3, then doubled it to $2(j + 3)$, then distributed it to become $2j + 6$, then added 10, and gotten the right answer. But say you forgot to distribute the 2, and $2(j + 3)$ became $2j + 3$, and you added 10 to get $2j + 13$. You could have chosen (C) and moved merrily along, unaware of your mistake, because ETS anticipated it.

Instead, you solved the problem using only arithmetic that you can double-check with your calculator if need be, and you avoided all of the traps. Try another.

If a machine working at a constant rate produces 3,000 golf balls per hour, how many golf balls can four of these machines make in y minutes?

○ $200y$

○ $\dfrac{200}{y}$

○ $750y$

○ $\dfrac{7500}{y}$

○ $\dfrac{720,000}{y}$

Here's How to Crack It

There are variables in the answer choices, so Plug In. Choose an easy number to plug in. There are 60 minutes in an hour, so make the math a little easier by choosing either a factor of 60, such as 30, or a multiple of 60. Plug in $y = 30$.

In 60 minutes, one machine makes 3,000 golf balls. In that case, in 30 minutes one machine would make 1,500 golf balls. The question asks how many golf balls four machines can make in 30 minutes, which is $1,500 \times 4 = 6,000$ golf balls. Write down 6,000 golf balls and circle it, as it is the target number. Now, check all the answer choices to see which one matches the target answer.

Replace x with 30 in each of the answer choices; the one that gives you an answer of 6,000 is the correct answer.

(A) $200(30) = 6,000$ Correct!

(B) $\dfrac{200}{30} = 6.66$ Nope.

(C) $750(30) = 22,500$ Nope.

(D) $\dfrac{7500}{30} = 250$ Nope.

(E) $\dfrac{720,000}{30} = 24,000$ Nope.

The correct answer is (A).

You might be asking yourself, "If I got a match right away, why did I have to spend that time checking all of the others?" And that's a good question, because your ultimate goal is to find the correct answer and scoot off to the next question as quickly as possible. Sometimes we may choose a number that works with multiple answer choices. For instance, say we had plugged in $y = 60$ instead. In that case, the four machines would have made 12,000 golf balls. Choice (A) still works: $200(60) = 12,000$. However, look at (E): $\frac{720,000}{60} = 12,000$. Had we picked 60, we would have had two answer choices that yielded the target number. If that happens, just pick a different number and check the remaining answers.

What to Plug In

When you plug numbers into a question, it's perfectly fine to choose almost any number you want, with a couple of exceptions that we will outline later, as long as the number doesn't violate restrictions that the problem stipulates. Usually, the first integer that pops into your head will work just fine, although as you get better at it you'll get a feel for picking numbers that make your math easier.

At Markham Academy, $\frac{2}{3}$ of the m faculty members live in housing on campus grounds. Of those living on campus, $\frac{3}{4}$ own a car. Which of the following represents, in terms of m, the number of faculty members who live in campus housing and do not own a car?

○ $\dfrac{m}{4}$

○ $\dfrac{m}{6}$

○ $\dfrac{m}{12}$

○ $\dfrac{2m}{3}$

○ $\dfrac{3m}{4}$

Here's How to Crack It

There are variables in the answer choices, so Plug In. Choose an easy number for the variable. This question has a lot of fractions in it, and fractions mean division. The fastest way to come up with a good number is to multiply the denominators, so try $m = 12$.

Now work through the problem in bite-sized pieces. Since $\frac{2}{3}$ of the 12 faculty members live on campus, $\frac{2}{3}(12) = \frac{2}{3} \times \frac{12}{1} = \frac{2}{1} \times \frac{4}{1} = 8$ people live on campus. The problem then states that of those 8 people living on campus, $\frac{3}{4}$ own a car. $\frac{3}{4} \times \frac{8}{1} = \frac{3}{1} \times \frac{2}{1} = 6$ people on campus own a car. The question asks how many people who live on campus *do not* own a car, which means that out of the 8 people on campus, 2 of them don't own a car. The target number is 2.

Check the answer choices. Replace m with 12 in each answer choice to find which one gives us our target number of 2.

(A) $\frac{12}{4} = 3$ Nope.

(B) $\frac{12}{6} = 2$ Correct!

(C) $\frac{12}{12} = 1$ Nope.

(D) $\frac{2(12)}{3} = \frac{24}{3} = 8$ Nope.

(E) $\frac{3(12)}{4} = \frac{36}{4} = 9$ Nope.

The correct answer is (B).

It Gets Easier with Practice

The more problems you work on, the better you'll get at choosing the numbers that will make the math easiest. If a problem involves percents, for example, you'll probably plug in a multiple of 100. Questions based on inches and feet might work best with a multiple of 12. If you're dealing with units of time, you might think in multiples of 60. Numbers like these often suggest themselves within the context of the problem. Just be careful to use multiples of conversion values because using the value itself is more likely to create multiple answer choices that match the target.

What *Not* to Plug In

Knowing the right number to choose for a Plug In problem is useful, but it's equally as important to know what numbers to avoid. These are the numbers that can have a strange effect on the algebra and are likely to result in more than one correct answer choice.

The following chart shows the numbers that cause trouble when you plug them in for variables. These numbers aren't forbidden, but it's best to avoid using them for most problems.

What	Why It's Trouble
0	Additive identity (anything plus 0 equals itself) Anything times 0 equals 0
1	Multiplicative identity (anything times 1 equals itself)
Any numbers that appear in the question	Lots of opportunity for duplicate answers; if $x = 2$, then answer choices "$2x$" and "x^2" both yield a target answer of 4

No Variables? No Problem!

Believe it or not, you can Plug In for a problem that doesn't appear to have any variables at all. In these cases, there might not be any x's or y's, but there will still be an unknown quantity that, if you knew it, would make the problem easier to solve.

During the first month after Johanna purchased stock in Amalgamedia Inc., the value of her shares fell by 20 percent. During the following month, however, Amalgamedia's stock price rose by 40 percent. By what percent did Johanna's shares of Amalgamedia change over those two months?

- ○ 4%
- ○ 12%
- ○ 20%
- ○ 50%
- ○ 68%

Here's How to Crack It

There are no variables here, but the problem would make a little more sense if you knew the price of a share of Amalgamedia when Johanna bought into it. So Plug In for the price of Johanna's shares. Because the question involves percents, it's best to plug in $100 for the price of the shares. Now solve the problem.

If the stock dropped by 20% during the first month, then the price dropped by $\frac{20}{100} \times 100$, or $20, and the price went from $100 to $80. After a 40% increase, the stock moved up by $\frac{40}{100} \times 80$, or $32, to $112. This represents a 12% increase from the original $100, so the correct answer is (B).

Plugging In Quick Quiz

Joshua is three times as old as Kali, and Kali's age is three years more than double Louella's age. If Joshua is j years old, then which of the following represents Louella's age?

○ $\dfrac{j-3}{6}$

○ $\dfrac{j+3}{3}$

○ $\dfrac{j-6}{9}$

○ $\dfrac{j+9}{3}$

○ $\dfrac{j-9}{6}$

Ana has a collection of books that are either fiction or nonfiction. Sixty percent of Ana's books are fiction, and 30 percent of the nonfiction books are about politics. What fraction of the books are nonfiction books that are not about politics?

○ $\dfrac{3}{25}$

○ $\dfrac{7}{25}$

○ $\dfrac{3}{10}$

○ $\dfrac{2}{5}$

○ $\dfrac{3}{5}$

A community park has two rectangular playgrounds—a little one for children younger than age 5, and a larger one for children aged 5 and older. The larger playground is twice as long and five times as wide as the smaller playground. If the area of the small playground is M, then, in terms of M, the area of the larger playground is how much larger than the area of the smaller playground?

- ○ $2M$
- ○ $5M$
- ○ $9M$
- ○ $10M$
- ○ $11M$

An Internet café offers Internet access at the rates of $3 per half hour for the first two hours and $2 for every half hour after that. If Charlene used the Internet at the café for $x + 5$ hours, how much money, in terms of x, did she have to pay?

- ○ $2x + 18$
- ○ $2x + 15$
- ○ $2x + 12$
- ○ $4x + 24$
- ○ $4x + 48$

Explanations for Plugging In Quick Quiz

1. There are variables in the answer choices, so Plug In. Try $l = 5$. If Kali is three years more than double Louella's age, then $k = 3 + (2 \times 5)$, or 13. Joshua is three times as old as Kali, so $j = 3 \times 13$, or 39. Louella's age (5) is the target number. Plug in $j = 39$ into the answer choices to find that (E), $\dfrac{39 - 9}{6} = 5$, is the only one that matches the target number and is the correct answer.

2. There is no variable in the problem, but plug in for the number of books that Ana has. Because the problem involves percents, plug in 100 for the number of books. If 60% are fiction, then the other 40 are nonfiction. Because 30% of those 40 books are about politics, then 12 books are about politics. That means the other 28 books are neither fiction nor about politics, and $\frac{28}{100}$ reduces to $\frac{7}{25}$. The correct answer is (B).

3 Plug In for the length and width of the smaller playground. If the length and width of the small playground are 8 feet and 10 feet, respectively, then the area of that playground is 8×10, or 80 square feet. Therefore, $M = 80$. The larger playground is twice as long ($2 \times 8 = 16$) and five times as wide ($5 \times 10 = 50$), so its area is 16×50, or 800 square feet. The difference in these areas is $800 - 80$, or 720 square feet, which is the target number. Plug in $M = 80$ to each answer choice, to find that the only answer choice that matches the target number is (C).

4. There are variables in the answer choices, so Plug In. Try $x = 6$. If $x = 6$, then Charlene used the Internet for 11 hours. She paid $12 for the first two hours (4 half hours at $3 each), and the remaining nine hours (18 half hours at $2 each) cost $36. The total is $12 + 36$, or $48, which is the target number. Plug $x = 6$ into the answer choices and find that the only choice that matches the target number is (D).

"Must Be" Problems

Every so often you'll see a question that contains variables and the phrase "must be." Must Be problems are looking for the answer choice that always works, so we may need to Plug In more than once to eliminate all the incorrect answers. The trick here is to use the numbers that most people don't think to use. We'll call those numbers FROZEN.

F – Fractions

R – Repeats

O – One

Z – Zero

E – Extremes

N – Negative

We won't have to try every single FROZEN number for Must Be problems, but we may have to try several. First, however, we'll try an easy number. It may be our usual easy numbers: 2, 3, 5, 10, or 100, but it could be any number that seems easy for the question. Don't think too hard about finding the perfect number at this point. We're just going to use the easy number to eliminate some or most of the answers. Once we've eliminated some answers, we'll Plug In using a FROZEN number to see which other answers we can eliminate.

1. **Recognize the Opportunity to Plug In.** If you have variables in the answer choices and the problem says "must be," Plug In.

2. **Set Up Your Scratch Paper.** Write down letters for each answer choice and any important information from the problem.

3. **Plug In an Easy Number for the Variable.** Choose an easy number, such as 2, 3, 5, 10, or 100, for one of the variables. If the problem gives you certain limitations for the value of the variable, such as "odd integer greater than 30," be sure to choose a number that follows those limitations. If there are multiple variables in a problem, see if you can solve for the other variables once you've Plugged In for one of them. If you can't, Plug In for those variables as well.

4. **Check All of the Answer Choices.** You're not looking for the right answer, but simply looking for any answers that you can eliminate.

5. **Try a FROZEN Number.** Pick a FROZEN number that may be able to help eliminate some of the remaining answer choices. Check all the remaining answers using that number. If necessary, try another FROZEN number.

If $|c| < 4$ and $d = 3c - 2$, then which of the following must be true?

○ $-2 \leq d < 10$

○ $d \neq -2$

○ $d < 0$

○ $c < d$

○ $-14 < d$

Here's How to Crack It

This is a Must Be problem, so Plug In more than once. Begin with an easy number, such as $c = 2$. If $c = 2$, then $d = 3(2) - 2 = 6 - 2 = 4$. Now check each answer. Choice (A) works, because $-2 \leq 4 < 10$, and (B) works, because $4 \neq -2$. Eliminate (C), because 4 is not less than 0. Keep (D) because $2 < 4$, and (E), because $-14 < 2$. There are still four answer choices remaining, so Plug In using a FROZEN number, such as $c = 0$, and check the remaining answer choices. If $c = 0$, then $d = 3(0) - 2 = -2$. Keep (A) because d is equal to -2. Eliminate (B) because *d* does equal −2. Eliminate (D), because 0 < −2 is not true. Keep (E), because −14 < −2. Plug in again using another FROZEN number to try to eliminate either (A) or (E). Since there's an absolute value in the problem, try a negative number for *c*. If *c* = −3, then *d* = 3(−3) − 2 = −9 − 2 = −11. Eliminate (A) because −11 is less than −2. The only answer left is (E), which is correct because −14 is less than −11. The correct answer is (E).

Here's what your scratch paper could look like:

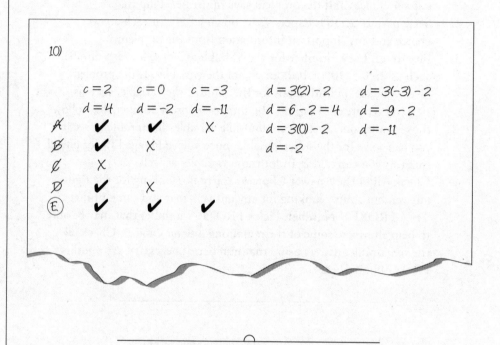

FROZEN numbers are the types of numbers people normally don't think of when working on GRE math problems. However, there may be numbers other than the FROZEN numbers that can work to eliminate answers on certain problems. For instance, a problem about even and odd numbers may require plugging in an even number and then an odd number. A problem about factoring may best be solved by plugging in prime numbers or perfect squares. FROZEN numbers will work most of the time, so stick with it unless you definitely see a different type of number that may be better suited to eliminate answer choices in the problem.

"Must Be" Quick Quiz

Question 1 of 4

If $xy \neq 0$ and y is even, then which of the following must also be even?

○ $\dfrac{2x}{y}$

○ $\dfrac{y}{2} + x$

○ $3y - 2x$

○ $\dfrac{y}{x} + \dfrac{x}{y}$

○ $2y - 3x$

Question 2 of 4

If b and c are negative integers, then which of the following must also be negative?

○ $b^3 - c^3$

○ $bc^2 - c$

○ $bc(b - c)$

○ $\dfrac{b}{c} + \dfrac{c}{b}$

○ $b^2c + bc^2$

Question 3 of 4

If $m > 0 > n$ and m is odd, then all of the following could be odd and positive EXCEPT

○ $(mn)^2$

○ $n^3 - m^3$

○ $(m - n)^2$

○ $m^2 + n^2$

○ $m(m + n)$

Question 4 of 4

If positive integer a is multiplied by integer b and the result is less than a, then it must be true that b is

○ equal to 1

○ greater than 0

○ greater than a

○ greater than 1

○ less than 1

Explanations for "Must Be" Quick Quiz

1. This is a Must Be problem, so Plug In more than once. If $xy \neq 0$ and y is even, you can set $x = 2$ and $y = 4$ and consider the results. Choice (A) is $\frac{2(2)}{4} = 1$, which is odd. Eliminate it. Choice (B) is $\frac{4}{2} + 2 = 4$, which is even. So keep (B). Choice (C) is $3(4) - 2(2) = 8$, which is even, so keep (C) as well. Choice (D) is $\frac{4}{2} + \frac{2}{4} = 2\frac{1}{2}$, which is not an integer, so eliminate (D). Choice (E) is $2(4) - 3(2) = 2$, which is even, so keep (E). Three answer choices remain, so Plug In again. Because the question asks about even and odd values, and the first round of Plugging In used all even numbers, it may be best to change one of the Plugged In numbers to an odd value. Try $x = 3$ and $y = 4$ and check the remaining answer choices. Choice (B) is $\frac{4}{2} + 3 = 5$, which is odd, so eliminate (B). Choice (C) is $3(4) - 2(3) = 2$, which is even, so keep (C). Choice (E) is $2(4) - 3(3) = -1$, so eliminate (E). The correct answer is (C).

2. This is a Must Be problem, so Plug In more than once. The problem states that b and c are negative, so plug in negative numbers for the variables. Let $b = -2$ and $c = -3$. Evaluate the answer choices one at a time. Choice (A) is $(-2)^3 - (-3)^3 = -8 + 27$, which is not negative, so eliminate (A). Choice (B) is $(-2)(-3)^2 - (-3) = -18 + 3 = -15$, which is negative, so keep (B). Choice (C) is $(-2)(-3)[-2 - (-3)] = 6$, which is not negative, so eliminate (C). Choice (D) is $\frac{-2}{-3} + \frac{-3}{-2} = \frac{13}{6}$, which is not negative, so eliminate (D). Choice (E) is $(-2)^2(-3) + (-2)(-3)^2 = -12 + -18 = -30$, which is negative, so keep (E) as well. Now, Plug In

again using FROZEN numbers for the two remaining answer choices. Try $b = -1$ and $c = -1$. Choice (B) is $(-1)(-1)^2 - (-1) = 0$, which isn't negative, so eliminate (B). Choice (E) is $(-1)^2(-1) + (-1)(-1)^2 = -2$, which is negative so keep (E). The correct answer is (E).

3. This is an EXCEPT question, which means that only one answer is never correct, so Plug In more than once. Because m is odd and positive, let $m = 3$. Plug in a value for n, such as $n = -2$, and evaluate the answer choices. This is an EXCEPT question, so look for the answer choice that could never be odd and positive. Choice (A) is $(3 \times -2)^2 = 36$, which is not odd and positive, so keep (A). Choice (B) is $(-2)^3 - 3^3 = -35$, which is not odd and positive, so keep (B). Choice (C) is $[3 - (-2)]^2 = 25$, which is odd and positive, so eliminate (C). Choice (D) is $3^2 + (-2)^2 = 13$, which is also odd and positive, so eliminate (D). Choice (E) is $3(3 + -2) = 3$, which is odd and positive, so eliminate (E). Plug In again for the two remaining answer choices. If $n = -3$, then (A) is $(3 \times -3)^2 = 81$, which is odd and positive, so eliminate (A). Choice (B) is $(-3)^3 - 3^3 = -54$, which is neither odd nor positive, so keep (B). The correct answer is (B).

4. This is a Must Be problem, so Plug In more than once. There are some restrictions in the problem, so work with the problem first. If $ab < a$, then either a or b must be negative and the other must be positive, or one of them must be zero. Since the question states that a is a positive integer, then b must be a negative integer or 0. Eliminate (A), (B), (C), and (D) because none of those suggest that b must be a negative integer. If b must always be less than 1, then b must be either a negative integer or zero. The correct answer is (E).

Plugging In on Quant Comps

Plugging In for Quant Comp questions is similar to Plugging In on Must Be questions. Make sure to Plug In more than once using FROZEN numbers until three of the answer choices have been eliminated.

Before we begin Plugging In on Quant Comp questions, let's review the answer choices for Quant Comp questions first.

(A)   means that Quantity A is *always* greater than Quantity B. Quantity B is never greater than Quantity A, and they are never the same.

(B)   means that Quantity B is *always* greater than Quantity A. Quantity A is never greater than Quantity B, and they are never the same.

(C)   means the two quantities are *always* equal. Quantity A is never greater than Quantity B, and Quantity B is never greater than Quantity A.

(D)   means sometimes Quantity A is greater than Quantity B, sometimes Quantity B is greater than Quantity A, or sometimes the values of the quantities are the same.

After Plugging In the first time, some information about the problem will be available and you will most likely be able to eliminate two answer choices. If Quantity A is greater than Quantity B, then eliminate (B) and (C), as Quantity B is not larger than Quantity A, and the two values are not equal. If Quantity B is greater than Quantity A, then eliminate (A) and (C) for the same reasons. If the two quantities are equal, then eliminate (A) and (B) because neither quantity is always greater than the other.

After Plugging In once and eliminating two answer choices, Plug In again using FROZEN numbers to try to eliminate another answer choice.

If there are no variables in the question, then eliminate (D). Choice (D) is correct only when there is more than one possible value for either or both of Quantity A and Quantity B. If there is only one possible value for each, then it is always possible to determine if one quantity is greater than the other, or if they are equal.

The Steps in Detail

- **Recognize the Opportunity to Plug In.** If it's a Quant Comp question with variables in both the Quantities, Plug In.
- **Use Your Scratch Paper.** Write down the question number, A B C D vertically on the left side of the paper, and any information given in the problem.
- **Plug In an Easy Number.** Choose an easy number to Plug In for the variable such as 2, 3, 5, 10, or 100. Work through the problem with the easy number. If you have multiple variables in the question, see if you can solve for the other variables once you've Plugged In for one of them. If not, Plug In for the other variable as well.
- **Cross off Two Answers.** Once you've solved the question with your first Plug In number, compare Quantity A and Quantity B. If Quantity A is greater, then eliminate (B) and (C). If Quantity B is greater, then eliminate (A) and (C). If the quantities are the equal, then eliminate (A) and (B).
- **Plug In Again Using FROZEN Numbers.** Plug in a FROZEN number for the variable and work the problem again. If Quantity A was greater after the first Plug In, then try a FROZEN number that you think could make Quantity B greater (and vice versa).
- **Continue Plugging In Until Only One Answer Choice Remains.** Plug in a couple of different FROZEN numbers until you are certain that one of the quantities is always greater than the other, the quantities are always equal, or both quantities have been greater than the other using different numbers.

	Quantity A	**Quantity B**
	$2x + 1$	$3x + 1$

○ Quantity A is greater.

○ Quantity B is greater.

○ The two quantities are equal.

○ The relationship cannot be determined
from the information given.

At first glance, you might think instinctively that Quantity B must always be greater, because 3 is greater than 2. The GRE is engineered to take advantage of these instincts, however. Follow our steps and you'll see what we mean.

This is a Quant Comp question with variables, so Plug In more than once. Plug in an easy number for the variable, such as $x = 3$. If $x = 3$, then Quantity A is $2(3) + 1 = 6 + 1 = 7$. Quantity B is $3(3) + 1 = 9 + 1 = 10$. Quantity B is greater than Quantity A, so eliminate (A) and (C).

Now Plug In again using FROZEN numbers to try to make Quantity B less than Quantity A. Try zero. If $x = 0$, then Quantity A is $2(0) + 1 = 0 + 1 = 1$. Quantity B is $3(0) + 1 = 0 + 1 = 1$. Now Quantity A equals Quantity B, so Quantity B is not always greater. Eliminate (B). Because two different numbers gave two different answers to the problem, the correct answer is (D).

Your scratch paper should look something like this:

6)

	A		B	$2(3) + 1 = 6 + 1 = 7$
	$2x + 1$		$3x + 1$	$3(3) + 1 = 9 + 1 = 10$
~~A~~	$2(3) + 1$	$x = 3$	$3(3) + 1$	
~~B~~	7		10 ✔	
~~C~~	$2(0) + 1$	$x = 0$	$3(0) + 1$	
Ⓓ	1		1	

Try another:

Quantity A	**Quantity B**
$1000x + 10$	x^2

○ Quantity A is greater.

○ Quantity B is greater.

○ The two quantities are equal.

○ The relationship cannot be determined from the information given.

Here's How to Crack It

This is a Quant Comp question with variables, so Plug In more than once. Start with an easy number such as $x = 2$. If $x = 2$, then Quantity A is $2,000 + 10 = 2,010$ and Quantity B is $2^2 = 4$. Since Quantity A is greater than Quantity B, eliminate (B) and (C).

Plug In again using FROZEN numbers and try to make Quantity B greater than Quantity A. Try $x = 0$. If $x = 0$, then Quantity A is $0 + 10 = 10$ and Quantity B is 0, so Quantity A is still greater.

Plug in another FROZEN number. Try a negative number, such as $x = -5$. If $x = -5$, then Quantity A is $1,000(-5) + 10 = -5,000 + 10 = -4,990$ and Quantity B is $(-5)^2 = 25$. Since Quantity A is negative and Quantity B is positive, Quantity B is now greater. Eliminate (A); the correct answer is (D).

Here's what your scratch paper should look like for this problem:

Many Quant Comp problems provide restrictions about what the value of certain variables can be. When Plugging In, make sure that the numbers chosen for the variable are allowed by the restrictions in the problem.

$$42 < m < 49$$

Quantity A

$\dfrac{m}{56}$

Quantity B

0.75

○ Quantity A is greater.

○ Quantity B is greater.

○ The two quantities are equal.

○ The relationship cannot be determined from the information given.

Here's How to Crack It

This is a Quant Comp question with variables, so Plug In more than once. The problem states that $42 < m < 49$, so plug in a number between 42 and 49, such as $m = 45$. If $m = 45$, then Quantity A is $\dfrac{45}{56} \approx 0.803$. This is greater than 0.75, so Quantity A is greater than Quantity B, so eliminate (B) and (C).

Now, Plug In again using FROZEN numbers. However, notice that because of the restrictions in the problem, not all FROZEN numbers are allowable. Because the goal is to find a way to make Quantity A less than Quantity B, the value for m needs to be as small as possible. Try an extreme value for m. The most extreme value for m possible is $m = 42$. Although the problem states that m is a value between 42 and 49, if the value of m is set at 42, then it is necessary that the least possible value of Quantity A has to be greater than if $m = 42$. If $m = 42$, then the value of Quantity A is 0.75, which is equivalent to Quantity B. Because m has to be greater than 42, it follows that Quantity A has to be greater than 0.75. Therefore, Quantity A is always greater than Quantity B. The correct answer is (A).

Some problems have multiple variables. In that case, Plug In for one variable at a time and try to solve for the other variables. If it's not possible to solve for the other variables, then Plug In again for the next variable to see if it's possible to solve for the remaining variables. If not, just continue Plugging In until all variables are assigned a number, or it's possible to solve for the remaining variables.

$$4a = 12b$$
$$2b = 10c$$

Quantity A	**Quantity B**
a	$15c$

○ Quantity A is greater.

○ Quantity B is greater.

○ The two quantities are equal.

○ The relationship cannot be determined from the information given.

Here's How to Crack It

This is a Quant Comp question with variables, so Plug In more than once. But first, begin by looking at the equations in the problem to determine if there is a good number to Plug In. To solve for the variables b and c, it will be necessary to divide by both 12 and 10, so begin by equating them to their product, 120. Set $4a = 120$, so $a = 30$. If $a = 30$, then $4(30) = 12b$ and $b = 10$. If $b = 10$, then $2(10) = 10c$, and $c = 2$. Now evaluate the quantities. Quantity A is 30, and Quantity B is also 30. The two quantities are equal, so eliminate (A) and (B). Now, Plug In again using FROZEN numbers. Try a negative number such as $a = -15$. In this case, $b = -5$, and $c = -1$. Quantity A is -15 and Quantity B is also -15. The quantities are still equal. In fact, no matter what number is plugged in for the quantities, the result is that the quantities are always equal. The correct answer is (C).

When you have to Plug In for multiple variables, make sure to plug in different numbers for each variable than from the first Plug In.

Quantity A	Quantity B
ab	$a + b$

○ Quantity A is greater.

○ Quantity B is greater.

○ The two quantities are equal.

○ The relationship cannot be determined
from the information given.

Here's How to Crack It

This is a Quant Comp question with variables, so Plug In more than once. Plug in an easy number for a, such as $a = 2$. This does not give any further information about the value of b, so plug in an easy number for b as well, such as $b = 3$. If $a = 2$ and $b = 3$, then Quantity A is $2 \times 3 = 6$. Quantity B is $2 + 3 = 5$. Quantity A is greater, so eliminate (B) and (C). Now Plug In again using FROZEN numbers. Try to make one number negative and one number positive. Plug in numbers such as $a = -4$ and $b = 5$. Now Quantity A is $(-4)(5) = -20$, and Quantity B is $(-4) + (5) = 1$, and Quantity B is greater, so eliminate (A). The correct answer is (D).

Quant Comp Plugging In Quick Quiz

Question 1 of 6

k is a negative integer.

Quantity A	Quantity B
$5 - 2k$	$2 - 5k$

○ Quantity A is greater.

○ Quantity B is greater.

○ The two quantities are equal.

○ The relationship cannot be determined
from the information given.

Quantity A	Quantity B
$(b - 15)(b + 15)$	$b^2 - 225$

○ Quantity A is greater.

○ Quantity B is greater.

○ The two quantities are equal.

○ The relationship cannot be determined from the information given.

h is a positive integer.

Quantity A	Quantity B
$h^2 - 16$	$h^2 + h - 12$

○ Quantity A is greater.

○ Quantity B is greater.

○ The two quantities are equal.

○ The relationship cannot be determined from the information given.

w, x, y, and z are consecutive even integers, and $0 < w < x < y < z$.

Quantity A	Quantity B
$2(w + x) + 2$	$y + z - 2$

○ Quantity A is greater.

○ Quantity B is greater.

○ The two quantities are equal.

○ The relationship cannot be determined from the information given.

Quantity A	Quantity B
The cost of m books, each of which costs $n - 3$ dollars	The cost of n books, each of which costs $m + 2$ dollars

○ Quantity A is greater.

○ Quantity B is greater.

○ The two quantities are equal.

○ The relationship cannot be determined from the information given.

Albert is a inches tall, Beatrice is b inches tall, Charlene is c inches tall, and c is the average (arithmetic mean) of a and b.

Quantity A	Quantity B
The combined height, in feet, of all three people	$\dfrac{c}{4}$

○ Quantity A is greater.

○ Quantity B is greater.

○ The two quantities are equal.

○ The relationship cannot be determined from the information given.

Explanations for Plugging In Quick Quiz

1. This is a Quant Comp question with variables, so Plug In more than once. The problem states that k is a negative integer, so plug in an easy number that meets those restrictions, such as $k = -2$. In that case, Quantity A is $5 - 2(-2) = 5 + 4 = 9$ and Quantity B is $2 - 5(-2) = 2 + 10 = 12$. Quantity B is greater than Quantity A, so eliminate (A) and (C). Now Plug In again using FROZEN numbers. Try $k = -1$. Quantity (A) is $5 - 2(-1) = 5 + 2 = 7$, and Quantity B is $2 - 5(-1) = 2 + 5 = 7$, so both quantities are equal. Eliminate (B); the correct answer is (D).

2. This is a Quant Comp question with variables, so Plug In more than once. However, begin first by recognizing the quadratic in Quantity A. FOIL, or recognize that the quantities are two sides of the common quadratic $(x + y)(x - y) = x^2 - y^2$ because $15^2 = 225$. Therefore, the two quantities are equal, and the correct answer is (C). This problem can be solved using Plugging In, but it always helps to know basic algebraic manipulation. In this case, if the common quadratic was recognized, this problem can be solved in a matter of seconds, as opposed to Plugging In, which may have taken a couple minutes.

3. This is a Quant Comp question with variables, so Plug In more than once. However, first begin by manipulating the quadratics in the quantities. Quantity A can be manipulated as a common quadratic to reveal that $h^2 - 16 = (h + 4)(h - 4)$. Quantity B can be factored to find that $h^2 + h - 12 = (h + 4)(h - 3)$. Both quantities contain the value $(h + 4)$, so cancel those values out. Now, Quantity A is $(h - 4)$ and Quantity B is $(h - 3)$. These equations are now simplified, so Plugging In is easy. Begin with an easy number for h, keeping in mind the restrictions of the problem, so plug in $h = 2$. Quantity A is -2 and Quantity B is -1. Quantity B is greater, so eliminate (A) and (C). Plug In again using FROZEN numbers. Try extreme numbers allowable by the problem, such as $h = 100$. Quantity A is 96 and Quantity B is 97. In fact, any value for h will always result in a greater Quantity B value. The correct answer is (B).

4. This is a Quant Comp question with variables, so Plug In more than once. Begin with easy numbers and keep in mind the restrictions of the problem. Plug in $w = 2$, $x = 4$, $y = 6$, and $z = 8$. Quantity A equals $2(2 + 4) + 2$, or 14, and Quantity B equals $6 + 8 - 2$, or 12. Quantity A is greater, so eliminate (B) and (C). Now Plug In again using FROZEN numbers. Try extreme numbers such as $w = 20$, $x = 22$, $y = 24$, and $z = 26$. Quantity A is $2(20 + 22) + 2$, or 86, while Quantity B is $24 + 26 - 2$, or 48. There are no more FROZEN numbers allowable by the problem and Quantity A has remained greater, so the correct answer is (A).

5. This is a Quant Comp question with variables, so Plug In more than once. Start with easy numbers such as $m = 4$ and $n = 8$. Quantity A is the price of 4 books at \$5 each, or \$20, while Quantity B is the price of 8 books at \$6 each, or \$48. Quantity B is greater so eliminate (A) and (C). Plug In again using FROZEN numbers. Try extreme numbers such as $m = 100$ and $n = 4$. Quantity A is the price of 100 books at \$1 each, or \$100. Quantity B is the price of 4 books at \$102, or \$408. Quantity B is greater. The correct answer is (B).

6.   This is a Quant Comp question with variables, so Plug In more than once. Just because the problem asks for heights does not mean the heights need to be realistic or average heights. Plug in numbers that make the math easy, such as $a = 11$ and $b = 13$. Therefore, c is 12. Quantity A, the combined height of all the people, is 11 + 13 + 12 = 36 inches. Convert this to feet by dividing by 12 to find the combined height in feet is 3. Quantity B is 3 as well. The two quantities are equal, so eliminate (A) and (B). Plug In again using FROZEN numbers. Combine three FROZEN numbers and plug in repeats, one, and extremes by plugging in $a = 1$ and $b = 1$. The value of c is also 1. Quantity A is $\frac{3}{12} = \frac{1}{4}$, and Quantity B is $\frac{1}{4}$. The quantities are still equal. The correct answer is (C).

PLUGGING IN THE ANSWER CHOICES

There is one more kind of Plugging In strategy. It is called PITA, which stands for Plugging In the Answers. It is one of the most powerful types of Plugging In because it can take some of the hardest problems on the GRE and turn them into simple arithmetic. The hardest thing about this technique, however, is remembering when to use it.

The steps for PITA are as follows:

1.   **Recognize the opportunity.** There are ways to know if a certain problem is a good candidate to Plug In the Answers:
     -   the question asks for a specific amount that the answer choices represent
     -   the question asks "how many" or "how much"
     -   it seems appropriate to write and solve an algebraic equation
2.   **Write out the answer choices on your scratch paper.** Write the numbers for each answer choice as well as the usual vertical A B C D E.
3.   **Label your answer choices.** If the question asks for the number of hats David has, label the column of answer choices as "David's hats." If it's asking for the value of x, label the column of answer choices with an x on top.
4.   **Plug In (C).** Since the answer choices are listed in ascending or descending order, it will be helpful to start with (C). If you have more or fewer than five answer choices, use the middle answer choice.

5. **Work the problem in bite-sized pieces, making a new column for each new step.** Use (C) to work through the problem in bite-sized pieces. As you come up with values for each step, make a new column next to your answer choices.
6. **POE.** If you end up with numbers that don't match up, then (C) is incorrect. This is why starting with (C) is so useful. Because the answer choices are listed in either ascending or descending numerical order, if it's possible to determine the value of (C) is either greater or less than needed, it's also possible to eliminate the answer choices that are greater or less than (C). Continue checking all the answer choices until one choice works.

If you're not sure whether your answer was too great or not, then pick another answer choice at random, preferably either (B) or (D). Once you've tried another answer choice, you'll be able to determine if that answer was further or closer away from the desired value than (C). This will inform you that the answer needs to be greater or less than the choice you just tried.

Finally, because you are using the answer choices as your number to plug in, for multiple-choice questions, once you have found one answer choice that works you do not need to check any other choices. If you Plug In the Answers and a choice works, that is the correct answer. Circle it and move on to the next problem.

———————————○———————————

When three consecutive integers are multiplied together, the result is 17,550. What is the greatest of these three integers?

○ 24

○ 25

○ 26

○ 27

○ 28

Here's How to Crack It

The question asks for a specific amount that the answer choices represent, and it seems reasonable to write an algebraic equation, so Plug In the Answers. Begin with (C). The problem states that there are three consecutive integers and the answer choices represent the greatest of those integers. If the greatest integer is 26, then the other two are 24 and 25.

The problem states that when the three integers are multiplied together, the result is 17,550. Multiply 26, 25, and 24 together to find that 24 × 25 × 26 = 15,600. This is less than 17,550, so the value of (C) is less than what is needed. Eliminate (C) and also eliminate (A) and (B) because they are less than (C) and would only make the final result less as well.

Now try (D). If the greatest integer is 27, then the other two consecutive integers are 25 and 26. Perform the necessary multiplication: $25 \times 26 \times 27 = 650 \times 27 = 17{,}550$. This matches the requirements of the problem. There is no need to check (E) because there can be only one correct answer. The correct answer is (D).

Here's what your scratch paper for this problem should look like:

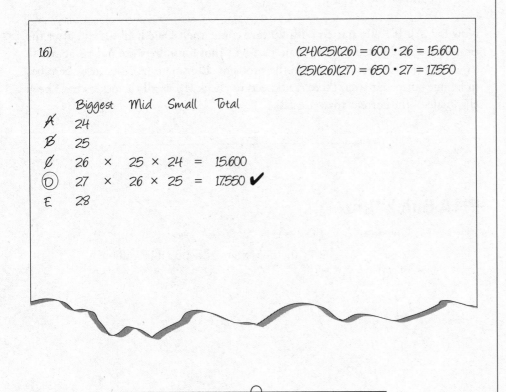

Try another one:

Dale and Kelly collect rare coins and Dale has twice as many rare coins as Kelly. If Dale gives Kelly 6 coins, leaving Dale with 10 more coins than Kelly, how many coins did Kelly have initially?

○ 20

○ 22

○ 28

○ 38

○ 44

Here's How to Crack It

The question asks for a specific amount that the answer choices represent, and it seems reasonable to write an algebraic equation, so Plug In the Answers. Start with (C). If Kelly had 28 rare coins initially, then Dale had twice as many, or 56. Dale then gave Kelly 6 coins and had 50 left; Kelly now has 6 additional coins, or 34 coins. The difference between 50 and 34 is 16, which is greater than the 10 specified in the problem. Eliminate (C); eliminate (D) and (E) as well, because they will also be too great.

Now try (A). If Kelly started with 20 rare coins, then Dale had 40, and after the transaction, Kelly had 26 and Dale had 34. Those numbers are only 8 apart, so (A) is less than necessary to solve the problem. Eliminate (A). Because there has to be one correct answer, there is no need to check (B) as all the others have been eliminated. The correct answer is (B).

PITA Quick Quiz

Question 1 of 4

If $3x^2 + 5x - 2 = 0$, then what is a possible value of x ?

○ −2

○ −1

○ 0

○ 1

○ 2

Question 2 of 4

If $3^x = 9^{x-4}$, then $x =$

○ 2

○ 4

○ 5

○ 8

○ 16

Margarita bought x identical sweaters for $300. If each sweater cost $7.50 less, she could have bought $x + 2$ sweaters for the same amount of money. How many sweaters did she buy?

○ 6

○ 8

○ 10

○ 12

○ 14

In the inventory at a certain car dealership, $\frac{2}{3}$ of the cars are four-door sedans and $\frac{2}{5}$ of the rest are SUVs. If the remaining 24 vehicles are pickup trucks, how many vehicles are in the inventory at the car dealership?

○ 60

○ 90

○ 120

○ 180

○ 240

Explanations for PITA Quick Quiz

1. This question looks like it could be solved algebraically and the question asks for a specific value that the answer choices represent, so Plug In the Answers. Start with (C). If $x = 0$, then the equation becomes $-2 = 0$, which is incorrect, so eliminate (C). It is impossible to know if (C) was too great or not, so plug in either (B) or (D) next. Try (D). If $x = 1$, then the resulting equation is $3 + 5 - 2 = 0$, or $6 = 0$, which is not correct, so eliminate (D). This is even further away from being correct than (C), so the value for x likely needs to be less. Try (A). If $x = -2$, then the resulting equation is $12 - 10 - 2 = 0$, or $0 = 0$. This is correct so there is no need to check (B). The correct answer is (A).

2. The question asks for a specific value and that value is represented by the answer choices, so PITA. But first, manipulate the equation to accurately compare the two sides of the equation. The prime factorization of 9 is 3^2, so rewrite this equation as $3^x = (3^2)^{x-4}$. Apply the Power-Multiply rule of exponents and rewrite the equation as $3^x = 3^{2x-8}$. Cancel the bases to find that $x = 2x - 8$. Simplify to reveal that $-x = -8$ and that $x = 8$. The correct answer is (D). It is always helpful to be able to do basic algebraic manipulation to simplify problems. In this case, the simplification leads directly the answer.

3. The question asks for a specific amount that is represented by the answer choices, so PITA. Try (C) first. If Margarita bought 10 identical sweaters for $300, then they cost $30 each. Two sweaters more would equal 12 sweaters, each of which would cost $\frac{300}{12}$, or $25. Because $30 and $25 are not $7.50 apart, eliminate (C). The difference between the prices needs to be greater, so a lesser number is needed. Eliminate (D) and (E) as well. Try (B). If she bought 8 sweaters, then they cost $37.50 each. An extra 2 sweaters would make 10, which would cost $30 each. The difference is $7.50. The correct answer is (B).

4. The question asks for a specific amount that is represented by the answer choices, so PITA. If the car dealership has 120 vehicles, then $\frac{2}{3}$ of those 120, or 80, are four-door sedans. Of the remaining 40, $\frac{2}{5}$ are SUVs. Because $\frac{2}{5} \times 40$ is 16, the number of cars that remain to be categorized is $40 - 16$, or 24. This matches the information in the problem. The correct answer is (C).

PITA and All That Apply

PITA also works on the other question types. With All That Apply questions, we'll typically be looking for the greatest and least answers that work, and crossing off any answers greater than the greatest answer that works and less than the least answer that works.

Last year, Company X spent between $\frac{1}{5}$ and $\frac{1}{4}$ of its yearly advertising budget on print ads. If Company X spent \$31,120 on print ads, then which of the following values could have been Company X's advertising budget last year?

Indicate <u>all</u> such values.

☐ \$106,720

☐ \$115,880

☐ \$121,960

☐ \$126,400

☐ \$138,240

☐ \$145,000

☐ \$157,100

Here's How to Crack It

The question is asking for specific values and the answer choices represent those values, so PITA. Begin with (D), as it is in the middle.

If the ad budget was \$126,400, then they must have spent between $\frac{1}{4}$ of \$126,400 = \$31,600 and $\frac{1}{5}$ of \$126,400 = \$25,280 on print ads. The problem states that Company X spent \$31,120 on ads, and \$25,280 < \$31,120 < \$31,600, so \$126,400 could have been the amount in Company X's advertising budget. Choice (D) is a possible answer.

Now work through the lesser answer choices until they no longer work. Work with (C) next. If the ad budget was \$121,960, then the company must have spent between $\frac{1}{4}$ of \$121,960 = \$30,490 and $\frac{1}{5}$ of \$121,960 = \$24,392 on print ads. Company X, however, spent \$31,120 on advertising, which is more than the \$30,490 allowed by (C). This is less than the necessary budget, so eliminate (C) as well as (A) and (B) as they will also be less than necessary.

Now try the greater answer choices. If the ad budget was $138,240, then the company must have spent between $\frac{1}{4}$ of $138,240 = $34,560 and $\frac{1}{5}$ of $138,240 = $27,648 on print ads. Since $27,648 < $31,120 < $34,560, the company's total budget could have been $138,240. Choice (E) is a correct answer.

For (F), if the total advertising budget was $145,000, then the company spent between $29,000 and $36,250 on print ads, which matches the information in the problem. Choice (F) is also a correct answer.

Check (G). If the company had $157,100 in its advertising budget, then it spent between $31,420 and $39,275 on print ads. That value is too great, so eliminate (G).

The answers are therefore (D), (E), and (F).

PITA Works for Quant Comp Too

Sometimes you can plug in some of the information that they give you in one of the Quantities in order to solve a problem.

On Monday, Dave's Car Emporium had h used cars in its inventory. Dave sold $\frac{1}{4}$ of the cars to his other dealership on Tuesday, and on Wednesday 7 people sold their used cars to Dave's. This brought the total number of used cars on the lot to 67.

Quantity A	Quantity B
h	84

○ Quantity A is greater.

○ Quantity B is greater.

○ The two quantities are equal.

○ The relationship cannot be determined from the information given.

Here's How to Crack It

This is a Quant Comp question with variables, so Plug In. Use the value in Quantity B as the value for h and determine whether the number of used cars in inventory is less than, greater than, or equal to 84. If Dave's had 84 cars on Monday and sold $\frac{1}{4}$ of them, then he would have had 63 cars left ($\frac{1}{4} \times 84 = 21$, and $84 - 21 = 63$). If he acquired 7 more on Tuesday, this would have brought his total up to 70. This is greater than the information provided in the problem. Therefore, the number h must be less than 84, and the correct answer is (B).

Quant Comp PITA Quick Quiz

Question 1 of 3

Mendel purchased three pairs of dress pants at a men's store. One pair cost $65, a second pair cost $85, and the average (arithmetic mean) price for all three is $73.

Quantity A	Quantity B
The price of the third pair of pants	$72

○ Quantity A is greater.

○ Quantity B is greater.

○ The two quantities are equal.

○ The relationship cannot be determined from the information given.

A rectangular swimming pool with a uniform depth is 20 feet long and 40 feet wide and holds a total of 9,600 cubic feet of water.

Quantity A	**Quantity B**
The depth of the swimming pool	12 feet

○ Quantity A is greater.

○ Quantity B is greater.

○ The two quantities are equal.

○ The relationship cannot be determined from the information given.

Question 3 of 3

A local movie theater normally sells individual tickets for $9 each, but it offers 20% discounts to all members of groups of 10 or more.

Quantity A	**Quantity B**
The total amount of money that a 16-person group spent at the movies	$112

○ Quantity A is greater.

○ Quantity B is greater.

○ The two quantities are equal.

○ The relationship cannot be determined from the information given.

Explanations for Quant Comp PITA Quick Quiz

1. Use PITA and assume that the third pair of pants cost $72. If that were the case, then the total cost of all three pairs of pants would be 65 + 85 + 72, or 222, and the average price would be 222 ÷ 3, or $74. Because the problem tells you the average price was $73, the average you calculated is too large, which means the $72 that you plugged into the problem is too large. Therefore, $72 must be greater than the price of the third pair of pants, and the answer is (B).

2. If the dimensions of the swimming pool are 20 by 40 by 12, the volume of the pool is 20 × 40 × 12, or 9,600 cubic feet. Because this matches the volume mentioned in the question, the answer is (C).

3. First, it's important to recognize that the group is large enough to qualify for the discount. If the group spent $112 at the movies, then each spent $112 ÷ 16, or $7. This is too little, because the discounted price of a ticket is 80% of $9, or $7.20. Therefore, they must have spent more than $112, and the answer is (A).

Plug In Early, Plug In Often

If you finish this book and take away just one new skill, make this the one. Plugging In is a million-dollar idea that can bring about solid score improvements right away, because of how efficiently it (1) makes problems more accessible and (2) reduces the chance that you'll make careless errors. You should practice Plugging In as much as you can until it becomes instinctive.

We've run through a number of examples in this chapter, and now it's your turn. As you practice these questions, train yourself to recognize patterns and determine the numbers that will either undermine or confirm your initial results.

Algebra Drill

$$ac < bc$$

Quantity A	**Quantity B**
a	b

○ Quantity A is greater.

○ Quantity B is greater.

○ The two quantities are equal.

○ The relationship cannot be determined from the information given.

A video game goes on sale for 15% off the original price and a customer can save an additional 10% on the sale price if she has a coupon. If Bailey buys the video game at the sale price and uses a coupon, what percent of the original price does she pay?

○ 12.5%

○ 25%

○ 75%

○ 76.5%

○ 83.5%

A merchant sold an equal number of 5-cent and 10-cent screws. If the total cost of the screws was $3.00, what was the total number of screws sold?

○ 25

○ 30

○ 40

○ 44

○ 50

At a constant rate of 12,000 rotations per hour, how many rotations does a spinning top make in p minutes?

○ $12,000p$

○ $200p$

○ $\dfrac{72,000}{p}$

○ $\dfrac{12,000}{p}$

○ $\dfrac{200}{p}$

If $3x = 12$, then $8 \div x =$

[   ]

$$st = -6$$

Quantity A	**Quantity B**
s	t

○ Quantity A is greater.

○ Quantity B is greater.

○ The two quantities are equal.

○ The relationship cannot be determined from the information given.

A contest winner receives $\frac{1}{4}$ of his winnings in cash and also receives four prizes, each worth $\frac{1}{4}$ of the remaining balance. If the total value of the cash and one of the prizes is $35,000, what is the total value of his winnings?

- ○ $70,000
- ○ $75,000
- ○ $80,000
- ○ $95,000
- ○ $140,000

Connie has more marbles than Joey, and Joey has fewer marbles than Mark.

Quantity A	**Quantity B**
The number of marbles Mark has	The number of marbles Connie has

- ○ Quantity A is greater.
- ○ Quantity B is greater.
- ○ The two quantities are equal.
- ○ The relationship cannot be determined from the information given.

If $2 < r < 8$ and $1 < s < \frac{5}{2}$, which of the following expresses all possible values of rs ?

- ○ $1 < rs < 5$
- ○ $2 < rs < 20$
- ○ $\frac{5}{2} < rs < 8$
- ○ $\frac{5}{2} < rs < 20$
- ○ $5 < rs < 10$

$$\text{Set } A = \{-1, 0, 1\}$$
$$\text{Set } B = \{-2, -1, 0, 1\}$$

If a is a member of Set A and b is a member of Set B, what is the least possible value of $a - b^2$?

- ○ 2
- ○ 0
- ○ −2
- ○ −5
- ○ −9

$12m^2 - 8m - 64 =$

- ○ $4(3m + 8)(m - 2)$
- ○ $4(3m - 8)(m + 2)$
- ○ $4(3m - 2)(m + 8)$
- ○ $4m^2 - 64$
- ○ $4m - 64$

If $a + b - 2c = 12$, and $3a + 3b + c = 22$, what is the value of c ?

- ○ −2
- ○ 0
- ○ 10
- ○ 17
- ○ 34

Kevin decided to consecutively number the T-shirts in his closet. He wrote one number on each of his T-shirts, starting with 1 on the first T-shirt. When he was finished numbering he had written a total of 59 digits.

Quantity A	**Quantity B**
35	The number of T-shirts in Kevin's closet

○ Quantity A is greater.

○ Quantity B is greater.

○ The two quantities are equal.

○ The relationship cannot be determined from the information given.

If the sum of x distinct, positive integers is less than 75, what is the greatest possible value of x ?

○   8

○   9

○   10

○   11

○   12

An office supply store sells staplers for $5 each, and boxes of staples for $2 each. On Monday, the store sold a total of 22 staplers and boxes of staples combined, for which it collected a total of $74. How many staplers did the store sell?

○   6

○   10

○   11

○   12

○   44

Carmen has 12 collectibles, and t, the value of Carmen's favorite collectible, is between 8 and 9 dollars.

Quantity A	**Quantity B**
$\dfrac{t}{\text{the number of Carmen's collectibles}}$	0.72

○ Quantity A is greater.

○ Quantity B is greater.

○ The two quantities are equal.

○ The relationship cannot be determined from the information given.

Which of the following is equivalent to $8a + (2ab - 4a)b - 4ab$?

○ $2a(b - 2)^2$

○ $2a(b^2 - 2b + 2)$

○ $4a(b^2 - 2b + b)$

○ $4ab(1 - 2b)$

○ $a^2(2b + 2b^2)b$

Timmie can buy his favorite pens in $10 packs that contain p pens, or he can buy the same pens individually at a cost of $1.12 each.

Quantity A	**Quantity B**
9	The largest possible value of p if it is cheaper to buy the pens individually rather than in packs

○ Quantity A is greater.

○ Quantity B is greater.

○ The two quantities are equal.

○ The relationship cannot be determined from the information given.

If $x = \dfrac{9y}{4}$ and $x \neq 0$, then $\dfrac{6y}{4x} =$

○ $\dfrac{27}{8}$

○ $\dfrac{9}{4}$

○ $\dfrac{3}{2}$

○ $\dfrac{2}{3}$

○ $\dfrac{1}{9}$

If x is an integer less than or equal to –2 and y is an integer with an absolute value greater than or equal to 5, which of the following statements must be true of xy ?

Indicate <u>all</u> such statements.

☐ xy is an integer

☐ xy is negative

☐ $xy \leq -10$

☐ $xy \geq 10$

☐ $xy = -10$

☐ $|xy| \geq 10$

Six years ago, Jim's age was four times Carol's age. Jim is now j years old, and Carol is now c years old.

Quantity A	**Quantity B**
c	$\dfrac{j+16}{4}$

○ Quantity A is greater.

○ Quantity B is greater.

○ The two quantities are equal.

○ The relationship cannot be determined from the information given.

Quantity A	**Quantity B**
$\dfrac{x^4}{x^3}$	x

○ Quantity A is greater.

○ Quantity B is greater.

○ The two quantities are equal.

○ The relationship cannot be determined from the information given.

$$2(a + b) = a^2 - b^2 = 32$$

Quantity A	**Quantity B**
$a + b$	$(a - b)^2$

○ Quantity A is greater.

○ Quantity B is greater.

○ The two quantities are equal.

○ The relationship cannot be determined from the information given.

If $a > 12$ and $b < 7$, which of the following must be true?

Indicate <u>all</u> such values.

☐ $a + b > 12$

☐ $a - b > 5$

☐ $a + b < 19$

☐ $a - b < 12$

☐ $ab > 84$

☐ $ab < 84$

$$x + y = 14$$
$$y + 4 = 10$$

Quantity A	**Quantity B**
x	y

○ Quantity A is greater.

○ Quantity B is greater.

○ The two quantities are equal.

○ The relationship cannot be determined from the information given.

If $x \neq 0$, which of the following must be true?

○ $x < x^2$

○ $\dfrac{1}{x} < x$

○ $x^2 < x^3$

○ $1 - x < x$

○ $x < x + 2$

If $x > 0$, $y > 0$, and $z > 0$, then $\dfrac{2}{x} + \dfrac{y + \dfrac{1}{z}}{2} =$

○ $\dfrac{2x}{2x + 2y}$

○ $\dfrac{4 + xy + x}{2x}$

○ $\dfrac{y + z}{2x}$

○ $\dfrac{xyz + 4}{x + y + z}$

○ $\dfrac{4z + xyz + x}{2xz}$

$$2x^2 + 3xy - 2y^2 = 0$$

Quantity A	**Quantity B**
$2x$	y

○ Quantity A is greater.

○ Quantity B is greater.

○ The two quantities are equal.

○ The relationship cannot be determined from the information given.

Pat has 4 teapots more than Judi, but 3 teapots fewer than Rudy. If Pat has y teapots, which of the following is an expression for the total number of teapots that Judi and Rudy have?

○ $2y - 7$

○ $2y - 1$

○ $2y + 9$

○ $y + 7$

○ $y + 9$

If $x \neq 0$ and one-half of x is equal to four times x^2, then $x =$

$$q \neq 0$$

Quantity A	**Quantity B**
$\dfrac{\left|q - 7\right|}{2}$	$\dfrac{\left|q\right| + \left|-7\right|}{2}$

○ Quantity A is greater.

○ Quantity B is greater.

○ The two quantities are equal.

○ The relationship cannot be determined from the information given.

For all non-zero numbers x and y, if $3x = 5y$, then $\dfrac{4x^2}{25y^2} =$

Terrence has $\dfrac{2}{3}$ as many cards as Phillip. If Terrence were to win one card from Phillip, he would have $\dfrac{3}{4}$ as many cards as Phillip. If Terrence wins an even number of cards from Phillip, which of the following could be the number of cards that Phillip has left? Indicate all such values.

☐ 24

☐ 20

☐ 19

☐ 18

☐ 17

☐ 14

$$40 < t < 50$$
$$10 < s < 12$$

Quantity A	**Quantity B**
$t - s$	39

○ Quantity A is greater.

○ Quantity B is greater.

○ The two quantities are equal.

○ The relationship cannot be determined from the information given.

If x and n are integers and $x^{(n + 2)} = 16x^2$, what is the least possible value of $16 + x$?

EXPLANATIONS FOR ALGEBRA DRILL

1. **D**

   Plug In. Let $a = 2$, $b = 5$, and $c = 1$. Quantity B can be greater than Quantity A, so eliminate (A) and (C). Now change the sign of c. Let $a = 5$, $b = 2$, and $c = -1$. Quantity A can be greater than Quantity B, so eliminate (B). Only (D) remains.

2. **D**

   Plug in $100 for the original price. The sale price is $100 − $15 = $85. The coupon reduces the price another $8.50, to $76.50. This is 76.5% of the original price, making (D) correct.

3. **C**

   Plug In the Answers, starting with (C). If there are 40 total screws, then there are 20 5-cent screws and 20 10-cent screws. The 5-cent screws cost 20 × $0.05 = $1.00, and the 10-cent screws cost 20 × $0.10 = $2.00. The total cost of the screws is $3.00. This information matches all of the information given in the problem, so (C) is correct.

4. **B**

   Plug In, and let $p = 30$ minutes. Because the top rotates 12,000 times per hour, it must rotate 6,000 times in 30 minutes, which is one half hour. Plug 30 for p into the answer choices to find the target answer of 6,000. You'll find it only in (B): 200 × 30 = 6,000.

5. **2**

   First, solve for x by dividing both sides of the equation by 3 to determine that $x = 4$. Next, answer the question: 8 ÷ 4 = 2.

6. **D**

   There are variables in the columns, so Plug In. Try $s = 2$ and $t = -3$. Quantity A is greater, so cross off (B) and (C). Now switch the numbers around and try $s = -3$ and $t = 2$. This time Quantity B is greater, so the correct answer is (D).

7. **C**

   Plug In the Answers, starting with (C). If the winnings were $80,000, the cash is $\frac{1}{4}$ × $80,000 = $20,000. Then take $\frac{1}{4}$ of the remainder of the prize, $60,000: $\frac{1}{4}$ × $60,000 = $15,000. The total of the cash and the first payment is $20,000 + $15,000 = $35,000. Because (C) is correct, there is no need to check the other answers.

8. **D**

   There are unknowns in the columns, so set up your scratch paper and Plug In more than once. Try 10 marbles for Connie, 5 marbles for Joey, and 7 marbles for Mark. Quantity B is greater, so cross off (A) and (C). Now try 10 marbles for Connie, 5 marbles for Joey, and 10 marbles for Mark. This time the quantities are equal, and you can eliminate (B). The correct answer is (D).

9. **B**

Break this problem into two parts, and use POE. Because $r > 2$ and $s > 1$, the product of rs must be greater than the product of 2×1. The only answer choice in which $2 < rs$ is (B). Alternatively, because $r < 8$ and $s < \dfrac{5}{2}$, the product of rs must be less than $8\left(\dfrac{5}{2}\right) = 20$. Choice (B) is also the only answer choice in which $rs < 20$. Either way, the correct answer is (B).

10. **D**

To make the value of $a - b^2$ as small as possible, make a as small as possible and b^2 as large as possible. The smallest number in Set A is -1, so that's the value for a. Use -2 for b because that makes $b^2 = 4$: $a - b^2 = -1 - 4 = -5$.

11. **B**

Plug In, and let $m = 3$. The equation is $(12 \times 3^2) - (8 \times 3) - 64 = 108 - 24 - 64 = 20$, and 20 is the target. Plug 3 for m into the answer choices, and match the target of 20. Only (B) matches the target: $4(3 \times 3 - 8)(3 + 2) = 4(9 - 8)(5) = 4(1)(5) = 20$.

12. **A**

Since you're looking for c, try to make a and b cancel out of the equations. Multiply the first equation by -3, giving you $-3a - 3b + 6c = -36$. Now add the equations. The a and b values cancel out, giving you $7c = -14$, so $c = -2$.

13. **A**

There is an unknown in one column and a number in the other, so PITA. If there were 35 T-shirts in Kevin's closet, that would be 9 digits for the first 9 T-shirts and $2 \times 26 = 52$ for the next 26 T-shirts. This is a total of 61 digits, which is more than 59 mentioned in the question, so the number of T-shirts must have been less than 35. The correct answer is (A).

14. **D**

Write down the integers starting with 1 and keep adding: $1 + 2 + 3 + 4 + 5 + 6 + 7 + 8 + 9 + 10 + 11 = 66$. If you added 12 to the total, you would reach 78. Thus, there are 11 distinct positive integers that have a sum less than 75.

15. **B**

The problem asks for a specific value that is represented by the answer choices, so Plug In the Answers. Begin with (C). The store sold 11 staplers, so, because the store sold a total of 22 staplers and boxes of staples, the store also sold 11 boxes of staples. If each stapler sells for $5, and each box of staples sells for $2, then the total collected from the sale of staplers and boxes of staples is $(11 \times \$5) + (11 \times \$2) = \$77$. This is greater than the $74 specified by the problem, so eliminate (C). Also eliminate (D) and (E) as they will make the total even greater. Try (B). If the store sold 10 staplers, then the store also sold 12 boxes of staples. The total collected from the sale of staplers and boxes of staples is $(10 \times \$5) + (12 \times \$2) = \$74$. The correct answer is (B).

16. **D**

Once you've set up your scratch paper to Plug In on a Quant Comp problem, start with $t = 8.1$. The value in Quantity A is 0.675; Quantity B is greater, so eliminate (A) and (C). Next, try $t = 8.9$. Now the value in Quantity A is about 0.74; this time, Quantity A is greater, so eliminate (B) and select (D).

17. **A**

Plug In. If $a = 2$ and $b = 3$, then $8a + (2ab - 4a)b - 4ab = 8(2) + (2(2)(3) - 4(2))(3) - 4(2)(3) = 16 + (12 - 8)(3) - 24 = 16 + 12 - 24 = 4$. Your target is 4. Plug $a = 2$ and $b = 3$ into all of the answers. Only (A) yields 4: $2(2)(3 - 2)^2 = 4(1) = 4$.

18. **A**

There's an unknown in one column and a number in the other, so Plug In the Answers. If p is 9, Timmie pays $9 \times \$1.12 = \$10.08$ to buy the pens individually; that's more than it would cost him to buy the pens in the pack, but it's supposed to be cheaper to buy the pens individually. Therefore, p must be less than 9, and the correct answer is (A).

19. **D**

Plug In. If $y = 8$, $x = \dfrac{(9)(8)}{4} = 18$. The problem asks for $\dfrac{6y}{4x}$, which is $\dfrac{(6)(8)}{(4)(18)} = \dfrac{48}{72} = \dfrac{2}{3}$. Choice (D) is the only match.

20. **A and F**

The product of two integers must be an integer, so (A) is correct. The requirement that $|y| \geq 5$ is equivalent to the following conditions: $y \geq 5$ or $y \leq -5$. If $y \geq 5$ and $x \leq -2$, then $xy \leq -10$; if $y \leq -5$ and $x \leq -2$, then $xy \geq 10$. Hence, $xy \leq -10$ or $xy \geq 10$, which is the same thing as saying $|xy| \geq 10$, so (F) is correct. Choice (B) is true of only some values of xy; (C) and (D) are partial answers along the way to (F), but are incomplete and hence incorrect. Of course, you can simplify this problem greatly by plugging in for x and y. First, make $x = -2$ and $y = 5$: $xy = -10$, so eliminate (D). Next, leave $x = -2$, but make $y = -5$: Now $xy = 10$, so eliminate (B), (C), and (E). No matter what value you plug in—as long as you meet the requirements—(A) and (F) will always work, so they *must* be true.

21. **A**

Plug in a few different rounds of numbers. The question states $j - 6 = 4(c - 6)$. If you choose $c = 7$, then $j = 10$. In that case, $7 > 6.5$ and Quantity A is greater, so you can eliminate (B) and (C). To decide between (A) and (D), choose a couple of very different numbers to plug in; however, don't use either negative numbers or zeros since neither work for ages. Let $c = 66$ to check the high end of the range. For $c = 66$, $j = 246$, and $66 > 65.5$, and Quantity A is still 0.5 greater. Choose one more number to be sure. If $c = 10$, $j = 22$. Once again Quantity A is 0.5 greater than Quantity B because $10 > 9.5$, so you can confidently select (A).

22. **C**

If you remember your exponent rules, you know that Quantity A reduces to x. However, you could also Plug In on this Quant Comp question, and when you're dealing with exponents or absolute values, you should plug in negative numbers. Go through FROZEN. If $x = 0$, then $0 = 0$ and the expressions are equal: Eliminate (A) and (B). If $x = 1$, then $1 = 1$. If $x = -2$, then $-2 = -2$. If $x = 100$, then $100 = 100$. If $x = \frac{1}{2}, \frac{1}{2} = \frac{1}{2}$. At this point you can be confident that (C) is the correct choice.

23. **A**

Recognize the common quadratic and this becomes easier. You are initially given $a + b$ and $a^2 - b^2$, and this may remind you of the common quadratic $(a + b)(a - b) = a^2 - b^2$. From the other given information, solve for $a + b$, which equals 16. Substituting 16 for $(a + b)$ and 32 for $(a^2 - b^2)$ in the quadratic, you can solve for $(a - b) = 2$. Now Quantity A is 16 and Quantity B is $2^2 = 4$, making Quantity A greater.

24. **B**

Solve this Must Be problem by Plugging In. Let $a = 13$ and $b = 6$. These numbers eliminate (C) and (E). Then try some extremes, such as $a = 100$ and $b = -100$. These new numbers eliminate (A) and (D). Try $a = 100$ and $b = 1$, which eliminates (F). Only (B) always works, because the values of a and b must be more than 5 apart.

25. **A**

Solve the second equation and you'll find that $y = 6$. Plug that in to the first equation, and you'll find that $x = 8$. Therefore, Quantity A is greater.

26. **E**

Plug in different numbers until there is only one answer choice left. If you try a simple number such as $x = 2$, you'll find that you can't eliminate any answer choices. That means it's time to start thinking about different kinds of numbers. If $x = \frac{1}{2}$, (A), (B), (C), and (D) are eliminated. Only (E) works.

27. **E**

Plug in $x = 2$, $y = 3$, and $z = 4$. Put these values into the equation: $\frac{2}{2} + \frac{3 + \frac{1}{4}}{2} = \frac{2 + 3 + \frac{1}{4}}{2} = \frac{5\frac{1}{4}}{2} = \frac{\frac{21}{4}}{2} = \frac{21}{4} \times \frac{1}{2} = \frac{21}{8}$. Now go through the answer choices and find $\frac{21}{8}$. The only one that works is (E).

28. **D**

You can effectively plug in (C) by assuming for a moment that $2x = y$. When you substitute this into the quadratic equation, it satisfies it and validates (C). Eliminate (A) and (B), neither of which can be the final answer if (C) is ever correct. Factor the quadratic equation: $(2x - y)(x + 2y) = 0$. This means $2x = y$ (which you proved above) or $x = -2y$. Plug in to this second scenario, which you have yet to examine. When $x = 0$, then $y = 0$ and the columns are still equal, validating (C). But when $x = 1$, $y = -0.5$, making Quantity (A) greater. So (D) must be the correct answer.

29. **B**

Plug In. If $y = 6$, then Pat has 6 teapots, Judi has 2 teapots, and Rudy has 9 teapots. The target answer, the number of teapots that Judi and Rudy have combined, is 11. Go to the answer choices, and plug in 6 for y. Choice (B) is the only answer choice that matches your target of 11.

30. $\dfrac{1}{8}$

Translate the words in the question into an equation: $\dfrac{1}{2}x = 4x^2$. Because the question states that $x \neq 0$, you can divide both sides of the equation by x to get $\dfrac{1}{2} = 4x$. Divide both sides by 4 to find that $x = \dfrac{1}{8}$.

31. **D**

Notice that the trap answer is (C). There are variables in the columns, so Plug In. Try $q = 7$. Quantity A is 0 and Quantity B is 7. Quantity B is greater, so cross off (A) and (C). Now try $q = -7$. This time both columns are 7. Different numbers gave different answers, so the correct answer is (D).

32. $\dfrac{4}{9}$

Plugging In is the easiest way to solve this question. Let $x = 5$ and $y = 3$. Plug those numbers into the expression: $\dfrac{4x^2}{25y^2} = \dfrac{4(5)^2}{25(3)^2} = \dfrac{(4)(25)}{(25)(9)} = \dfrac{4}{9}$.

33. **C and E**

The first sentence tells you that $T = \dfrac{2}{3}P$, and the second tells you that $(T + 1) = \dfrac{3}{4}(P - 1)$. Simplify the second equation to get $T = \dfrac{3}{4}P - \dfrac{7}{4}$. Because both equations express the value of T, set them equal to one another: $\dfrac{2}{3}P = \dfrac{3}{4}P - \dfrac{7}{4}$. Multiply by 12 to get rid of the fractions, and you're left with $8P = 9P - 21$; P, therefore, equals 21. If Phillip has 21 cards and loses an even number of them, he could have $21 - 2 = 19$ cards or $21 - 4 = 17$ cards left. Choices (C) and (E) are correct.

34. **D**

If you simply subtract the second inequality from the first, it can appear as if (B) should be the answer. Be careful of merely doing the obvious on a question like this. Because there are variables, set up to Plug In on a Quant Comp. Choose something easy to start with, like $t = 45$ and $s = 11$. Then, $t - s = 45 - 11 = 34$. Eliminate (A) and (C). Your task is to now attempt to make the value of Quantity A greater than (or equal to) 39. This appears difficult at first, because of the limited amount of range you're given. FROZEN isn't particularly helpful: You can't plug in 0, 1, or negatives for this problem, but you can try fractions. Let $t = 49$ and $s = 10.5$ so $49 - 10.5 = 38.5$. You're closer, but still not quite there. This time, let $t = 49.5$ and keep $s = 10.5$ so $49.5 - 10.5 = 39$. Eliminate (B) and select (D).

35. **12**

To find the least possible value of $16 + x$, first find the least possible value of x. Rewrite the equation as $(x^n)(x^2) = 16x^2$. Divide both sides by x^2 to get $x^n = 16$. If both x and n are integers, then there are only a very few values for x and n. Minimize $16 + x$ by using a negative value for x. Because $(-4)^2 = 16$, then $x = -4$ is the least possible value for x. The least possible value of $16 + x$ is $16 - 4 = 12$.

Chapter 6
Charts and Graphs

THE JOY OF VISUAL DATA

GRE chart questions are pretty straightforward; you read a couple of charts and/or graphs and then you answer some questions about them.

Chart questions appear on a split screen; the chart(s) appear on the left, and the questions are on the right. When a chart question pops up, be sure to start by hitting the scroll bar to see just how much data you're dealing with. There might be a second chart hidden below the first one, so don't get thrown off if you see questions about a chart you don't think exists.

Chart questions test four primary skills:

- how well you read charts
- how well you approximate percentage and percentage change
- how well you calculate exact percentage and percentage change
- how well you synthesize related data from two separate sources

When you have to answer chart questions, there are a couple things to remember.

1. **Read all the charts.** Before you answer any questions about a set of charts, look over the charts. Make sure you pay particular attention to the units involved. Is each axis in terms of a number of people, a percentage, a dollar amount? **Look for a legend for the charts.** Are we talking about 100 people, or 100 million people? **Check to see if you need to scroll down for any additional charts.** If there are multiple charts, spend a minute or so figuring out how the charts relate to each other. Do the charts show different aspects of the same information? For instance, does one chart show the jobs of a group of people, whereas the other chart shows the education level of those same people? Does one chart give more detail about a limited sliver of information from the previous chart? Spending time understanding the charts now will pay off later.
2. **Find the information you need.** Once you read a Charts question, figure out which chart and which data points you need to look at.
3. **Use your scratch paper and label your information.** Find the data points you need to answer the question, and write each one down on your scratch paper. Include units and a name for each data point. Don't just write "23." Write "2004 imports – 23 mil tons." It adds only an extra couple of seconds of time, and makes it much less likely that you will make a mistake or get lost in the problem.
4. **Estimate before you calculate.** Look to eliminate answers before doing too many calculations. If 226 of the 603 employees were fired, and the question wants to know what percentage were fired, then do

a quick estimation: $\frac{226}{603} \approx \frac{200}{600} = \frac{2}{6} = \frac{1}{3} \approx 33\%$. Since we rounded

226 down to 200, our answer will probably be a bit larger than 33%.

Cross off any answers that are 33% or less, or much greater than 40%.

If we can't choose an exact answer based on our estimation, then we

can go back and calculate afterwards.

Percentage Change Quick Quiz

Remember all the reading you did about percentages and percent change in Chapter 3? Well, here are some questions. Let's see how much skill you've retained:

Question 1 of 5

If a stock portfolio grew from $1,200 to $1,600, then by what percent did the portfolio increase?

○ 25%

○ 33%

○ 40%

○ 67%

○ 75%

Question 2 of 5

If a stock portfolio with $1,600 in it has 30% of the money withdrawn, then how much money is left in the stock portfolio?

○ $360

○ $480

○ $720

○ $840

○ $1,120

A certain stock portfolio is worth $1,120.

Quantity A	**Quantity B**
$1,120	The amount of money in the portfolio if the value of the portfolio increases by 25% and then immediately decreases by 25%.

○ Quantity A is greater.

○ Quantity B is greater.

○ The two quantities are equal.

○ The relationship cannot be determined from the information given.

Question 4 of 5

If a stock portfolio worth $1,050 increase by 200%, then what is the value of the portfolio after the increase?

```
┌─────────┐
│         │
└─────────┘
```

Question 5 of 5

A stock portfolio increased in value from $1,200 to $3,150. What is the percent increase of the stock portfolio?

○   32%

○   49%

○   62%

○   163%

○   213%

Explanations for Percentage Quick Quiz

1. If a stock portfolio grew from \$1,200 to \$1,600, then the change is 1,600 – 1,200, or \$400. The percent change is $\frac{400}{1200} \times 100$ or **33%**. The correct answer is (B).

2. If a portfolio with \$1,600 in it has 30% of the money withdrawn, then the amount of money withdrawn is $\frac{30}{100} \times 1,600$, or \$480. The portfolio has \$1,600 – \$480, or **\$1,120** remaining. This can be solved in one fewer step by recognizing that withdrawing 30% is the same thing as leaving 70%. 70% of 1,600 is 1,120. The correct answer is (E).

3. The stock portfolio is worth \$1,120. Quantity A is the value of the portfolio. Quantity B states the portfolio increased by 25% then decreased by 25%. If a stock portfolio worth \$1,120 increase by 25%, then the stock portfolio increases by $\frac{25}{100} \times 1120$, or \$280, to **\$1,400**. Then, if it lost 25% the value of the stock portfolio drops from \$1,400 to $\frac{75}{100} \times 1400$, or **\$1,050**. Quantity A is greater than Quantity B, so the correct answer is (A).

4. This problem states that a stock portfolio worth \$1,600 increases by 200%. Because 200% of \$1,050 is \$2,100, the new value of the portfolio is \$1,050 + \$2,100, or **\$3,150**.

5. A portfolio that began with \$1,200 and ended with \$3,150 increased in value by \$3,150 – \$1,200 = \$1,950. To determine the percent increase, divide \$1,950 by \$1,200 and multiply the result by 100. The portfolio grew 163%. The correct answer is (D).

FOCUS MINIMIZES CARELESSNESS

Reading charts is a lot like interpreting points that are graphed on the coordinate plane. It's a process that anyone can learn with practice. The worst thing about GRE charts, however, is that they are often intentionally confusing and/or difficult to read, so it's easy to make careless mistakes under stressful conditions. Above all else, resolve to be calm and systematic when you navigate the data that the GRE throws at you. If you can manage that, the rest should fall into place nicely.

The Formats

Most chart questions come in three formats: bar or line graphs, pie charts, and data tables. Additionally, the test often gives you two separate charts that are somehow related, however remotely.

Data tables are made up entirely of numbers, so all you need to do is crunch the numbers. Graphs and charts can be a little trickier because they require you to interpret them visually.

Bar Graphs

On bar graphs, data points are indicated with rectangular bars that can run either horizontally or vertically. Bar graphs get tricky when one bar contains two or more bits of data that are often colored or patterned differently, like this:

COMPANY *X*'S GROSS PROFITS,
IN MILLIONS, 2001–02

Line Graphs

Line graphs are very similar to bar graphs except they link data points with lines that can indicate overall trends.

AVERAGE TRAFFIC DELAY ACROSS
MCCOY BRIDGE

Pie Charts

Pie charts divide up all data into wedges, each of which indicates a percentage of the whole. All of the percentages should total to 100%, and the bigger the wedge, the bigger the percentage.

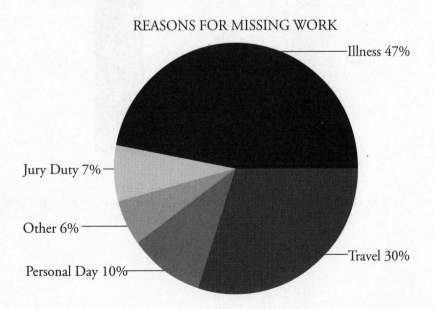

REASONS FOR MISSING WORK

Data Tables

Sometimes the GRE does away with graphics altogether and simply presents raw data in several rows and columns.

Number of Driver's Licenses Applied For, in millions

	California	Michigan	New Jersey	Maine
2000	5.41	2.26	1.21	.061
2001	4.96	1.05	0.95	.039
2002	4.92	1.96	1.06	.044
2003	4.88	2.33	1.15	.052

Ballparking, Redux

Many times, the numbers you'll work with will be approximations rather than exact calculations. Working well with these approximations is an important skill.

Let's look at an example: About how much bigger, in terms of a percentage, is the bar on the left than the bar on the right?

Pretty hard to tell, isn't it? Now look at those same bars placed next to each other:

When the bars are adjacent, it's a little easier to compare their relative size. The bar on the left is about half again as big, or 50% bigger. You can confirm this when the two bars are next to a vertical scale:

Now you have a very good (though not necessarily exact) idea of how large each bar is, and you can crunch some numbers to determine the percent decrease from Bar A to Bar B or the percent increase from Bar B to Bar A. Let's work that into a sample question, shall we?

Quantity A

The percent increase from
Bar A to Bar B

Quantity B

The percent decrease from
Bar B to Bar A

○ Quantity A is greater.

○ Quantity B is greater.

○ The two quantities are equal.

○ The relationship cannot be determined
from the information given.

Here's How to Crack It

For this question, you can estimate the value of each bar. Bar A is approximately
55; the value of Bar B is approximately 85. Now you can use the percent change
formula (divide the change by the original value and then multiply by 100) to find
your answer.

The change from A to B is 30, and the original value is 55, so the percent increase

is $\frac{30}{55} \times 100$, or approximately 50%. Conversely, the percent decrease from B to A

is $\frac{30}{85} \times 100$, or approximately 33%. The answer is (A).

The Power of Guesstimation

Have you ever heard the expression *"Almost* only counts in hand-grenades and horseshoes"? Well, you can add "GRE charts" to that list. Approximating values is an important skill when you're interpreting charts, because as you saw in the previous example, the value might not necessarily sit directly on a calibration line.

If the test asks you to estimate something, the answer choices will not be very close together. If the right answer is 47%, for example, you won't see 44% or 50% among the answer choices because they're too close to the right answer. Someone could easily be just a little off in his estimations and get 44% rather than 47%. ETS doesn't want to leave any room for dispute, because they don't want complaints from test takers.

If you don't feel confident in your abilities to estimate, resolve to practice on as many chart questions as you can until you're more confident. Greater skill will come with time, diligence, and patience.

Here's an example of how a series of chart questions might look.

PRESIDENT'S FAVORABLE AND
UNFAVORABLE RATINGS, 2002

For which of the following months was the difference between the percentages of the favorable and unfavorable ratings of the president greater than 10% ?

○ March

○ April

○ May

○ August

○ November

Here's How to Crack It

The favorable/unfavorable ratings are displayed in the line chart. Look at the line chart for the months in question and determine which month has a difference between favorable and unfavorable ratings greater than 10%. The only month of the answer choices for which is the difference is greater than 10% is March, so the correct answer is (A).

How many people who were polled in November identified themselves as members of party *Y* ?

- ○ 413
- ○ 536
- ○ 603
- ○ 723
- ○ 891

Here's How to Crack It

Now look at the pie charts, because they're the ones that reference the party affiliations of those polled. The November pie is on the far right, and 45% of the 1,340 people said they belonged to party *Y*. Because 1,340 × 0.45 = 603, the answer is (C).

And that's the basic idea behind Charts questions. The wall of data is supposed to be intimidating, especially under test-taking pressure. But if you pay attention, keep your cool, and work methodically—and keep practicing—you'll find they can be very approachable.

Charts and Graphs Drill

Questions 1–5 refer to the following graphs.

EXPENDITURES ON METAL BY COMPANY X

DISTRIBUTION OF SPENDING ON METALS BY COMPANY X IN 1990

Year	Price of Aluminum Per Ton
1975	$1,900
1980	$2,200
1985	$2,700
1990	$3,400

Approximately how much did Company X spend on aluminum in 1980 ?

- ○ $675,000
- ○ $385,000
- ○ $330,000
- ○ $165,000
- ○ $139,000

Approximately what was the percent increase in the price of aluminum from 1975 to 1985 ?

- ○ 8%
- ○ 16%
- ○ 23%
- ○ 30%
- ○ 42%

In 1990, if Company X spent $3,183,000 on metals, what was the approximate price per ton of iron?

- ○ $1,040
- ○ $2,000
- ○ $2,800
- ○ $3,400
- ○ $4,670

Approximately how many tons of aluminum and copper combined were purchased by Company X in 1985 ?

- ○ 75
- ○ 265
- ○ 325
- ○ 375
- ○ 470

Which of the following can be inferred from the graphs?

Indicate <u>all</u> such statements.

☐ Company *X* spent more on copper than it did on iron in 1975.

☐ The price per ton of copper was more than that of aluminum in 1990.

☐ Company *X* purchased fewer tons of iron in 1990 than it did "Other" metals in 1990.

Questions 6–10 refer to the following graphs.

PRODUCT SALES AND EMPLOYEES OF FOUR LEADING ELECTRONIC COMPANIES IN 1988

■ Sales (top scale)
▨ Employees (bottom scale)

DISTRIBUTION OF SALES RECEIPTS BY PRODUCT FOR COMPANY *W*, 1988 (in millions of dollars)

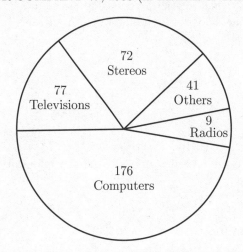

<u>Note</u>: Not drawn to scale.

In 1988, what was the approximate revenue from sales, in millions of dollars, for Company *Y* ?

○ 110

○ 235

○ 310

○ 375

○ 475

In 1988, how many of the four leading electronics companies employed at least 4,000 people?

○ None

○ One

○ Two

○ Three

○ Four

In 1988, which of the four leading electronics companies had the highest revenue from sales per employee?

○ *W*

○ *X*

○ *Y*

○ *Z*

○ It cannot be determined from the information given.

What was the approximate average (arithmetic mean) of revenue from sales, in millions of dollars, for the four leading electronics companies in 1988 ?

○ 290

○ 345

○ 375

○ 420

○ 460

By what percentage were receipts from computer sales greater than receipts from stereo sales for Company *W* in 1988 ?

○ 7%

○ 59%

○ 104%

○ 144%

○ 244%

Questions 11–15 refer to the following graphs.

EXPORTS BY SCANDINAVIAN COUNTRIES IN YEAR X
Total — $270 billion
By Country

By Product

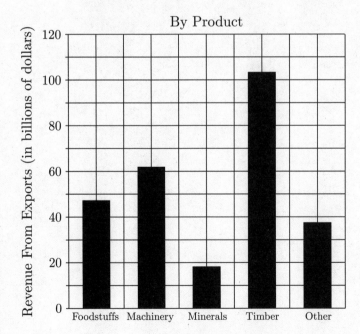

In Year X, which of the following products represented between 15 percent and 20 percent of the total revenue from all Scandinavian exports?

○ Foodstuffs

○ Machinery

○ Minerals

○ Timber

○ Other

If Sweden, Denmark, and Finland exported 30, 18, and 6 billion dollars worth of machinery, respectively, approximately how many billion dollars worth of machinery did Norway export in Year X ?

○ 62

○ 43

○ 19

○ 12

○ 8

Approximately how many billions of dollars worth of minerals did Denmark export in Year X ?

○ 5

○ 18

○ 48

○ 67

○ It cannot be determined from the information given.

In Year X, if foodstuffs accounted for 15 percent of the revenue from all Swedish exports, and if the revenue from foodstuffs exported by Norway was 40 percent less than the revenue from foodstuffs exported by Sweden, then foodstuffs accounted for approximately what percent of the revenue from all Norwegian exports?

○   8%

○   20%

○   28%

○   44%

○   60%

If, on average, 10 pounds of exported timber were worth $1, and 4 pounds of exported foodstuffs were worth $1, what was the approximate ratio of the number of pounds of exported timber to the number of pounds of exported foodstuffs for the four Scandinavian countries in Year X ?

○   5 : 4

○   2 : 1

○   5 : 2

○   4 : 1

○   5 : 1

EXPLANATIONS FOR CHARTS AND GRAPHS DRILL

1. **C**

   There were 200 tons of aluminum and 125 tons of copper purchased in 1985. The sum is 325.

2. **B**

   There were 175 tons purchased in 1980. Multiply 175 by the price per ton: 175 tons × $2,200 per ton = $385,000.

3. **E**

   The price per ton of aluminum was $1,900 in 1975 and $2,700 in 1985. Therefore,

   $$\frac{difference}{original} \times 100 = \frac{800}{1900} \times 100 = 42\%.$$

4. **C**

   If Company X spent $3,183,000 on metals and 11% of that on iron, then 3,183,000 × .11, or $350,130, was spent on iron. Divide $350,130 by 125 tons of iron to find that the price per ton of iron is approximately $2,800.

5. **B**

   Statement (A) cannot be inferred because you do not have information on the price of copper or iron in 1975, and Statement (C) cannot be inferred because you do not have information on the number of tons of "Other" metals that were purchased in 1990, so Statement (B) must be true because all that apply questions must have at least one correct answer. Although the ratio of aluminum spending to copper spending is 36 to 24, the ratio of amount of aluminum purchased to amount of copper purchased (295 tons to 175 tons) exceeds the 36 to 24 ratio. This means that copper cost more per ton than did aluminum.

6. **B**

   The bar graph indicates that Company Y had sales of approximately $235 million in 1988.

7. **C**

   The bar graph shows that Company W and Company X have more than 4,000 employees.

8. **C**

   Set up fractions of revenue over employees: Company $W = \frac{375}{5.5}$, Company $X = \frac{470}{8.0}$, Company $Y = \frac{235}{2.2}$, and Company $Z = \frac{305}{3.8}$. Company Y has the highest revenue from sales per employee.

9. **B**

Company W had $375 million in sales, X had $470 million, Y had $235 million, and Z had $305 million. The average is the total (375 + 470 + 235 + 305 = 1,385) divided by 4, or approximately $345 million.

10. **D**

Stereo receipts were $72 million, and computer receipts were $176 million. The percent change is $\dfrac{difference}{original} \times 100 = \dfrac{104}{72} \times 100$, which is 144%.

11. **A**

Foodstuffs make up about $48 billion of the $270 billion total Scandinavian exports. 15% of 270 is 40.5 and 20% of 270 is 54. Foodstuffs are the only export that falls within that range.

12. **E**

Sweden, Denmark, and Finland account for $54 billion in machinery exports out of a total of $62 billion. Therefore, Norway must account for the remaining $8 billion.

13. **E**

Denmark accounts for approximately 25% of the revenue from total Scandinavian exports, but you cannot assume that Denmark accounts for 25% of each of the different products. There is no way to determine what Denmark produces in terms of minerals for export.

14. **C**

Revenue from all Swedish exports was approximately $132 billion, and 15% of 132 is $19.8 billion. Revenue from Norwegian food stuffs is 40% less than $19.8 billion, or approximately $12 billion. $12 billion out of a total of $42 billion is approximately 28%.

15. **E**

If $1 buys you 10 pounds of timber, then $103 billion buys you about 1,000 billion pounds of timber. Similarly, if $1 buys you 4 pounds of foodstuffs, then $48 billion buys you about 200 billion pounds of foodstuffs. Therefore, the ratio of pounds of exported timber to pounds of exported foodstuffs is 1,000 to 200, or 5 to 1.

Chapter 7
Math in the
Real World

TRYING TO RELATE

The most common critique against the GRE is that it tests topics that have no direct connection to the topics most graduate school students will use. So the Educational Testing Service, makers of the GRE, decided not to test too much abstract math. Instead, they try to make questions have actual, real-life connections.

Of course, for people who spend their entire day writing standardized tests, "real-life situations" means something very different than it does for most normal people. For the GRE, this is a real-world problem:

Rhoda deposited money into her savings account for four consecutive months: March, April, May, and June. For each of the last three months, the amount she saved each month was double the amount she saved in the previous month. If the amount she saved in June was $227.50 more than the amount she saved in March, how much did she save in March?

○ $260.00

○ $130.00

○ $97.50

○ $65.00

○ $32.50

Here's How to Crack It

A typical, real-world situation that we've all been in. You save and save, but then forget how much you have in your account. When you ask your bank how much you have, you are informed that you put $227.50 more in your account this month than you did three months ago. "But how much do I actually have in my account?" you ask. The bank teller types some numbers into her computer, answers "you put double the amount into your account each month for the past four months. Since that answers your question, thank you for banking with Oblique Bank, and remember to sign up for an Obfuscation Checking Account," and hangs up.

You mean you've never been in that situation? But it's a perfectly *common* situation.

Okay, so it's not a common situation at all. However, it is a common style of GRE question, and one that you may have seen before. Notice all those numbers in the answers, and how the question is asking for a specific amount? You may have recognized the opportunity to PITA. If so, good for you. If not, feel free to look over Chapter 5 to learn more about Plugging In the Answers.

Write down A B C D E on your scratch paper, copy the answers, and label the column "March." Start with (C). If she saved $97.50 in March, then she saved double that in April ($195), doubled again in May ($390), and doubled once more in June ($780). The amount she saved in June was ($780 − $97.50) = $682.50 more than what she saved in March, which is way more than $227.50. Because (C) is too big, cross off (C), (B), and (A).

Try (D). If she saved $65 in March, she saved $130 in April, $260 in May, and $520 in June. She therefore saved ($520 − $65) = $455 dollars more in June than in March, which means (D) is too large as well. Cross off (D), and pick (E), the only answer left.

Fictional World Examples

So the questions on the GRE won't actually apply to the real world. However, they'll frequently use certain real-world topics. You should know exactly what to do when any of these topics come up, so you don't get lost in all the extra word problem garbage.

As always, focus on learning what you need to recognize in a problem to know what to start writing on your scratch paper.

THE THREE M'S

When it comes to crunching numbers, there are three statistical terms that every GRE student should recognize and distinguish from each other.

- The **mean,** or "arithmetic mean," is just another word for the average.
- The **median** is the middle number in a list of numbers when the numbers are listed in order from lowest to highest.
- The **mode** is the term that occurs *most* frequently in a list of numbers.

To remember these last two terms, you can think that (1) the *median* of a highway is in the *middle* of the highway, and (2) if you say the word *most* as if you have a terrible head cold, it comes out sounding like *mode*.

One final term you should know is **range;** the range of a set of numbers is the difference between the greatest and smallest numbers in the set.

The Mean (Average)

You calculate the average value of a list of numbers by finding their total value and dividing by the quantity of numbers in that list. To find the average of 12, 29, 32, 8, and 19, for example, add them all up (12 + 29 + 32 + 8 + 19 = 100) and divide by the number of terms (five). The answer is $\frac{100}{5}$, or 20.

A basketball player scores 12 points during her first game, 29 during her second, 32 in her third, 8 in her fourth, and 19 in her fifth game. What was her average (arithmetic mean) score per game during that week?

○ 14

○ 17

○ 20

○ 25

○ 33

Here's How to Crack It

Based on the work you just did, you know the answer is (C). However, it's worth pointing out that you can eliminate a few answer choices right away. In particular, (E) stands out, because the average of a list of numbers cannot be greater than the greatest number in the list. To solve problems like these, you can use the Average Pie.

The Average Pie

All average problems involve three quantities—the *Total* value, the *Number* of things, and the *Average* value of those things. You can relate them in a diagram we call the Average Pie, which looks like this:

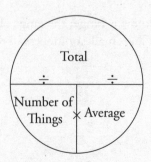

The Average Pie helps you visualize the relationship between the three numbers. It also helps you organize your thoughts by giving you three discrete compartments in which to put your information.

In order to solve the previous problem, you would add up the elements to get 100, recognize that there were five numbers, and place that information in the Average Pie like this:

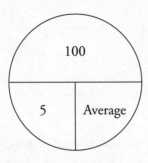

When you divide 100 by 5, you see that the answer is 20.

Try another example:

During the six weeks between Thanksgiving and New Year's Eve, an average (arithmetic mean) of 12.6 million people rode mass transit in City X each week.

Quantity A	**Quantity B**
The number of people who rode mass transit in City X between Thanksgiving and New Year's Eve	75 million

○ Quantity A is greater.

○ Quantity B is greater.

○ The two quantities are equal.

○ The relationship cannot be determined from the information given.

Here's How to Crack It

Here you have two of the three elements that go in the Average Pie. You know the Average and the Number of things, and you're looking for the Total, so set up your Average Pie like this:

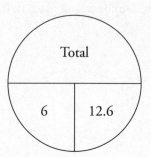

To find the Total, multiply the two bottom numbers: 6 × 12.6 = 75.6 million, which is slightly larger than the 75 million in Quantity B. The answer is (A).

Averages Quick Quiz

Question 1 of 4

Day	# of Eggs
Sunday	43
Monday	56
Tuesday	39
Wednesday	31
Thursday	46
Friday	49
Saturday	37

Farmer Brown took note of the quantity of eggs produced by the hens on his farm and compiled the chart above. What was the average (arithmetic mean) number of eggs that his hens produced each day?

○ 43

○ 44

○ 45

○ 46

○ 47

On average, each laying hen lays 255 eggs per year. If Farmer Jones has 21 hens, how many eggs can she expect her hens to lay over the course of a year?

$$\boxed{}$$

During a particularly productive month, Farmer Green's hens laid a total of 572 eggs. If each hen laid an average (arithmetic mean) of 22 eggs that month, how many hens did Farmer Green have that month?

○ 18

○ 22

○ 26

○ 32

○ 45

Over a certain month, the average (arithmetic mean) of eggs laid among 12 hens was 9. If Farmer Dobbs removes the eggs laid by the top three producers, the average of the remaining hens is 7.

Quantity A	Quantity B
The average number of eggs laid by the top three producers	11

○ Quantity A is greater.

○ Quantity B is greater.

○ The two quantities are equal.

○ The relationship cannot be determined from the information given.

Explanations for Averages Quick Quiz

1. During the seven days, the hens produced a total of 301 eggs. The Average Pie, therefore, looks like this:

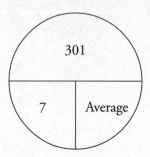

   The average value equals 301 ÷ 7, or 43. The answer is (A).

2. You know the number and the average, so set up your Average Pie like this:

   Farmer Jones can expect to get 21 × 255, or 5,355 eggs over the course of a year.

3. This time, you know the total and the average, so the Average Pie looks like this:

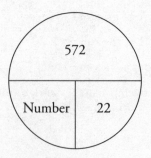

   The number of hens equals 572 ÷ 22, or 26 hens. The answer is (C).

4. Average is used three times, so set up three Average Pies and then start filling in what information is known to solve for what is not. If 12 hens lay an average of 9 eggs apiece, then the total number of eggs is 12 × 9, or 108. Once the top three egg-layers are disqualified, there are 9 hens left that lay an average of 7 eggs. They account for 7 × 9, or 63 of the eggs. The top three layers must therefore account for 108 − 63, or 45 eggs. The average value among the top three is 45 ÷ 3, or 15.

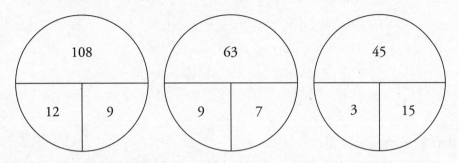

Because 15 is greater than 11, the answer is (A).

Sequences: A Helpful Hint

The GRE likes to make certain average questions seem more difficult and time-consuming than they are by having them involve huge sequences of numbers. The good news is that if the elements in a list are evenly spaced, there's a lot less work involved than you might think.

> The average of any sequence of evenly spaced elements is either
>
> *   the middle number (if the number of elements is odd); or
> *   the average of the middle two numbers (if the number of elements is even).

Quantity A	Quantity B
The average (arithmetic mean) of the first 20 even numbers	The average (arithmetic mean) of the first 21 odd numbers

○ Quantity A is greater.

○ Quantity B is greater.

○ The two quantities are equal.

○ The relationship cannot be determined from the information given.

Here's How to Crack It

The decoy answer is (B), because it looks like 21 numbers would lead to a greater answer than 20 numbers. Keep in mind that because there are no variables, you can eliminate (D).

The first 20 even numbers are 2, 4, 6, 8, 10, 12, 14, 16, 18, 20, 22, 24, 26, 28, 30, 32, 34, 36, 38, and 40. Once you list them all out, you might panic at the thought of having to add them all up and divide by 20. However, these numbers are evenly spaced, and there are 20 of them. Therefore, the average value is the average of the middle two numbers, 20 and 22. This average is 21.

Calculate Quantity B in a similar way. There are 21 terms in the sequence, so the middle number, the 11th, is the average. If you count along the sequence of odd numbers, the 11th number is 21. Therefore, the answer is (C).

The Median

As you know, the median of a list of numbers is the middle value when the numbers are placed in order of increasing size. One of the most common places to find median values is in a grad-school brochure, which often displays its "median" GRE score.

Once again, the number of elements in the list is important. Once you've ordered them from least to greatest, the median will be either the middle value (if the number of elements is odd) or the average of the middle two values (if the number of elements in the set is even).

Set D = {the first 15 positive integers}

Set F = {the prime elements in Set D}

Quantity A	Quantity B
The median of Set D	The median of Set F

○ Quantity A is greater.

○ Quantity B is greater.

○ The two quantities are equal.

○ The relationship cannot be determined from the information given.

Here's How to Crack It

Set D contains 15 elements (numbers 1 through 15), so the median is the middle number, or 7. The prime elements in Set D are 2, 3, 5, 7, 11, and 13, so the median is the average of the middle two numbers, 5 and 7. Their average is 6, so the answer is (A).

Three M's Quick Quiz

Questions 1 through 5 refer to the following list.

List G = (4, 8, 5, 9, 8, 3, 8, 5, 4)

Question 1 of 5

What is the average (arithmetic mean) of List G ?

Question 2 of 5

Quantity A	Quantity B
The median of List G	5

○ Quantity A is greater.

○ Quantity B is greater.

○ The two quantities are equal.

○ The relationship cannot be determined from the information given.

Quantity A	**Quantity B**
The mode of List G	The median of List G

○ Quantity A is greater.

○ Quantity B is greater.

○ The two quantities are equal.

○ The relationship cannot be determined
from the information given.

Question 4 of 5

What is the range of List G ?

Question 5 of 5

The addition of which of the following numbers
leaves the median of List G unchanged?

Indicate <u>all</u> such numbers.

☐ 1

☐ 3

☐ 4

☐ 5

☐ 6

☐ 7

☐ 9

Explanations for Three M's Quick Quiz

1. The sum of all of the elements in List G is $4 + 8 + 5 + 9 + 8 + 3 + 8 + 5 + 4$, or 54. There are nine elements, so the average value is $54 \div 9$, or **6**.

2. When the elements are arranged in order, List G looks like this: (3, 4, 4, 5, 5, 8, 8, 8, 9). The middle value is 5, so the answer is (C).

3. The element that occurs most often is 8, which is greater than the median (5). The answer is (A).

4. The least value in List G is 3, and the greatest value is 9. Therefore, the range of the list is $9 - 3$, or **6**.

5. The addition of a tenth number to the list means that the new median is the average of the fifth and sixth elements. Any number that is less than or equal to 5 makes both the fifth and sixth elements 5, effectively keeping the median at 5. Therefore, any of the first four values (1, 3, 4, and 5) works.

RATIOS

Ratios are a lot like fractions and decimals, with one important difference: Fractions and decimals compare parts to the whole, while ratios are more concerned with comparing two or more parts that together don't necessarily represent the whole. Most of the time, ratios are denoted with a colon, as in "the ratio of boys to girls in the classroom was 4 : 3." This means that for every four boys in the room, there were three girls. The actual number of boys is therefore a multiple of 4, the number of girls is a multiple of 3, and the number of children is a multiple of 7.

Most of us have been trained to use algebra when solving ratio questions, but the Ratio Box lets you throw algebra out the window.

The Ratio Box

Rather than deal with variables when you encounter a ratio problem, you can use the Ratio Box to organize your data in nice little columns:

	PART	PART	WHOLE
Ratio			
Multiplier			
Actual Number			

The Ratio Box is a great tool because it lets you compare the parts within the whole at a glance and it clearly relates the ratio (along the top row) to the actual number of elements you have (the bottom row). Here's how to use it.

In a certain used-car showroom, the ratio of hardtop cars to convertibles is 7 : 2. If there are 16 convertibles, how many cars are in the showroom?

- ○ 2
- ○ 7
- ○ 9
- ○ 56
- ○ 72

Here's How to Crack It

Set up your Ratio Box, label your Parts columns, and enter all the information you know:

	Hardtops	Convertibles	Whole
Ratio	7 +	2	= 9
Multiplier			
Actual Number		16	

Notice that the first thing to do with the numbers in the ratio row is to put their sum in the far-right column. Now, from the top row, you know that for every 9 cars, 7 of them are hardtops and 2 are convertibles.

The next step is to make the connection between the ratio of the cars and the actual number of cars, which are separated by a multiplier. The link is in the convertible column; there are 16 actual convertibles, and the ratio value is 2. Therefore, the multiplier for the whole box is 16 ÷ 2, or 8. Enter 8 across the entire multiplier row, like this:

	Hardtops	Convertibles	Whole
Ratio	7	2	9
Multiplier	8	8	8
Actual Number	56	16	72

Finish the box by multiplying down each of the other columns.

You now know that there are 56 hardtops and 16 convertibles, for a total of 72 vehicles so the answer is (E).

———————○———————

It's Expandable!

Not all ratio questions have just two parts, and you can expand your Ratio Box to include as many parts as necessary. Here's how that works:

———————○———————

A contractor mixes cement, water, sand, and gravel in a ratio of 1 : 3 : 4 : 2 by weight to make concrete. How many pounds of sand are needed to make 28 pounds of concrete?

○ 2.8

○ 5.6

○ 8.4

○ 11.2

○ 13.6

Here's How to Crack It

The formula has four parts, so create a column for each one, like this:

	C	W	S	G	Total
Ratio	1	3	4	2	10
Multiplier			2.8		2.8
Actual Number			11.2		28

The total is 1 + 3 + 4 + 2, or 10 parts. If the actual amount is 28 pounds, then the multiplier is 28 ÷ 10, or 2.8. Don't bother filling in every column; all you need is the amount of sand. Place the 2.8 in the sand column, multiply by 4, and you get 11.2 pounds. The answer is (D).

———————○———————

Ratios Quick Quiz

The ratio of boys to girls in a hospital maternity ward is 3 : 4. Which of the following CANNOT be the number of babies in the ward?

○ 28

○ 35

○ 38

○ 42

○ 63

If there are only tulips and daffodils in a garden and the ratio of tulips to daffodils is 3 : 5, what percent of the flowers in the garden are daffodils?

○ 37.5%

○ 40%

○ 60%

○ 62.5%

○ 133.3%

At a certain restaurant, the ratio of line cooks to waiters is 2 : 3 and the ratio of waiters to busboys is 4 : 3.

Quantity A	Quantity B
The number of line cooks at the restaurant	The number of busboys at the restaurant

○ Quantity A is greater.

○ Quantity B is greater.

○ The two quantities are equal.

○ The relationship cannot be determined from the information given.

If there are 120 workers in an office, each of the following could be the ratio of men to women EXCEPT

○ 2 : 1

○ 3 : 1

○ 4 : 1

○ 6 : 1

○ 7 : 1

Explanations for Ratios Quick Quiz

1. When you fill in the Ratio Box with the given ratio, the sum of the two parts is 7.

	Boys	Girls	Whole
Ratio	3	4	7
Multiplier			
Actual number			38

Therefore, the number of babies in the maternity ward must be a multiple of 7. Each of the answer choices except 38 is a multiple of 7. The answer is (C).

2. If the ratio of tulips to daffodils is 3 : 5, your Ratio Box looks like this:

	Tulips	Daffodils	Whole
Ratio	3	5	8
Multiplier			
Actual Number			

Because the total is 8, the fractional amount of daffodils is 5 out of 8, or $\frac{5}{8}$. Because $\frac{5}{8}$ is equivalent to 62.5%, the answer is (D).

3. Line up the ratios like this, so that you can compare all three parts at once.

line cooks		waiters		busboys
2	:	3		
		4	:	3
8	:	12	:	9

There are two separate ratios listed here, and the only way to compare line cooks and busboys is to relate them to a common number of waiters. If you multiply the two numbers you have for waiters, you get 12—a lowest common denominator. From here, you can convert the ratio of line cooks to waiters from 2 : 3 to 8 : 12, and the ratio of waiters to busboys from 4 : 3 to 12 : 9. This makes the ratio of line cooks to busboys 8 : 9. There are more busboys than line cooks, so the answer is (B).

4. When you fill in the Ratio Box, the value in the Whole column of the ratio row must be a factor of 120. Because 6 + 1 = 7, and 7 is not a factor of 120, the answer is (D).

PROPORTIONS

Proportions are related to ratios, because a ratio between two elements is proportional to the actual values. If you know the ratio of two quantities and you have to extrapolate that ratio onto some actual values, you'll probably end up writing a proportion.

The Setup

Proportions are comparisons of two things in a fixed ratio. There are two very important considerations to keep in mind when you set proportions up.

*   **Make sure your elements are consistent.** If you're comparing miles per hour and you decide that miles are in the numerator, make sure they're always in the numerator.
*   **Make sure your units are consistent.** If you're comparing distances, and one distance is given in feet while the other is in inches, convert one of those distances so that the units are the same.

Once your proportion is ready, you can cross-multiply and solve for the missing value.

If a train maintains a constant speed of 80 miles per hour, how far does the train travel in 24 minutes?

Here's How to Crack It

The first ratio compares miles and hours, so your first instinct might be to set up a proportion like this:

$$\textbf{WRONG:} \quad \frac{miles}{hours} \quad \frac{80}{1} = \frac{x}{24}$$

The elements are aligned, but the units aren't consistent because the question mentions 24 *minutes*, not hours. To solve this, convert 1 hour to 60 minutes, and you'll be ready to cross-multiply:

$$\frac{miles}{minutes} \quad \frac{80}{60} = \frac{x}{24}$$

$$60x = 80 \times 24$$

$$60x = 1{,}920$$

$$x = 32$$

Proportions Quick Quiz

A muffin recipe that calls for 2 cups of flour yields 25 muffins. If Yvonne needs to make 40 muffins, how many cups of flour should she use?

- ○ $1\dfrac{1}{4}$

- ○ $2\dfrac{1}{3}$

- ○ $2\dfrac{4}{5}$

- ○ $3\dfrac{1}{5}$

- ○ $5\dfrac{1}{3}$

Question 2 of 4

A greenskeeper wants to fertilize the eighteenth hole of a golf course, which has an area of 12,000 square feet. If the fertilizer he wants to use suggests using one bag for every 10 square yards, how many bags should he purchase?

- ○ 48
- ○ 133
- ○ 134
- ○ 266
- ○ 1,200

Question 3 of 4

If 75 percent of a certain number is 1,200, then what is 10 percent of that number?

- ○ 90
- ○ 120
- ○ 160
- ○ 240
- ○ 480

Arturo saves $1,490 in 8 months.

Quantity A	**Quantity B**
The number of months, at the same rate, it would take Arturo to save 3.5 times the amount he has already saved	28

○ Quantity A is greater.

○ Quantity B is greater.

○ The two quantities are equal.

○ The relationship cannot be determined from the information given.

Explanations for Proportions Quick Quiz

1. Set up the proportion that compares cups of flour to muffins.

$$\frac{2}{25} = \frac{x}{40}$$

When you cross-multiply, your equation becomes $25x = 80$, and $x = 3.2$. Because this is equivalent to $3\frac{1}{5}$, the answer is (D). Note: Just because you can use your calculator doesn't mean you should forget all about fractions, which can still appear in answer choices.

2. First, an important conversion: Because one yard equals three feet, one square yard is the same as *nine* square feet. Therefore, if each bag fertilizes 10 square yards, it fertilizes 90 square feet. Set up your proportion, comparing bags to square feet of coverage:

$$\frac{1}{90} = \frac{x}{12,000}$$

When you cross-multiply, $90x = 12,000$ and $x = 133.3$. Because he has to buy full bags, he must buy 134 for complete coverage. The answer is (C).

3. You can find the value of the number, but you really don't need to. Just set up the proportion that compares percentages to numbers.

$$\frac{75}{1,200} = \frac{10}{x}$$

From this proportion, you can cross-multiply to find that $75x = 12,000$, and $x = 160$. The answer is (C).

4. Even though the quantities are proportional, there's no need to set up a proportion. If Arturo wants to save 3.5 times the amount, he'll need 3.5 times more time. When you multiply 8 by 3.5, you get 28 months. The two quantities are equal, so the answer is (C).

Naturally, statistics can get a little more complicated, but we'll wait until Chapter 9 to delve into the world of combinations, probability, and standard deviation. In the meantime, here are some more practice questions about ratios, proportions, and real-life math situations.

Math in the Real World Drill

A machine punches x plates per hour for 4 hours and then y plates per hour for 2 hours. Which of the following is an expression for the average number of plates punched per hour by the machine for the entire 6 hours?

- ○ $2x + 4y$

- ○ $\dfrac{2x + 4y}{6}$

- ○ $\dfrac{3xy}{2}$

- ○ $\dfrac{4x + 2y}{6}$

- ○ $4x + 2y$

Twenty bottles contain a total of 8 liters of apple juice. If each bottle contains the same amount of apple juice, how much juice, in liters, is in each bottle?

$$\boxed{}$$

If 12 equally priced melons cost a total of $9.60, then what is the cost of 9 of these melons?

- ○ $7.00
- ○ $7.20
- ○ $8.00
- ○ $8.45
- ○ $8.65

If $2a = 3b = 4c = 72$, then what is the average (arithmetic mean) of a, b, and c ?

- ○ 39
- ○ 26
- ○ 24
- ○ 18
- ○ 9

Jenny notices a consistent, increasing pattern in the number of geese she sees flying over her house each day. If she sees 5 geese on Monday, 8 geese on Tuesday, 11 geese on Wednesday, and 14 geese on Thursday, and the next week starts on Sunday, on which of the following days of the next week will she see a prime number of geese if the pattern continues?

Indicate all such values.

- ☐ Sunday
- ☐ Monday
- ☐ Tuesday
- ☐ Thursday
- ☐ Friday
- ☐ Saturday

Set B contains only positive, even integers. Which of the following could be the median of set B ?

Indicate all such values.

- ☐ –2
- ☐ 0
- ☐ 1
- ☐ 3
- ☐ 3.5
- ☐ 4

A car manufacturer has 2,992 forklifts, which is approximately one forklift for every 48.9 employees. Which of the following is the closest approximation, in thousands, of the number of employees employed by the manufacturer?

- ○ 60
- ○ 100
- ○ 150
- ○ 175
- ○ 300

A recipe for 4 loaves of bread requires $\frac{3}{4}$ cup of sugar. If Chris wants to make 2 loaves of bread, which of the following calculations yields the amount of sugar he needs?

Indicate all such values.

- ☐ $\frac{3}{4} \times \frac{1}{2}$
- ☐ $\frac{3}{4} \times 2$
- ☐ $\frac{3}{4} \div \frac{1}{2}$
- ☐ $\frac{3}{4} \div 2$

V is a sequence of numbers in which every term after the first two is the average of the two previous terms. If the first term x is 16 more than the second term y, then which of the following represents the fifth term of the sequence, in terms of y ?

- ○ $y - 2$
- ○ y
- ○ $y + 2$
- ○ $y + 4$
- ○ $y + 6$

Set A contains only even integers. Which of the following CANNOT be the median of set A ?

- ○ –2
- ○ –1
- ○ 0
- ○ 0.5
- ○ 1

A violinist needs 2 hours to tune a violin made in the twentieth century. To tune violins made before the twentieth century, the violinist needs twice as long, and for violins made after the twentieth century, she needs half as long. Which of the following groups of violins could she tune in 6 hours?

Indicate all such groups.

- ☐ Two violins made before the twentieth century
- ☐ Three violins made during the twentieth century
- ☐ One violin made during the twentieth century, one made before, and two made after
- ☐ Two violins made after the twentieth century, and one made before
- ☐ Two violins made after the twentieth century, and two made during the twentieth century

$$2g = 6h$$

Quantity A	Quantity B
The ratio of g to h	$\frac{1}{3}$

- ○ Quantity A is greater.
- ○ Quantity B is greater.
- ○ The two quantities are equal.
- ○ The relationship cannot be determined from the information given.

If 6 students have an average (arithmetic mean) score of 88 on an exam, and one of those students scored a 93 on the exam, what is the average score on this exam for the other 5 students?

○ 84

○ 85

○ 86

○ 87

○ 89

Let H be a sequence, h_1, h_2, h_3 ... h_n, such that each term after the first is two less than one-third of the previous term. If the fourth term in the sequence is 0, which of the following is the sum of the first and fifth terms of the sequence?

○ −2

○ $25\frac{1}{3}$

○ 26

○ 76

○ 78

A bag of jellybeans has red and yellow jellybeans in a ratio of $c : d$. If there are r red jellybeans in the bag, which of the following represents the number of yellow jellybeans in the bag?

○ $\dfrac{cd}{dr}$

○ $\dfrac{dr}{c}$

○ $\dfrac{cd}{r}$

○ $d(c + r)$

○ $d(r - d)$

Miguel's bowling team bowled a practice round in preparation for their upcoming league game. The team's average (arithmetic mean) score for the practice round was 180. Miguel scored 190, Janice scored 200, and Thad scored 210. If no team member scored less than 165, and none of the remaining team members scored greater than 170, what is one possible value for the number of members on Miguel's team? (Note: Bowling scores are always positive integers.)

EXPLANATIONS FOR MATH IN THE REAL WORLD DRILL

1. **D**

    Plug In, and let $x = 6$ and $y = 3$. If the machine punches 6 plates per hour for 4 hours, you know that it punches 24 plates in that time. If the machine punches 3 plates per hour for 2 hours, you know that it punches 6 plates in that time. In 6 hours the machine punches a total of 30 plates. If you divide 30 by 6, you'll get 5 plates per hour, your target answer. The only answer that matches the target is (D): $\dfrac{(4 \times 6) + (2 \times 3)}{6} = \dfrac{24 + 6}{6} = 5$.

2. **0.4**

    Twenty bottles hold a total of 8 liters of juice. Each bottle contains the same amount, so you need to divide the amount of juice by the number of bottles: $8 \div 20 = 0.4$.

3. **B**

    Divide the total cost of $9.60 by 12 melons to get the per-melon cost of $0.80. Now calculate the cost of 9 melons at the same price per melon: $9 \times \$0.80 = \$7.20$.

4. **B**

    Break the expression into three equations. Since $2a = 72$, $a = 36$. Since $3b = 72$, $b = 24$. Since $4c = 72$, $c = 18$. The average of 36, 24, and 18 is $\dfrac{36 + 24 + 18}{3} = 26$. You could estimate that (E) is incorrect because the value of each of the three variables is greater than 9, and the average will be greater than 9.

5. **A, C, and F**

    Once you deduce the pattern, you'll be able to predict the number of geese for each day of the next week and select the prime numbers. The number of geese increases by 3 each day: If she saw 14 on Thursday, she'll see 17 on Friday, 20 on Saturday, 23 on Sunday, 26 on Monday, 29 on Tuesday, 32 on Wednesday, 35 on Thursday, 38 on Friday, and 41 on Saturday. Sunday, Tuesday, and Saturday have a prime number of geese, so (A), (C), and (F) are correct.

6. **D and F**

    If the set contains only positive integers, then there's no way numbers 0 or less can be the median, so eliminate (A) and (B). For 1 to be the median, there has to be a number in the set less than 1, so eliminate (C). Don't eliminate (D) just because it's odd—remember that in a set with no unique middle term, the median is the average of the two middle terms; the set could be {2, 4}, for instance, which would have a median of 3. The same set could be extended to {2, 4, 6}, which would have a median of 4, or (F). Since 3.5 itself cannot be in the set, the only remaining question is whether 3.5 can be the average of two even numbers: It can't, because $3.5 \times 2 = 7$, and two even numbers can't add up to 7. Eliminate (E) and select (D) and (F).

7. **C**

Estimate. 2,992 is almost 3,000, and 48.9 is almost 50. The number of employees is approximately 3,000 × 50, or 150,000. Only (C) is close.

8. **A and D**

Because Chris is making only 2 loaves, he needs half as much sugar as he does for 4 loaves. You can multiply $\frac{3}{4}$ by $\frac{1}{2}$ to find how much sugar he needs, or you can divide the quantity by 2.

9. **E**

When you see variables in the answer choices, Plug In. Start by choosing your y. Since x is 16 more than y, let y be some small positive integer like 2. That makes $x = 18$. Average the two together, and the third term in the sequence (remember, x and y are the first *two* terms of the sequence) is 10. Take the second and third terms, average them together, and you get 6 ((10 + 2) ÷ 2 = 6) as the fourth term. Do it one more time to get 8 ((6 + 10) ÷ 2 = 8) as the fifth term. Plug In to your answer choices, and eliminate all but (E).

10. **D**

Come up with possible sets that could have the medians of the answer choices. Choices (A) and (C) are eliminated because –2 and 0 are even numbers and you could easily have a set with those choices as the center number. Both –1 and 1 are a bit more difficult to eliminate, but keep in mind that if your set has two middle terms, rather than just one, the median of the set is the average of those two middle terms. So, for a median of –1, the set could be –2 and 0; for a median of 1, the set could be 0 and 2. Eliminate (B) and (E). Select your only remaining choice, (D).

11. **B, D, and E**

First, figure out how long it will take the violinist to tune each type of instrument. Violins made before the 20th century take twice as long to tune, so they take 4 hours. Violins made after the 20th century take half as long to tune, so they take 1 hour. Add up the total time needed to tune the violins in each answer choice. The total time for (A) is 4 + 4 = 8 hours, so (A) can be eliminated. For (B), the total time is 3 × 2 = 6 hours. Choice (B) is correct. For (C), 2 + 4 + 1 + 1 = 8 hours. Choice (C) can be eliminated. For (D), 1 + 1 + 4 = 6 hours. Choice (D) is correct. For (E) 1 + 1 + 2 + 2 = 6 hours. Choice (E) is correct.

12. **A**

Since there are variables involved, this is an opportunity to Plug In. First, simplify the equation by dividing both sides by 2 to get $g = 3h$. Plug in a number for h and solve for g to see the ratio. For example, if you plug in 1 for h, then $g = 3$. Quantity A asks for the ratio of g to h, which is now 3 to 1. Quantity A is greater.

13. **D**

The average for 6 students is 88. Set up an Average Pie and use 6 for the number of things and 88 for the average. Therefore, the 6 students scored a total of 6 × 88 = 528 points. One student scored a 93, so the remaining 5 students scored a total of 528 – 93 = 435 points. Set up another Average Pie, using 435 as the total and 5 as the number of things. Divide 435 by 5 to find that these 5 students scored an average of 87 points. The answer is (D).

14. **D**

With sequence questions, PITA typically works well. This problem makes that a little more difficult by asking you for a sum of two terms, rather than the term itself (i.e., you would still have to guess about the terms, even if you attempted to begin at a certain answer choice and work from there). You are given the fourth term, so try to move back and forth from there. Each following term is one-third of the previous term minus 2. So, $\frac{1}{3}$ of 0 equals 0, and 0 – 2 equals –2, your fifth term. To find the previous terms, simply invert the sequence: Add 2 and then multiply by 3. The third term is (0 + 2) × 3 = 6, the second term is (6 + 2) × 3 = 24, and the first term must be (24 + 2) × 3 = 78. Add together your first and fifth terms: 78 + –2 = 76, which is (D).

15. **B**

Use the Ratio Box and plug in some values. If $c = 2$, $d = 3$, and $r = 20$, then there will be 30 yellow jellybeans. Circle 30 as your target and check all five choices. Choices (A) and (C) are way too small, but (B) works. Choices (D) and (E) do not match, leaving (B) as your correct answer.

16. **7, 8, or 9**

Use the Average Pie. Label the number of additional team members t. Assume that all of these t people scored 165. These t people therefore scored a total of $165t$ points. Miguel, Janice, and Thad scored a total of 600 points. Therefore, the total number of points scored by the team is $165t + 600$. Put this in the top segment of the pie. The total number of people on the team is $t + 3$, which should go in the bottom left segment. Put the average, 180, in the bottom right segment. At this point you can see that $\frac{165t + 600}{t + 3} = 180$, or total divided by number of things equals average. Solve algebraically. First, $165t + 600 = 180t + 540$. Subtract 540 from both sides to find that $165t + 60 = 180t$. Subtract $165t$ from both sides to find that $60 = 15t$. Therefore, $t = 4$. Remember that t is the number of *additional* people on the team, and the question asks for total people; therefore if $t = 4$, there are 7 people on the team. The problem also gives you an integer for t if you use 170 ($t = 6$, and the total number of team members is 9) and 168 ($t = 5$, and the total number of team members is 8).

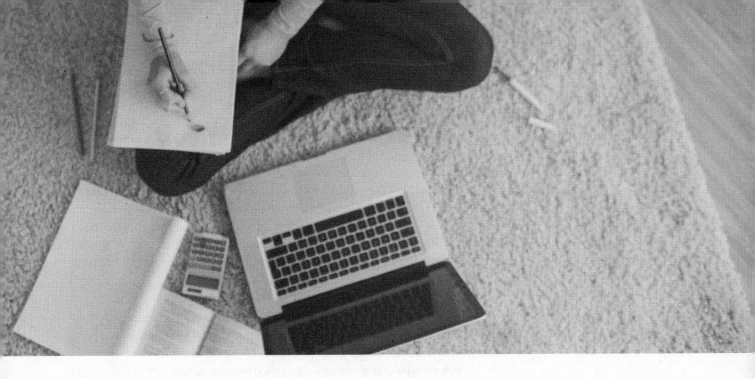

Chapter 8
Geometry

ANGLING FOR A BETTER GRADE?

Now that you've reached this chapter, you may be having a flashback to your freshman year in high school when you first came in contact with theorems, postulates, and definitions, all woven together to form the geometric proof. Well, relax. GRE geometry questions have little to do with deductive reasoning. You're much more likely to be tested on the basic formulas involving area, perimeter, volume, and angle measurements. As you work through the GRE Math, you'll find that there is a basic battery of terms and formulas that you should know for the geometry questions that do come your way. Before we get to those, let's look at some techniques.

- **Plug In.** If a problem tells you that a rectangle is *x* inches long and *y* inches wide, plug in some real numbers to help the question take on a more tangible quality. (And if there is more than one variable, remember to plug in a different number for each one.)
- **Use Ballparking.** If a diagram is drawn to scale, you can sometimes estimate the right answer and eliminate all the answer choices that don't come close.
- **Redraw to Scale.** If a diagram is not drawn to scale—and for problem solving questions you'll know because you'll see the words "Note: Figure not drawn to scale" right below the picture—redraw it to make it look like it's supposed to look like. Drawings like this are meant to confuse you by suggesting that the figure looks how it's represented in the problem. Redrawing the figure to scale helps you avoid falling into that trap.

BASIC HINTS FOR GEOMETRY QUESTIONS

Geometry is a special science all its own, but that doesn't mean it marches to the beat of an entirely different drummer. Many of the techniques you've learned for other problems will work here as well.

So let's start with our pal Euclid and his three primary building blocks of measured space: points, lines, and planes.

LINES AND ANGLES

Two points determine a line, and two intersecting lines form an angle measured in degrees. There are 360° in a complete circle, so halfway around the circle forms a straight angle, which measures 180°, and half of that is a right angle, which measures 90°.

Two lines that intersect in a right angle are perpendicular, and perpendicularity is denoted by the symbol "⊥." Two lines that lie in the same plane and never intersect are parallel, which is denoted by "∥." Take a look at two parallel lines below:

If one line intersects two parallel lines, it is called a transversal. It may look as though this transversal creates eight angles with the two lines, but there are actually only two types: big angles and small angles. All the big angles have the same degree measure, and all the small angles have the same degree measure. The sum of the degree measures of one big angle and one small angle is always 180°.

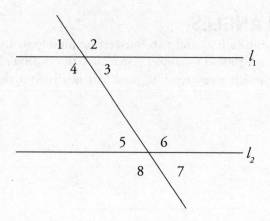

$$l_1 \| l_2$$

Notice that for the figure above, the acute (small) angles labeled 1, 3, 5, and 7 are all the same, because l_1 is parallel with l_2. You also know that the angles labeled 2, 4, 6, and 8 are all the same for the same reason. Whenever the GRE states that two lines are parallel, look to see if the question is actually testing this concept.

TRIANGLES

Three points determine a triangle, and all triangles have three sides and three angles. The sum of the measures of the angles inside a triangle is 180°. The sides and angles are related. Just remember that the longest side is always opposite the largest angle, and the shortest side is always opposite the smallest angle.

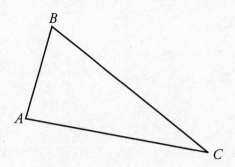

Types of Triangles

The properties of triangles start to get more interesting when some or all of the sides have the same length.

- **Isosceles Triangles:** If two sides of a triangle have the same length, the triangle is isosceles. The relationship between sides and angles still goes; if two sides of a triangle are the same length, then the angles opposite those sides have the same degree measure.
- **Equilateral Triangles:** Equilateral triangles have three equal sides and three equal angles. Because the sum of the angle measures is 180°, each angle in an equilateral triangle measures $\frac{180}{3}$, or 60°.

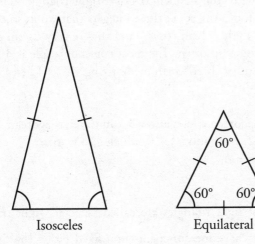

Isosceles   Equilateral

Right Triangles

Right triangles contain exactly one right angle and two acute angles. The perpendicular sides are called legs, and the longest side (which is opposite the right angle) is called the hypotenuse.

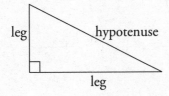

The Pythagorean Theorem

Whenever you know the length of two sides of a right triangle, you can find the length of the third side by using the Pythagorean Theorem.

$$a^2 + b^2 = c^2$$

Most of the time, one of the side lengths of a right triangle is irrational and in the form of a square root. Any set of three integers that works in the Pythagorean Theorem is called a "Pythagorean triple," and they're very useful to know for the GRE because they come up often. The most common triple is 3 : 4 : 5 (because $3^2 + 4^2 = 5^2$), but the other three worth memorizing are 5 : 12 : 13, 7 : 24 : 25, and 8 : 15 : 17.

All multiples of Pythagorean triples also work in the Pythagorean Theorem. If you multiply 3 : 4 : 5 by 2, you get 6 : 8 : 10, which also works.

Special Triangles

Two specific types of right triangles are called "special" right triangles because their angles and sides have measurements in a fixed ratio. The first, an isosceles right triangle, is also referred to as a 45 : 45 : 90 triangle because its angle measures are 45°, 45°, and 90°. The ratio of its side lengths is $x : x : \sqrt{2}$. The second is a 30 : 60 : 90 triangle, which has side lengths in a ratio of $x : x\sqrt{3} : 2x$.

ETS likes to use special triangles because they can confuse test takers into thinking they don't have enough information to answer a question. The fact is, though, if you know the length of one side of a special triangle, you can use the ratios to find the lengths of the other two sides.

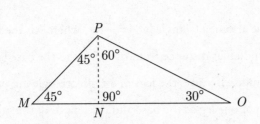

In the figure shown above, if the height of triangle *MPO* is 4 inches, what is the perimeter, in inches, of triangle *MPO* ?

○ $8 + 4\sqrt{2} + 4\sqrt{3}$

○ $12 + 8\sqrt{3}$

○ $12 + 4\sqrt{2} + 4\sqrt{3}$

○ $20 + 8\sqrt{3}$

○ $20 + 4\sqrt{2} + 4\sqrt{3}$

Here's How to Crack It

The figure consists of two special triangles; consider the 45 : 45 : 90 triangle on the left. If $PN = 4$, then $MN = 4$ and $MP = 4\sqrt{2}$. The height PN also helps you find the lengths of the 30 : 60 : 90 triangle on the right. Because PN is the short side, the hypotenuse PO is twice as long, or 8 inches long. The other side, *NO*, measures $4\sqrt{3}$. The perimeter of triangle *MPO* is therefore $4 + 4\sqrt{2} + 8 + 4\sqrt{3}$, so the answer is (C).

Area

The formula for the area of a triangle is $A = \frac{1}{2}bh$, where b is the length of the base and h is the perpendicular distance from the vertex to the base (also known as the height, or the altitude). Because the legs of a right triangle are perpendicular, you can use the length of one leg as the base and the length of the other as the height.

In the diagram above, each of the triangles has the same base and a height of the same measure. Therefore, each triangle has the same area.

How Long Is the Third Side?

If you know the lengths of two sides of a triangle, you can use a simple formula to determine how long and how short the third side could possibly be.

> If the lengths of two sides of a triangle are x and y, respectively, the length of the third side must be less than $x + y$ and greater than $|x - y|$.

The townships of Addington and Bordenview are 65 miles apart, and Clearwater is 40 miles from Bordenview. If the three towns do not lie on a straight line, which of the following could be the distance from Addington to Clearwater?

○   15

○   25

○   35

○   105

○   125

Here's How to Crack It

This is a "third-side" problem disguised as a word problem about three towns. Because the towns do *not* lie along a straight line, they form a triangle; one side is 65 miles long, and the other is 40 miles long. Therefore, the third side (the length between towns A and C) must be greater than 65 – 40, or 25, and less than 65 + 40, or 105. (Remember, the distance has to be *greater than* 25, so it can't be *equal* to 25, nor can it be equal to 105.) Therefore, the correct answer is (C).

Triangle Quick Quiz

Question 1 of 6

If the degree measures of two angles of $\triangle ABC$ are 50° and 65°, what is the degree measure of the third angle?

○   15°

○   50°

○   65°

○   115°

○   165°

Question 2 of 6

If isosceles $\triangle DEF$ has sides of length 11.5 and 13.7, which of the following could be the perimeter of the triangle?

Indicate <u>all</u> such values.

☐   2.1

☐   12.0

☐   25.2

☐   36.7

☐   50.4

The base of a triangle is twice its height, which is 5 cm. What is the area, in square centimeters, of the triangle?

○   6.25

○   10

○   12.5

○   25

○   50

What is the perimeter of triangle *XYZ* shown above?

On his way home from shopping, Mike must travel due south for 5 miles and then due east for another 12 miles to reach his house. If Mike could travel in a straight line from the store to his house, how many fewer miles would he travel?

○   1

○   4

○   8

○   13

○   17

If the lengths of all 3 sides of triangle *RST* are distinct, single-digit prime numbers, then which of the following could be the perimeter of triangle *RST* ?

Indicate <u>all</u> such values.

- ☐ 6
- ☐ 10
- ☐ 12
- ☐ 14
- ☐ 15
- ☐ 19

Explanations for Triangle Quick Quiz

1. The first two measures are 50° and 65°, so their total measure is 115°. The third angle must measure 180 − 115, or **65°**. The answer is (C).

2. Since the triangle is isosceles, then the third side must be either 11.5 or 13.7. If the third side is 11.5, then the perimeter is 36.7. If the third side is 13.7, then the perimeter is 38.9. The answer is (D).

3. The height is 5 cm so the base is 10 cm. The area is therefore $\frac{1}{2}(5)(10)$, or **25 cm²**. The answer is (D).

4. Using the Pythagorean Theorem, you can find the third side. $25^2 - 15^2 = 400$, and the square root of 400 is 20. The perimeter equals 15 + 20 + 25, or 60. You can also find the third side based on the 3 : 4 : 5 Pythagorean triple (just multiply the whole ratio by 5). The answer is 60.

5. Draw out the right triangle described in the question. By traveling due south and then due east, you get a right triangle with legs of length 5 and 12. Now you can solve for the length of the hypotenuse, or the distance from the store to the house. It equals 13 from the 5 : 12 : 13 Pythagorean triple. The question asks how many fewer miles Mike would travel if he could travel in a straight line. Mike travels a total of 5 + 12 = 17 miles as opposed to 13 miles if he could travel in a straight line. 17 − 13 = 4, so he would save 4 miles, which is (B).

6. The only single-digit prime numbers are 2, 3, 5, and 7; remember, though, that triangles must conform to the Third Side Rule, which states that the largest side of a triangle must be less than the sum of the other two sides. Only (E) is the sum of 3 sides that meet both requirements: 3, 5, and 7. Choices (B), (C), and (D) can also be reached by adding 3 distinct single digit primes—2, 3, and 5; 2, 3, and 7; and 2, 5, and 7, respectively—but all violate the Third Side Rule. If you selected (A) or (F), remember to use only *distinct* values for the sides. The answer is (E).

QUADRILATERALS

A quadrilateral is any figure that has four sides, and the same types of quadrilaterals—parallelograms, rectangles, and squares—show up over and over again on the GRE. Regardless of their shape or size, however, one thing is true of all four-sided figures: They can be divided into two triangles. From this, you can determine a couple of things:

Degrees: Because every quadrilateral can be divided into 2 triangles, all quadrilaterals obey what we call the **Rule of 360:** There are 180° in a triangle, so there are 2 × 180, or 360, degrees in every quadrilateral.

Area: The area of a triangle is $\frac{1}{2}bh$, so the area of a parallelogram is $2 \times \frac{1}{2}bh$, or bh.

Properties, Area, and Perimeter

Quadrilaterals are often referred to as a "family" because they share lots of characteristics. For example, every rectangle is a parallelogram, so rectangles have every characteristic that a parallelogram has, and they also happen to have four right angles. Ditto for a square, which is just a rectangle that has four equal sides.

Here is a handy chart to help you keep track of all the various properties and the formulas for area and perimeter.

Quadrilateral	Properties	Area	Perimeter
Parallelogram	Opposite sides are parallel Opposite sides have the same length Opposite angles have the same measure Diagonals are not the same length (unless it's a rectangle)	$A = b \times h$	Sum of the sides
Rectangle	All the properties of parallelograms, plus: Diagonals have the same length All angles have the same measure (90°)	$A = l \times w$	$P = 2l + 2w$
Square	All the properties of rectangles, plus: All sides have the same length	$A = s^2$	$P = 4s$

Quadrilateral Quick Quiz

If the degree measures of two angles in a quadrilateral are 70° and 130° and the remaining two angles are equal to each other, what is the degree measure of one of these angles?

- ○ 60°
- ○ 80°
- ○ 100°
- ○ 160°
- ○ 200°

If the length of a rectangular garden is five times its width, and the perimeter of the garden is 36 feet, what is the garden's width?

- ○ 3
- ○ 12
- ○ 15
- ○ 18
- ○ 30

If the base and height of a parallelogram are 10 cm and 15 cm, respectively, what is the area, in square cm, of the parallelogram?

- ○ 25
- ○ 50
- ○ 75
- ○ 150
- ○ It cannot be determined from the information given.

Explanations for Quadrilateral Quick Quiz

1. The sum of the given angles is 70° + 130°, or 200°, so the sum of the remaining angles must be 360° − 200°, or 160°. These angles are the same size, so they must each measure $\frac{160}{2}$, or 80°. The answer is (B).

2. If the width of the garden is w, then the length is five times that, or $5w$. Plug these into the formula for perimeter ($2l + 2w$) and solve: $2(5w) + 2w = 36$, so $12w = 36$ and $w = 3$. The garden is 3 feet wide. The answer is (A).

3. The area of a parallelogram is base × height, so the parallelogram's area is 10 × 15, or 150 cm². The answer is (D).

CIRCLES

A circle represents all the points that are a fixed distance away from a certain point (called the center). The fixed distance from the center to the edge is the radius, and all radii are equal in length. When a radius is rotated 360° around the center, the circumference (the perimeter of the circle) is formed; any segment connecting two points on the circumference is called a chord. The diameter is the longest chord that can be drawn on a circle; it goes through the center and is twice as long as the radius.

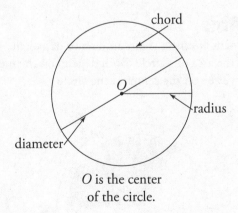

O is the center
of the circle.

Area and Circumference

Circles are wondrous things, because they gave us π. One day, a Greek mathematician with a lot of time on his hands began measuring circumferences (C) of circles and dividing those distances by the diameters (d), and he kept getting the same number: 3.141592…. He thought this was pretty cool, but also hard to remember, so he renamed it "p." He was Greek, though, so he used the Greek letter p, which is π.

From this discovery we find that $\dfrac{C}{d} = \pi$, and this can be rewritten as $C = \pi d$. This is the most common formula for finding the circumference of a circle. A diameter is twice as long as a radius ($d = 2r$), so you can also write the formula as $C = 2\pi r$. The formula for the area of a circle is $A = \pi r^2$.

- Area of a circle = πr^2
- Circumference of a circle = $2\pi r$

Notice that the radius, r, is in both of those formulas? The radius is the most important part of a circle to know. Once you know the radius, you can easily find the diameter, the circumference, or the area. So if you're ever stuck on a circle question, find the radius.

One quick note about π. Although it is true that $\pi \approx 3.1415$ (and so on and so on), you won't have to use that too often on the GRE. Don't worry about memorizing π beyond the hundredths digit: It's 3.14. Even that is more precise than the GRE typically requires. Most answers are going to be in terms of π, which means that the GRE is much more likely to have 5π as an answer choice than it is to have 15.707. So don't multiply out π unless you absolutely have to. Most of the time, each individual π will either cancel out or be in the answer choices.

Sectors and Arcs

An arc is a measurement around the circumference of a circle, and a sector is a partial measurement of the area of a circle. Both depend on the measure of the central angle, which has its vertex on the center of the circle.

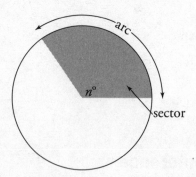

You can figure out the length of an arc or the area of a sector by comparing it to the entire circle. If the central angle is 180°, then the arc must be half of the circumference, because 180° is half of the total 360° in the central angle of a circle. A sector made up of a 90° angle must be $\frac{1}{4}$ of the total area, because 90° is one fourth of 360°.

$$\frac{angle}{360°} = \frac{arc}{circumference} = \frac{sector}{area}$$

In the diagram above, the clock shows that it is five minutes after 9 o'clock. If the radius of the clock is 9 inches, what is the area of the sector created by the hands of the clock starting at 9 and moving clockwise?

○ 6π

○ 13.5π

○ 27π

○ 81π

○ 54π

Here's How to Crack It

There are 360° in a circle and 12 numbers on the face of a clock. Therefore, the measure of the central angle between each numeral on the clock (say, between the 12 and the 1) is $\dfrac{360}{12}$, or 30°. There are four such central angles between the 9 and the 1, so the central angle is 4 × 30, or 120°. The radius of the circle is 9 inches, so the area of the whole clock is $\pi(9)^2$, or 81π. To find the area of the sector, use the formula: $81\pi \times \dfrac{120}{360} = 27\pi$. The correct answer is (C).

Circle Quick Quiz

Question 1 of 4

What is the radius of a circle that has a circumference of 6π inches?

- ○ 2
- ○ 3
- ○ 4
- ○ 6
- ○ 12

Question 2 of 4

What is the area of a circle that has a circumference of 6π ?

- ○ 3π
- ○ 6π
- ○ 9π
- ○ 12π
- ○ 36π

A cherry pie with a radius of 8 inches is cut into six equal slices. What is the area, in square inches, of each slice?

○ $\dfrac{8\pi}{3}$

○ $\dfrac{16\pi}{3}$

○ $\dfrac{32\pi}{3}$

○ $\dfrac{64\pi}{3}$

○ $\dfrac{128\pi}{3}$

Question 4 of 4

A cherry pie with a radius of 8 inches is cut into six equal pieces. What is the degree measure of the central angle of each piece of pie?

○ 15°

○ 30°

○ 60°

○ 90°

○ 120°

Explanations for Circle Quick Quiz

1. Because $C = \pi d$, the diameter of a circle with a circumference of 6π inches is 6 inches and thus the radius is 3 inches. The answer is (B).

2. The diameter of the circle is 6, so the radius is half that, or 3. The area of the circle is $\pi(3)^2$, or 9π square inches. The answer is (C).

3. The area of the pie is πr^2, or 64π, so each slice has an area of $\dfrac{64\pi}{6}$ square inches. This converts to $\dfrac{32\pi}{3}$. The answer is (C).

4. There are 360° in a circle, so the measure of each central angle is $\dfrac{360}{6}$, or 60°. The answer is (C). (Notice that you did not have to use the radius measurement to answer this question.)

THE COORDINATE PLANE

You might find a smattering of questions about the *xy*-plane, otherwise known as the Cartesian or rectangular coordinate plane on the GRE. The primary skill you'll need to possess in order to answer these questions is the ability to plot points by using the calibrations on the *x*- and *y*-axes. These two lines divide the space into four quadrants.

> When plotting the point (*x*, *y*) on the coordinate plane
>
> - start at the point (0, 0), which is also known as the "origin"
> - move *x* units to the right (if *x* is positive) or left (if *x* is negative)
> - move *y* units up (if *y* is positive) or down (if *y* is negative)

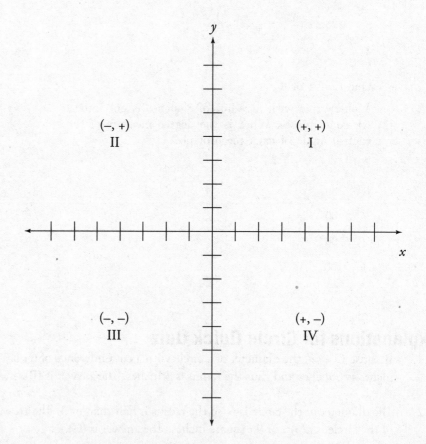

When you plot points on the Cartesian plane, you'll most likely be asked to (1) find the distance between two of them, (2) find the slope of the line that connects the two points, or (3) find the equation of the line they define.

Distance in the Coordinate Plane

If you need to find the distance between two points in the coordinate plane, draw a right triangle. The hypotenuse of the triangle is the distance between the two points, and the legs are the differences in the *x*- and *y*-coordinates of the two points.

If point A is at (2, 3) in the rectangular coordinate plane, and point B is at (–3, 15), what is the length of line segment $\overline{AB}$?

Here's How to Crack It

Start by drawing a simple coordinate plane on your scratch paper. You don't need to mark out each and every tick mark; this is just to get a rough idea of where the points are. Your drawing will probably look something like this:

Now find the length of each leg. The bottom leg is the distance between the two *x*-coordinates. From –3 to 2 is a total of 5 units (or, $|-3-2|=5$). The height is the distance between the two *y*-coordinates. From 3 to 15 is 12 units (or, $|3-15|=12$). So you have a triangle with sides of length 5 and 12. You can either use the Pythagorean Theorem to find the hypotenuse, or use the fact that you have a 5 : 12 : 13 triangle (one of the Pythagorean triples), which means that the line is 13 units long.

Many two-dimensional distance problems are really Pythagorean Theorem problems in disguise. The GRE will often hide this using questions in which people travel north/south and east/west.

Mark and Kim are at the post office. To get home, Kim walks 3 miles north and 2 miles west and Mark walks 8 miles south and 2 miles east. What is the approximate straight-line distance between Kim's house and Mark's house?

- ○ 10.1 miles
- ○ 11.7 miles
- ○ 12 miles
- ○ 13.2 miles
- ○ 15 miles

Here's How to Crack It

Draw a diagram, first. Nothing fancy, just enough to show us the location of the post office relative to the two houses. It will probably look something like this:

Now that you've got that drawn, make a triangle. The trick here is that you can now completely ignore the post office. You just want to know the distance from Kim's house to Mark's house, so those will be the two points of the triangle, like so:

The total east/west distance is 4 miles, and the total north/south distance is 11 miles. Those are the legs of our triangle. You can plug those into the Pythagorean Theorem to get $4^2 + 11^2 = c^2$; $16 + 121 = c^2$; $137 = c^2$; $c = \sqrt{137} \approx 11.7$, (B).

Slope Formula

To find the slope of a line, you need two distinct points on that line: (x_1, y_1) and (x_2, y_2). Notice the subscripts that designate the first point from the second point. It doesn't matter which points you assign to which values as long as you're consistent.

$$\text{Slope of a line} = \frac{rise}{run} = \frac{y_2 - y_1}{x_2 - x_1}$$

The most important part of slope, however, is to understand what it means. The slope is a measure of how much a line goes up or down on the *y*-axis (rise) as it goes over on the *x*-axis (run). In simpler language, the slope measures how slanted the line is. A positive slope means that the line rises up from left to right. A negative slope means that the line goes down from left to right. Notice that you always read the line from left to right, like reading a sentence. A slope of zero means that as you go over, the line never rises: It just remains a level, flat line. An undefined slope means that the line never runs over; it just goes up and up and up. (The slope is undefined because the difference in *x*-coordinates for any two points is 0, and you can't divide by 0.)

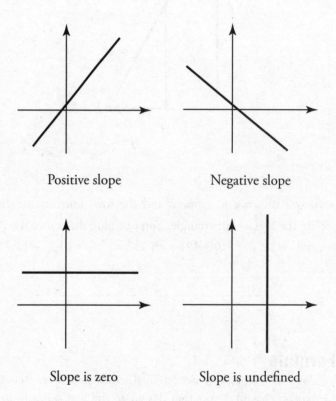

Positive slope   Negative slope

Slope is zero   Slope is undefined

Equation of a Line

Any line on the coordinate plane can be represented in the form $y = mx + b$, in which m is the slope of the line and b is the y-intercept. For example, the line $y = 3x - 6$ has a slope of 3 and intersects the y-axis at the point $(0, -6)$.

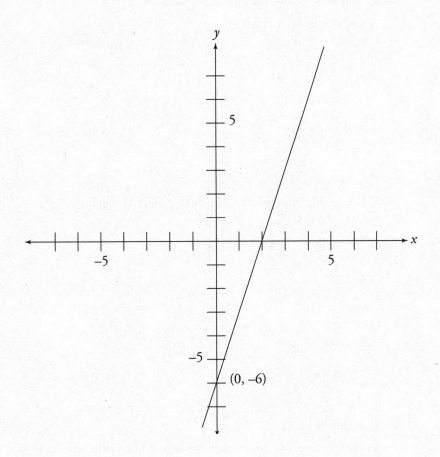

Point-Slope Formula

If you know the slope m of a line and the coordinates of one of the points on that line (x_0, y_0), you can use the point-slope formula to determine the equation of the line: $y - y_0 = m (x - x_0)$.

Coordinate Plane Quick Quiz

What is the equation of a line that has a slope of −3 and that passes through the point (2, 1) ?

○ $y = -3x + 1$

○ $y = -3x + 7$

○ $y = -3x + 11$

○ $y = 3x + 1$

○ $y = 3x + 5$

What is the slope of the line that passes through the points (−4, 3) and (6, −2)?

○ −2

○ $-\dfrac{1}{2}$

○ $\dfrac{1}{2}$

○ 2

○ 4

In the rectangular coordinate system, what is the distance between (−4, 3) and (6, −2)?

○ $5\sqrt{2}$

○ $5\sqrt{5}$

○ $6\sqrt{3}$

○ $6\sqrt{5}$

○ $7\sqrt{2}$

What is the equation of the line that passes through the points $(-4, 3)$ and $(6, -2)$?

- $\bigcirc\quad y = -\dfrac{1}{2}x + 1$

- $\bigcirc\quad y = -\dfrac{1}{2}x + 2$

- $\bigcirc\quad y = \dfrac{1}{2}x + 5$

- $\bigcirc\quad y = \dfrac{1}{2}x + 7$

- $\bigcirc\quad y = \dfrac{1}{2}x + 8$

At what point does the line $y = 2x + 6$ intersect the x-axis?

- $\bigcirc\quad (0, -3)$

- $\bigcirc\quad (0, 6)$

- $\bigcirc\quad (-6, 0)$

- $\bigcirc\quad (-3, 0)$

- $\bigcirc\quad (3, 0)$

Explanations for Coordinate Plane Quick Quiz

1. You have a point and the slope, so use the point-slope formula: $(y - 1) = -3(x - 2)$. Simplified, this becomes $y - 1 = -3x + 6$. Add 1 to both sides, and your final answer is $y = -3x + 7$. The answer is (B).

2. Use the slope formula: $\dfrac{-2 - 3}{6 - (-4)} = \dfrac{-5}{10} = -\dfrac{1}{2}$. The answer is (B).

3. Draw a triangle on your scratch paper. The bottom of the triangle goes from -4 to 6, so the base is 10 units long. The height of the triangle goes from -2 to 3, so it is 5 units long. Plugging these lengths into the Pythagorean Theorem, $a^2 + b^2 = c^2$, gives you $5^2 + 10^2 = c^2$; $25 + 100 = c^2$; $125 = c^2$; $c = \sqrt{125} = \sqrt{25} \times \sqrt{5} = 5\sqrt{5}$, (B).

4. You know the slope, and you can choose either point you were given. Use the point-slope formula: $y - (-2) = -\dfrac{1}{2}(x - 6)$. This simplifies to $y = -\dfrac{1}{2}x + 1$. The answer is (A).

5. You are given the formula for the line, $y = 2x + 6$. When the line crosses the x-axis, the value of y, at that point, will be 0. Eliminate (A) and (B). Now plug 0 in for y in the equation for the line and solve for x: $x = -3$. Therefore, the point is $(-3, 0)$, and the answer is (D).

VOLUME FORMULAS

Volume problems on the GRE are rare and will involve only a select few geometric solids. Formulas for those solids are below, and it's best simply to memorize them, just in case a volume problem comes up.

Solid	Volume Formula
Rectangular prism	$V = l \times w \times h$
Right circular cylinder	$V = \pi r^2 h$

Space Diagonal

If you know the dimensions of a rectangular prism, you can determine the length of the greatest distance between any two points in that prism. This distance is called the space diagonal, which can be found using what looks like an extension of the Pythagorean Theorem.

> If the dimensions of a rectangular prism are a, b, and c, then the space diagonal d can be found using the formula $d^2 = a^2 + b^2 + c^2$.

SURFACE AREA

Predictably, the surface area of a three-dimensional figure is the sum of the area of each of its surfaces. Almost all surface area questions on the GRE deal with rectangular solids. Here is the formula for the surface area of a rectangular solid.

$$SA = 2lw + 2wh + 2lh$$

Geometry Drill

Lines X, Y, and Z intersect to form a triangle. If line X is perpendicular to line Y and line X forms a 30-degree angle with line Z, which of the following is the degree measure of the angle formed by the intersection of lines Y and Z?

- ⭕ 20°
- ⭕ 30°
- ⭕ 45°
- ⭕ 50°
- ⭕ 60°

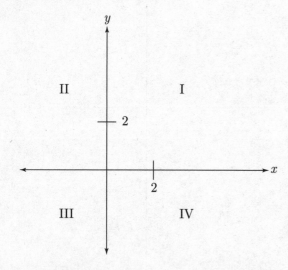

Points $(x, 5)$ and $(-6, y)$, not shown in the figure above, are in Quadrants I and III, respectively. If $xy \neq 0$, in which quadrant is point (x, y)?

- ⭕ IV
- ⭕ III
- ⭕ II
- ⭕ I
- ⭕ It cannot be determined from the information given.

In the triangle above, what is the degree measure of the smallest angle?

- ⭕ 10°
- ⭕ 40°
- ⭕ 45°
- ⭕ 50°
- ⭕ 60°

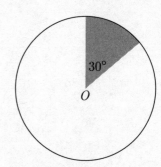

The area of the shaded region is 3π. What is the radius of the circle with center O?

- ⭕ 3
- ⭕ 6
- ⭕ 9
- ⭕ 12
- ⭕ 36

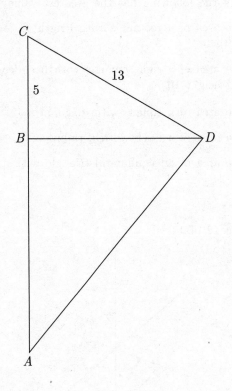

In the figure above, if BD is perpendicular to AC and $AC = 21$, then $AD =$

○ 12

○ 13

○ 20

○ 21

○ 25

Which of the following expresses the area of a square region in terms of its perimeter p ?

○ $\dfrac{p}{4}$

○ $\dfrac{p^2}{4}$

○ $\dfrac{p}{16}$

○ $\dfrac{p^2}{16}$

○ $\left(\dfrac{4p}{p}\right)^2$

The figure above is a rectangular solid in which $JK = 2$, $KL = 9$, and $LM = 9$. What is the total surface area of the rectangular solid?

○ 234

○ 162

○ 134

○ 117

○ 20

The four vertices of a face of a cube have coordinates (a, b), (a, d), (c, b), and (c, d). If $a = 2$ and c is an even number between 6 and 11, which of the following could be the surface area of the cube?

○   96

○   150

○   294

○   384

○   600

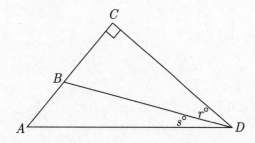

In the figure above, if $AC = CD$, then $r =$

○ $45 - s$

○ $90 - s$

○ s

○ $45 + s$

○ $60 + s$

Triangle ABC is an isosceles right triangle. If $AB = AC$, then the area of a square with a side length equal to twice the length of BC is how many times the area of triangle ABC ?

Which of the following has the greatest value?

○   The area of a rectangle with length 11 and width 6

○   The area of a right triangle with base length 10 and height 10

○   The area of a square with diagonal $8\sqrt{2}$

○   The area of a circle with a radius of 5

○   The area of an equilateral triangle with a side of 12

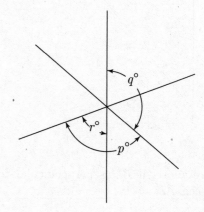

In the figure above, if $q = 130$ and $p = 120$, then $r =$

○   20°

○   60°

○   70°

○   80°

○   90°

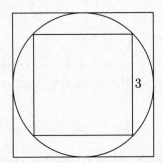

In the figure above, a square with side of length 3 is inscribed in a circle that is inscribed in a square. What is the area of the larger square?

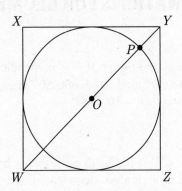

In the figure above, a circle with center O is inscribed in square $WXYZ$. If the circle has radius 3, then $PZ =$

○ 6

○ $3\sqrt{2}$

○ $6 + \sqrt{2}$

○ $3 + \sqrt{3}$

○ $3\sqrt{3}$

EXPLANATIONS FOR GEOMETRY DRILL

1. **E**

   Draw the figure. If X is perpendicular to Y, and X and Z form a 30° angle, you have a triangle with one 90° angle and one 30° angle. There are 180° in a triangle, so the remaining angle must be 180° − 90° − 30° = 60°.

2. **A**

   If $(x, 5)$ is in Quadrant I, then x has a positive value. If $(−6, y)$ is in Quadrant III, then y is negative. A point with a positive x-coordinate and negative y-coordinate is in Quadrant IV. For example, if $x = 3$ and $y = −5$, $(x, y) = (3, −5)$, which is in Quadrant IV.

3. **B**

   Because there are 180° in a line, the value of x is 180° − 140° = 40°. Because the internal angles of a triangle add up to 180°, determine that $9y + 5y = 140°$. Thus, $y = 10$, the angle represented by $5y$ is 50°, and the angle represented by $9y$ is 90°. That angle represented by x, which is 40°, is the smallest angle, making (B) the correct answer.

4. **B**

   Because $\dfrac{30}{360} = \dfrac{1}{12}$, the shaded region is $\dfrac{1}{12}$ of the circle. Multiply 3π by 12 to find the area of the entire circle, 36π. Now put the values you know into the formula for the area of the circle: $36\pi = \pi r^2$. Solve for r to find the radius is 6. The answer is (B).

5. **C**

   Since BD is perpendicular to AC, it cuts the large triangle into two right triangles. The small triangle on top, BCD, is the familiar 5 : 12: 13 triangle, so $BD = 12$. Since $AC = 21$ and $CB = 5$, $AB = 16$. Now you have the two short sides of ABD, 12 and 16; use the Pythagorean Theorem or recognize the multiple of the 3 : 4 : 5 triangle to find that $AD = 20$.

6. **D**

   Plug In, letting $p = 8$. If the perimeter of the square is 8, then each side of the square equals 2. If a square has sides of length 2, then its area is 4. Therefore, 4 is the target. Put $p = 8$ into the answer choices. Choice (D) is the only one that matches the target of 4: $\dfrac{8^2}{16} = \dfrac{64}{16} = 4$.

7. **A**

   To find surface area, add the areas of each face. The rectangle facing outward has sides of $KL = 9$ and $LM = 9$, so it has an area of 9 × 9 = 81. The face opposite this front face is identical, and the area of those two faces totals 162. Now look at the face on the left of the solid: It has sides of 2 and 9. The area of this face is 2 × 9 = 18, and again, the opposite face is the same, for a total area of 36. Finally, the bottom and top faces are each 2 × 9, for a total area of 36. Add up the areas of all faces to find the total surface area: 162 + 36 + 36 = 234, (A). Alternatively, the measurements can be plugged into the surface area formula, which also gives 234 as the total. In either case, (A) is correct.

8. **D**

First, draw the face of the cube in the coordinate plane.

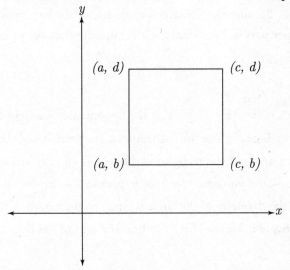

Because $a = 2$ and c could be 8 or 10, one side of the square face of the cube could measure 6 or 8. Now take the possible areas for a single face, found by squaring the side, and multiply by 6 to account for the 6 equal faces of the cube: $6^2 \times 6 = 36 \times 6 = 216$ and $8^2 \times 6 = 64 \times 6 = 384$. Only 384 is an option, so the answer is (D).

9. **A**

$\Delta BCD + \Delta ABD$ make the big ΔACD. The problem tells you that $AC = CD$. These are the legs of the big ΔACD. Because $\angle ACD$ is a right angle, and you know the two smaller angles of ΔACD are equal (because the sides are equal), then each of the angles must be 45°. There are variables in the answer choices, so Plug In for s and r. If $s = 20$, then $r = 25$. Only (A) works.

10. **16**

First, draw triangle ABC, and plug in sides; *isosceles right triangle* is another way of saying 45 : 45 : 90 triangle, so make the legs 10 and the hypotenuse, or BC, $10\sqrt{2}$. Now the area of triangle ABC is 50. Since $BC = 10\sqrt{2}$, the square has a side of $20\sqrt{2}$, and an area of 800. To find how many times the area of the triangle this represents, calculate $800 \div 50 = 16$ times the area of triangle ABC.

11. **D**

Unfortunately you will have to calculate them all. Choice (A) is length multiplied by width, which equals 66. Choice (B) is $\frac{1}{2}bh$, which is 50. Eliminate (B). The square in (C) has a side length of 8 because the diagonal of a square is the hypotenuse of a right isosceles triangle with a ratio of sides of $x : x : x\sqrt{2}$, so the area of the square is 64. Eliminate (C). Choice (D) has an area of πr^2 which in this case is 25π, which will be something slightly north of 75. Eliminate (A). For (E), the height of an equilateral triangle is the middle side of a 30 : 60 : 90 triangle, which has a ratio of sides of $x : x\sqrt{3} : 2x$. In this case, the area of the triangle, $\frac{1}{2}bh$, is $\frac{1}{2}(12)(6\sqrt{3})$. Since $\sqrt{3}$ is less than two and 36×2 is still less than (D), you can eliminate (E). The answer is (D).

12. **C**

If $p = 120°$, then by the Rule of 180 for lines (see the explanation for question 3), the lower unnamed angle in the figure must be $180° - 120° = 60°$. Because this unnamed angle is also the lower part of $\angle q$, then the lower part of $\angle q$ is 60° and the upper part is 70°. Because $\angle r$ is opposite the upper portion of $\angle q$, r is also 70°.

13. **18**

Start by drawing the diagonal of the smaller square. This diagonal is the hypotenuse of a right triangle created by the diagonal and two sides of the small square. Use the Pythagorean Theorem to find the length of the hypotenuse: $c = \sqrt{3^2 + 3^2} = 3\sqrt{2}$. Alternatively, if you recognized this as a 45 : 45 : 90 triangle, you would know the ratio of the sides is $x : x : x\sqrt{2}$, and you could find the hypotenuse using the ratio. This length is also the diameter of the circle, and the diameter of the circle is equal to the length of the sides of the big square. Use the formula for the area of a square, $A = s^2$, to find the area of the larger square: $A = \left(3\sqrt{2}\right)^2 = 18$.

14. **E**

Draw a diameter across the circle. The diameter is the same length as a side of the square. The radius of the circle is 3, the diameter is 6, and the side of the square is also 6. Line segment XZ forms a diagonal of the square, and it divides the square into two 45 : 45 : 90 right triangles. Because you know the side of the square is 6, you can use the 45 : 45 : 90 ratio $(x : x : x\sqrt{2})$ to find that the length of the diagonal is $6\sqrt{2}$. Finally, PZ can be the hypotenuse of a right triangle, with legs OP and OZ. Line segment OP is equal to the radius of the circle, 3. Line segment OZ is equal to half the diagonal of the square, or half of $6\sqrt{2}$. Use the Pythagorean Theorem to find PZ, which equals $3\sqrt{3}$, (E).

Chapter 9
The Rest of
the Story

TYING UP LOOSE ENDS

So here it is, the last chapter about quantitative topics on the GRE. Most of the material we review in this chapter will probably appear less frequently on the GRE, and most of it deals with data analysis. There are a lot of formulas in this chapter that you'd do well to memorize, because it will save you a considerable amount of time when you sit down to take the test. Let's begin.

FUNCTIONS

Sometimes the GRE will make up a mathematical operator. You will see some weird shape, which you've never seen in a math problem, and be asked to solve a problem using this weird shape. This is simply the GRE trying to confuse you.

These questions are asking about functions. A function is simply a set of directions. For instance, think of the word "chop" in a recipe. The word chop is actually telling you to do many things: take out a cutting board, rinse the vegetable or fruit to be chopped, take out a knife, place the vegetable on the cutting board, etc. If a recipe says "Chop 3 carrots," then you must do all those things that chopping entails, but using carrots. If the recipe says "Chop 2 stalks of celery," then you must do all of those chopping things, but with celery.

A function is the same way. It is a set of rules, and the GRE will ask you to perform those rules on a certain number. If the GRE invents some function, for instance that $\blacklozenge x = 4x + 2$, and then asks what $\blacklozenge 5$ is, then figure out what rules you need to follow. The original function was $\blacklozenge x$, but notice how $\blacklozenge 5$ replaced the x that was after the $\blacklozenge$ with a 5? Well, do the same thing with the equation given for $\blacklozenge x$: Replace each x with a 5. You get $\blacklozenge 5 = 4(5) + 2 = 20 + 2 = 22$.

Try a practice problem. Look for what numbers you'll need to place in the original function, and where each number will go.

If $x \sim y$ is defined as the sum of all of the prime integers between x and y, which of the following is equal to 17 ?

Indicate __all__ such values.

- ☐ 1~10
- ☐ 4~10
- ☐ 6~12
- ☐ 14~18

Here's How to Crack It

Here you have a completely made-up mathematical operator. This question says that whenever you see a ~, you must find the sum of all the prime integers between those two numbers. Rather than write out all the primes and figure out which numbers you could pick to get 17, try PITA. As you plug in each answer choice, find the sum of all the prime integers between those two numbers. So 1~10 is the sum of all the prime integers between 1 and 10, which is 2 + 3 + 5 + 7 = 17, so (A) is an answer. Since 4~10 = 5 + 7 = 12, cross off (B). Since 6~12 = 7 + 11 = 18, cross off (C). For the last answer, the only prime integer between 14 and 18 is 17, and since the sum of 17 and nothing is 17, (D) is also an answer. The answers are therefore (A) and (D).

You may also see function questions of the form $f(x) = x^2 + 5$. In that case, if they ask for $f(3)$, then wherever there used to be an x in the original function, put a 3: $f(3) = 3^2 + 5 = 9 + 5 = 14$.

Whenever you see something unfamiliar on a GRE question, look to see if the question itself tells you what to do, and follow those directions.

FACTORIALS!

The term $n!$ is referred to as "n factorial," and whenever a factorial shows up on the GRE, it pertains to the number of ways a number of elements can be chosen, or *arranged*. We'll discuss this further when we get to the section on arrangements and combinations, a little later. But for now:

> The term $n!$ (read as "n factorial") represents the product of all integers from n to 1, inclusive. For example, $5! = 5 \times 4 \times 3 \times 2 \times 1$, or 120.

Factorial questions can look like they require more work than they really do. This is because you can usually cancel a lot of numbers and make a huge sequence of multiplications into something much more manageable. Here's an example:

---○---

Quantity A	**Quantity B**
$\dfrac{24!}{23!}$	$4!$

○ Quantity A is greater.

○ Quantity B is greater.

○ The two quantities are equal.

○ The relationship cannot be determined from the information given.

Here's How to Crack It

When evaluating Quantity A, it might look like you're about to spend 10 minutes multiplying all those numbers on your calculator. Break the fraction down first, though, and you'll see that all but one of the numbers cancels out.

$$\frac{24!}{23!} = \frac{24 \times 23 \times 22 \times 21 \times \ldots \times 3 \times 2 \times 1}{23 \times 22 \times 21 \times \ldots \times 3 \times 2 \times 1} = 24$$

As you can see, you can cancel out everything from the 23 on, and you're left with 24. Quantity B also equals 24 ($4 \times 3 \times 2 \times 1$), so the answer is (C).

---○---

Sometimes, however, a GRE question will involve adding or subtracting factorials. In that case, you're going to have to factor.

---○---

What is the value of the expression $\dfrac{15! - 14!}{13!}$?

Here's How to Crack It

15! is too large to enter into the calculator, so factor out what 15! and 14! have in common. Since 15! is the same as $15 \times 14 \times 13 \times 12 \times 11 \times 10\ldots$ and 14! is $14 \times 13 \times 12 \times 11\ldots$, rewrite 15! as 15(14!). Both 15(14!) and 14! contain 14!, so rewrite the fraction as $\dfrac{14!(15-1)}{13!}$. Note that if you distributed the 14! to each term within the parentheses, you'd have back the original numerator: 15! − 14!. You can simplify the 15 − 1 inside the parentheses to get $\dfrac{14!(14)}{13!}$. Now it's time to cancel out the two factorials, as you did with the previous example question.

$$\frac{14(13!)(14)}{13!} = \frac{14(14)}{1} = 196.$$

Factorials Quick Quiz

Question 1 of 4

$$\frac{25!}{23!} \times \frac{1}{4!} =$$

☐

Question 2 of 4

Each of the following is equivalent to 6! EXCEPT

○ 3! × 5!

○ 4! × 30

○ $6^2 \times 20$

○ $\dfrac{7!}{7}$

○ $\dfrac{12!}{2!}$

Quantity A	Quantity B
17! − 14!	4078 × 14!

○ Quantity A is greater.

○ Quantity B is greater.

○ The two quantities are equal.

○ The relationship cannot be determined from the information given.

Question 4 of 4

If $n > 2$, then what is the value of $\dfrac{(n+1)!}{(n-2)!}$?

○ 0

○ $n!$

○ $n^3 - n$

○ $n^3 - 4n$

○ $(2n)!$

Explanations for Factorials Quick Quiz

1. The first term, $\dfrac{25!}{23!}$, is equivalent to 25×24, and the second term equals $\dfrac{1}{24}$. Therefore, the final term is $\dfrac{25 \times 24}{24}$, or 25.

2. All of the answer choices are equivalent to 6!, or 720, except (E), because $\dfrac{12!}{2!}$ is the same as $\dfrac{12 \times 11 \times 10 \times 9 \times 8 \times 7 \times 6 \times 5 \times 4 \times 3 \times 2 \times 1}{2 \times 1}$. Because $12 \times 11 \times 10$ is already 1,320, it's possible to see that this is far bigger than 720 without even bothering with your calculator. The answer is (E).

3. Since there are no variables in this question, eliminate (D). There are factorials combined with subtraction, so you're going to have to factor. 17! is the same as $17 \times 16 \times 15 \times 14!$. You can therefore rewrite Quantity A as $17 \times 16 \times 15 \times 14! - 14!$. Since you have 14! in both terms, factor out 14! to get $14!(17 \times 16 \times 15 - 1)$. Now it's time for a bit of calculator work, which gives you $14!(4{,}080 - 1) = 14!(4{,}079)$. Both quantities have 14!, so focus on the other parts. Since 4,079 is larger than 4,078, $14!(4{,}079)$ is larger than $4{,}078 \times 14!$, and the answer is (A).

4. There are variables in the answer choices and question stem, so Plug In. Pick a number that is easy to work with for n, such as $n = 5$. If $n = 5$, then the target answer can be found by reducing the expression in the question stem. The question stem now reads $\dfrac{6!}{3!}$ which, if expanded, reduces to $6 \times 5 \times 4 = 120$, which is the target answer. Now, plug in 5 for all values of n in the answer choices and see which results in a value of 120. Choice (A) is clearly incorrect, so eliminate (A). Choice (B) is 5!, which expands to $5 \times 4 \times 3 \times 2 \times 1 = 120$, so keep (B). Choice (C) is $5^3 - 5 = 125 - 5 = 120$, which is also correct so keep (C). Choice (D) is less than (C) because $4(5) = 20$, and $125 - 20 = 105$, so eliminate (D). Choice (E) is 10!, which is too great, so eliminate (E). Now Plug In again for (B) and (C), but this time use a FROZEN number. Try an Extreme number such as $n = 10$. If $n = 10$, then the question stem now reads $\dfrac{11!}{8!}$, which, if expanded, reduces to $11 \times 10 \times 9$, which equals 990. With 990 as the new target answer, plug in 10 for (B) and (C) to see if either of these equals 990. Choice (B) is now 10!. Since 10! is a great number, try to do some of the beginning stages of the calculation. 10! expands to $10 \times 9 \times 8 \times 7 \times 6 \times 5 \times 4 \times 3 \times 2 \times 1$. Well, $10 \times 9 = 90$ and $90 \times 8 = 720$. Since 720×7 is going to be way greater than 990, which makes (B) greater than 990, eliminate (B). Choice (C) is now $10^3 - 10$. Since $10^3 = 1{,}000$ and $1{,}000 - 10 = 990$, the correct answer is (C).

PROBABILITY

In probability questions, something that you *want* to happen is a "favorable out-come," and all of the things that *could* happen are "possible outcomes." So for these types of questions, your job is to figure out the chance that a favorable out-come—an outcome you want to happen—will occur.

The probability of a favorable outcome is found by dividing the number of possible favorable outcomes by the total number of possible outcomes.

- If a favorable outcome is impossible, then the probability that it will happen is 0.
- If a favorable outcome is a certainty, then the probability that it will happen is 1.
- The probability that something will happen plus the probability that it will not happen is equal to 1.
- If more than two outcomes are possible, the sum of the prob-abilities of all outcomes is equal to 1.

Quantity A	Quantity B
The probability of randomly selecting the blue marble from a bag of 50 red marbles and 1 blue marble.	The probability of randomly selecting the blue marble from a bag of 51 red marbles and 1 blue marble.

○ Quantity A is greater.

○ Quantity B is greater.

○ The two quantities are equal.

○ The relationship cannot be determined from the information given.

Here's How to Crack It

For Quantity A, there is only 1 blue marble in a bag of 51 marbles (50 red marbles + 1 blue marble), so the probability of selecting the blue marble is $\frac{1}{51}$. For Quan-tity B, there is only 1 blue marble in a bag of 52 marbles (51 red marbles + 1 blue marble), so the probability of selecting the blue marble is $\frac{1}{52}$. Because the denominator in Quantity B is greater, the fraction must be smaller. Therefore, the answer is (A).

Multiple Probabilities

If you're asked to find the probability that two specific events will occur one after the other, first find the individual probabilities that each event will occur, and then multiply them. There are two different scenarios on problems like these; sometimes the odds of an individual event are different from another event, and sometimes they aren't.

Probability of A and B = Probability of A × Probability of B

For example, if a problem involves flipping a coin, the probability that it will come up heads will always be $\frac{1}{2}$. It will never change, because there will always be heads on one side of the coin and tails on the other. Here's a typical problem you might see on the GRE.

If a six-sided die with faces numbered one through six is rolled three times, what is the probability that 5 faces upward for all three rolls?

○ $\frac{1}{6}$

○ $\frac{1}{36}$

○ $\frac{1}{96}$

○ $\frac{1}{126}$

○ $\frac{1}{216}$

Here's How to Crack It

There is only one 5 on the six-sided die, so the chance of rolling a 5 is $\frac{1}{6}$. When you roll the die a second or third time, you still have a $\frac{1}{6}$ chance of rolling a 5, so the chance remains $\frac{1}{6}$. Therefore, the chance of rolling three 5's in a row is $\frac{1}{6} \times \frac{1}{6} \times \frac{1}{6} = \frac{1}{216}$. The answer is (E).

Removing Items Changes the Probability

So far, the total, the denominator of our fraction, has always stayed constant. However, there will be some questions in which items are removed as you go. These problems often contain the phrase *without replacement,* because items are taken without replacing them. In that case, the total will change. At each point, figure out the next probability by assuming that what the problem wants to happen has happened.

For instance, imagine there are 3 red marbles and 1 green marble in a bag. What's the probability of selecting 2 red marbles in a row? When you first reach into the bag, you'll have a $\frac{3}{4}$ chance of pulling out a red marble: There are 3 red marbles, out of a total of 4 marbles. But what about when you reach in again? You'll have to assume that you pulled out that first red marble. (Otherwise, who cares if you pull out a second red marble? You wanted two red marbles in a row, not a something else and then a red marble.) That means you have only 2 red marbles left, out of a total of 3 marbles, and your chance to pull that second red marble is $\frac{2}{3}$. Now you can combine your two probabilities by multiplying them together: $\frac{3}{4} \times \frac{2}{3} = \frac{1}{2}$.

Try a harder problem that uses a changing total.

A shopping bag contains 5 green peppers and 4 red peppers. A grocer removes three of the peppers from the bag at random.

Quantity A	**Quantity B**
The probability that the first two peppers are green and the third is red	The probability that the first pepper is green and the last two are red

○ Quantity A is greater.

○ Quantity B is greater.

○ The two quantities are equal.

○ The relationship cannot be determined from the information given.

Here's How to Crack It

This question is different because multiple peppers are removed, so the odds change after each pepper leaves the bag. Work with Quantity A first: When the grocer reaches in the first time, he has a $\frac{5}{9}$ chance of selecting a green pepper. The second time, there are only 4 green peppers out of a total of 8, so the chance of getting a second green pepper is $\frac{4}{8}$. The third time, there are only 7 peppers left and 4 of them are red. The chance of getting a red is $\frac{4}{7}$, and the composite probability is $\frac{5}{9} \times \frac{4}{8} \times \frac{4}{7}$.

Before you multiply, look at Quantity B. The probabilities are $\frac{5}{9}$ (green), $\frac{4}{8}$ (first red), and $\frac{3}{7}$ (second red), so the composite probability is $\frac{5}{9} \times \frac{4}{8} \times \frac{3}{7}$. When comparing the two quantities, the denominators are the same but the numerator in Quantity B is smaller. Therefore, Quantity B itself must be smaller, and the answer must be (A).

At Least Probabilities

Some questions will not ask for the probability of a single event, but instead ask for the probability that "at least" a certain number of events will happen. For instance, let's go back to the bag of marbles. Say there are 4 red marbles and 5 green marbles, and you're asked the likelihood of reaching in, taking out 3 marbles, and getting at least 1 red marble.

You *could* find that out by figuring out the probability of getting 1 red marble and then 2 green marbles, and adding that to the probability of getting a green, a red, and a green, plus the probability of getting a green, a green, and a red. But you could get more than just one red, right? You'd also have to find the chance of RRG, RGR, and GRR, and then the probability of getting RRR, and add all of those different ways of getting at least one red marble together.

But there's an easier way. Think of it this way: If there's a 30% chance of rain, what's the chance it won't rain? 70%. Since any two mutually exclusive probabilities always add up to 100%, you can sometimes find the probability that something *won't* happen rather than find the probability it will happen. Once you do, subtract it from 1, because 100% = 1.

Going back to the marble example, if you were asked "Did you pull at least 1 red marble from the bag?" and you answered "No," then what marbles did you pull? If you didn't pull at least 1 red marble, then you pulled all green marbles. The probability of pulling all green marbles is $\frac{5}{9} \times \frac{4}{8} \times \frac{3}{7} = \frac{5}{42}$. But you don't want to pull all green marbles; you want the opposite of that. Therefore, the probability of getting at least one red marble is $1 - \frac{5}{42} = \frac{37}{42}$.

Probability Quick Quiz

Question 1 of 5

Of the 50 U.S. states, 23 border a major body of salt water.

Quantity A	Quantity B
The probability of randomly selecting a state with a saltwater border	The probability of randomly selecting a state that does not have a saltwater border

○ Quantity A is greater.

○ Quantity B is greater.

○ The two quantities are equal.

○ The relationship cannot be determined from the information given.

If the numbers 1, 2, 3, and 4 are randomly selected, and no number can be selected more than once, then what is the probability that the numbers are selected in ascending numerical order?

○ $\frac{1}{24}$

○ $\frac{1}{12}$

○ $\frac{5}{24}$

○ $\frac{9}{24}$

○ $\frac{2}{3}$

Fred has three dimes, two nickels, and four quarters in his pocket. If he selects two coins, at random and without replacement, what is the probability that he selects two dimes?

○ $\frac{1}{12}$

○ $\frac{1}{6}$

○ $\frac{1}{4}$

○ $\frac{1}{3}$

○ $\frac{1}{2}$

Harry throws two fair, six-sided dice both with faces numbered one through six.

Quantity A	**Quantity B**
The probability that he will roll numbers that sum to 8	The probability that he will roll numbers that sum to 7

- ○ Quantity A is greater.
- ○ Quantity B is greater.
- ○ The two quantities are equal.
- ○ The relationship cannot be determined from the information given.

Question 5 of 5

The probability of event J occurring is 0.63, while the probability that both events J and K occur is 0.42. What is the probability that event K will occur?

Give your answer as a fraction.

$$\boxed{} \over \boxed{}$$

Explanations for Probability Quick Quiz

1. There are 50 different states; these are the *possible* outcomes. There are 23 states with a saltwater border, and these are the desired outcomes for Quantity A. Therefore, the probability that a randomly selected state will have a saltwater border is $\frac{23}{50}$. If 23 have saltwater borders, then 27 states do not. This is the desired outcome for Quantity B. The number of possible outcomes remains the same, so the probability for Quantity B is $\frac{27}{50}$. This fraction is greater, so the correct answer is (B).

2. There are 24 (or 4!) ways to randomly select the numbers 1, 2, 3, and 4. There is only 1 way to select them in ascending numerical order, so the probability is $\frac{1}{24}$. The correct answer is (C).

3. There are 9 coins in Fred's pocket, 3 of which are dimes, so the probability that he will get a dime the first time is $\frac{3}{9}$. The second time, there are only 2 dimes out of 8 coins, so the probability drops to $\frac{2}{8}$. The composite probability is $\frac{3}{9} \times \frac{2}{8}$, or $\frac{6}{72}$. This reduces to $\frac{1}{12}$, so the correct answer is (A).

4. When two fair, six-sided dice are thrown, there are 36 possible rolls. Of these, 5 will sum to 8 (2 and 6, 3 and 5, 4 and 4, 5 and 3, and 6 and 2) and 6 will sum to 7 (1 and 6, 2 and 5, 3 and 4, 4 and 3, 5 and 2, and 6 and 1). Because there are more ways to roll 7, Quantity B is greater so the correct answer is (B).

5. Remember that the probability of two events happening is probability of $A \times$ probability of B. Since you know that probability of $J \times$ probability of $K = 0.42$, and you know the probability of J is 0.63, you know that $0.63 \times$ probability of $K = 0.42$. Dividing both sides by 0.63 gives the probability of K: $\frac{0.42}{0.63} = \frac{42}{63} = \frac{2}{3}$.

As we near the homestretch, here are two more topics that could appear on the GRE. These topics occur very rarely, and when they do appear you'll see at most one question about them per section. Therefore, it pays to reference them here, at the end of the chapter.

GROUPS

There are two basic types of group questions: those that involve overlap between two groups, and those that involve groups in which there is no overlap. The group questions with overlap can be represented visually using the classic Venn diagram below, but you may find it easier, and more straightforward, to use an equation.

> **Group Formula:**
> Total = [Group 1] + [Group 2] − [Both] + [Neither]

The first thing you'll have to do with this sort of question is to recognize that you need to use the Group Formula. What are your clues? If there are any elements that overlap between two of the groups, then you will need to use the Group Formula. You may not have any elements that are in neither group (Neither = 0), but if you have any overlapping elements, then those elements are being counted twice: once because they belong to Group 1, and again because they belong to Group 2. To eliminate one of the times those Both elements are being counted, subtract the Both. Note that Group 1 includes everything in Group 1, including those that are in Both. The same applies to Group 2.

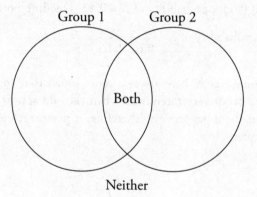

Try a problem using the Group Formula:

Of the 213 people who responded to a genealogical poll, 82 said they have French ancestors and 113 said they have Italian ancestors. If 51 of the respondents said they have neither French nor Italian heritage, how many have both?

○ 33

○ 52

○ 69

○ 101

○ 124

Here's How to Crack It

Assign the groups (Group 1 is French, Group 2 is Italian), and plug the numbers you know into the formula: $82 + 113 - B + 51 = 213$. Because $246 - B = 213$, B must equal 33. The answer is (A).

Either/Or Group Problems

The Group Formula is great, but it works only on problems in which there is some overlap between two groups. The GRE will also sometimes ask group questions in which there is no overlap between groups. These questions involve elements that are in either group A or B, *and* in either group X or Y. Since nothing is in both groups A and B, or in both groups X or Y, instead use a simple chart, which looks like this:

	Group *X*	Group *Y*	Total
Group *A*			
Group *B*			
Total			

These questions often involve elements that have two different qualities. For instance, cupcakes that are either vanilla or chocolate, and either frosted or unfrosted. Notice that there's no overlap within each group: A cupcake can't be both vanilla and chocolate, and it can't be both frosted and unfrosted. You could have vanilla frosted cupcakes, vanilla unfrosted cupcakes, chocolate frosted cupcakes, or chocolate unfrosted cupcakes.

Here's an either/or question example.

Out of the 12,000 students and faculty at a certain university, there are 5 times as many students as there are faculty. There are 200 more female faculty members than there are male faculty members. If the university contains a combined total of 6,425 male students and faculty, how many female students are there?

```
┌─────────────┐
│             │
└─────────────┘
```

Here's How to Crack It

Since you can be either a student or faculty and either male or female, and there's no overlap in the question, draw a Group Table. It should look like this:

	Male	Female	Total
Students			
Faculty			
Total			12,000

Now take the question apart in bite-sized pieces. The first thing you find out is that there are 5 times as many students as faculty. If there are f total members of the faculty, then $5f = s$. Now that you know there's a total of 12,000 faculty and students, $12,000 = f + s$. Substituting in the earlier equation gives you $12,000 = f + 5f$. Since $12,000 = 6f$, $f = 2,000$. Since there are 2,000 faculty members, there are 10,000 students.

	Male	Female	Total
Students			10,000
Faculty			2,000
Total			12,000

Now you can use the next piece of information: There are 200 more female faculty members than there are male faculty members. There are 2,000 total, so $m + w = 2{,}000$. You know that $w = 200 + m$, which you can plug into the earlier equation to get $m + 200 + m = 2{,}000$, so $m = 900$. If there are 900 male faculty, there are $(2{,}000 - 900)$ 1,100 female faculty.

	Male	Female	Total
Students			10,000
Faculty	900	1,100	2,000
Total			12,000

Okay, there is one more piece to use: There's a total of 6,425 males. There's a total of 12,000 students and faculty, which means there are $12{,}000 - 6{,}425 = 5{,}575$ females. Fill that into the chart.

	Male	Female	Total
Students			10,000
Faculty	900	1,100	2,000
Total	6,425	5,575	12,000

Now you can easily fill in the rest of the table with simple subtraction: The $6{,}450 - 900 = 5{,}550$ males, and the number of female students is $5{,}575 - 1{,}100 = 4{,}475$. The answer to the question is 4,475. (You don't need to know the number of male students to answer the question, but for the sake of completeness, $6{,}425 - 900 = 5{,}525$ male students.)

	Male	Female	Total
Students	5,525	4,475	10,000
Faculty	900	1,100	2,000
Total	6,425	5,575	12,000

STANDARD DEVIATION

Standard deviation means almost exactly what it looks like it means: deviation from the "standard," or mean, value of a set of numbers. A normal distribution of data means that most of the numbers in the data are close to the mean, while fewer values spread out toward the extremes. The bigger the deviation from the norm, the wider the spectrum of numbers involved.

The Bell Curve

A normal distribution is best displayed in the form of a regular bell curve, which looks like this:

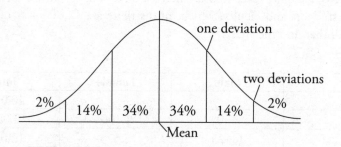

The mean is the middle number, right at the 50% mark. The GRE will either just present you with the mean straight up, or it will be one quick calculation away. The rest of the lines on the curve represent standard breakpoints at 34%, 14%, and 2% of the data values. These mean that, within a normal distribution, 68% of the values (34% on the left, 34% on the right) are within one standard deviation from the mean.

To explain the normal distribution, use a sample data set. Say we asked 1,000 people to see how long they could hold their breath. After measuring all those people, and watching all those faces turn purple, we calculated that the average (arithmetic mean) number of seconds that people could hold their breath was 50. We then handed our data to a statistician friend, who calculated that our data followed a normal distribution and the standard deviation was 15 seconds.

Since the mean time was 50 seconds, half of the people were able to hold their breath for less than 50 seconds and half the people were able to hold their breath for longer. Our data would look something like this:

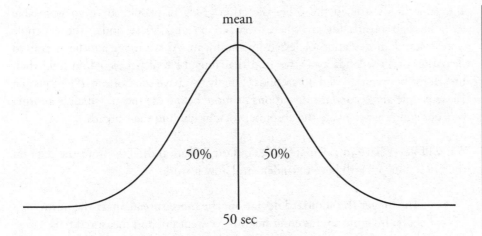

mean

50%   50%

50 sec

Most people were able to hold their breath close to 50 seconds, and as we get farther away from 50 seconds, the number of people drops off substantially in both directions. That's what's important about a normal distribution. The data points are distributed in this nice, predictable bell curve shape.

Here's where our standard deviation and 34-14-2 pattern comes into play. Since our standard deviation is 15 seconds, that means that 34% of people held their breath between 50 and 65 seconds. Those people were 1 standard deviation or less from the mean. When we move another standard deviation (another 15 seconds) away, we find that only 14% of people could hold their breath for anywhere between 65 and 80 seconds. Only 2% of people (all of whom have excellent lungs and do plenty of cardio) could hold their breath for more than 80 seconds.

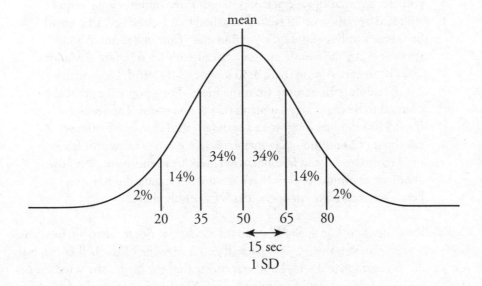

mean

2% 14% 34% 34% 14% 2%

20   35   50   65   80

⟷
15 sec
1 SD

The same holds true in the other direction. 34% of people surveyed were able to hold their breath for anywhere between 35 and 50 seconds. Those people were 1 standard deviation or less from the mean. As we move another standard deviation of 15 seconds away, we find that only 14% of people could hold their breath for between 20 and 35 seconds. Finally, we have the bottom 2% of people. These people are 2 standard deviations or more below the mean, which is another way of saying that they are the absolute worst at holding their breath.

You will never have to calculate the standard deviation directly from the data on the GRE, but you will have to understand how it works.

- **The bigger the standard deviation, the more spread apart the numbers.** Imagine an unkempt field. If we went out and measured the height of the grass in that field, we'd probably get a standard deviation of about 20 centimeters or so: We'd have some really tall grass, but also some young, short grass. Due to those variations in height, we'd have a large standard deviation. The height of grass wouldn't always be too close to the mean. Now imagine we took a lawnmower to that field. The lawnmower wouldn't cut every blade of grass to the exact same height, but it would make every blade fairly close to the same height. Our standard deviation would shrink from 20 cm to 1 cm. Sure, some grass is a little taller than our mean height and some is a little shorter, but overall the heights of the blades of grass are very close to being the same. There aren't many variations in height, so we have a small standard deviation. Lots of tall grass, short grass, and medium grass meant a large standard deviation, but when all of our grass was close to the same height, we had a small standard deviation.
- **The more standard deviations away from the mean, the "stranger" you are.** Say that the average pop song is three minutes long, with a standard deviation of 30 seconds. A song that is 3:30 isn't that weird, because it's only 1 standard deviation away from the mean. A song that's 3:45 is a little more unusual, because it's 1.5 standard deviations from the mean. A song that's 4:30 long is really weird, because that's 3 standard deviations away from the mean. For a pop song, it's really unusual to be that long. Compare that to the opera. The average opera is 90 minutes long, with a standard deviation of 25 minutes. A two-hour (120 minute) long opera, therefore, isn't that weird: It's a little more than 1 standard deviation away from the mean. But how about a five-minute opera? That's around 3.5 standard deviations below the mean. For an opera, that's freakishly short.

That's all you need to know about standard deviation. Sometimes, in fact, the GRE will even give you the 34-14-2 pattern and a drawing of the bell curve, but you should still memorize 34-14-2 and remember that the bigger the standard deviation, the more spread apart the numbers, and that the more standard deviations away from the mean, the "stranger" you are.

The average age among members of a retirement community is 61, and the standard deviation is 2.5 years. Under a normal distribution, what percent of the community members are younger than 56 years old?

○   2%

○   16%

○   32%

○   34%

○   50%

Here's How to Crack It

If the average age is 61 and the standard deviation is 2.5 years, then a person who is 56 years old is 2 deviations from the mean (2×2.5 is 5, and $61 - 5 = 56$). This means that only the bottom 2% of the group are less than 56 years old. The answer is (A).

Your scratch paper should look like this:

In this type of question, expect to see phrases like "arrangements," "permutations," "combinations," "different ways," "many ways," or "different groups."

ARRANGEMENTS AND COMBINATIONS

We've got one last topic to cover. It doesn't come up often, so if you're not completely comfortable with Plugging In, PITA, and all those other topics, you should go back and review those first.

Comfortable so far? Okay, so let's talk about arrangements and combinations. Arrangements and combinations questions typically ask about the number of different ways of either arranging things or grouping things. For these questions, we'll pretend that we're arranging or grouping our items piece by piece, item by item, element by element.

Each time we have to choose something, we'll figure out how many options we have. Then we'll pretend we chose one, and now have to choose the next thing. Once we've figured out how many choices we had at each point, we'll multiply those numbers together.

Let's do an easy example first. Pretend you have three pictures, one of Groucho, one of Harpo, and one of Chico, that you need to place on a shelf. To find the number of different ways to arrange those pictures, you could simply write out all the different possibilities. We could have Groucho, Harpo, and then Chico, or we could have Groucho, Chico, then Harpo. We could also have Harpo, Groucho, Chico, or Harpo, Chico, Groucho, or Chico, Harpo, Groucho, or Chico, Groucho, Harpo. That's six different ways of arranging those pictures.

So let's look at how we listed our original set of three pictures, and do some math. We have three different choices we have to make: Who is going in the first spot on the wall, who is going in the second, and who is going into the third. Because we have three choices to make, draw three slots (short horizontal lines to put numbers in) on our scratch paper, like so:

——— ——— ———

The first thing we had to decide was whether to put Groucho, Harpo, or Chico first. We had three different options of whom to place in that first spot, so put three in the first slot on our scratch paper:

_3_ ——— ———

Notice that once we choose Groucho to go first, we have only two options left: Does Harpo go next, or does Chico? The same is true whether we put Harpo or Chico first; we have only two options for that second slot. Put a 2 on that second spot.

_3_ _2_ ———

Once we've put Groucho in the first spot, and Harpo in the second, we've got to put Chico last, right? Or, say we put Harpo in the first spot and Chico in the second: In that case, Groucho's got to be last. Since, no matter whom we place in the first two spots, we have only one option (whoever is left) for the last spot, put a 1 in the last slot.

$$\underline{\quad 3 \quad} \quad \underline{\quad 2 \quad} \quad \underline{\quad 1 \quad}$$

Now multiply those numbers together: $3 \times 2 \times 1 = 6$. Six different ways, exactly how we calculated when we listed everything out earlier.

Each time we had a choice to make, we looked at the number of options we had for that choice. As we moved through our choices, we had fewer options, because we pretended that the previous choices had been made.

Try the next problem.

———————————◯———————————

> Eight horses compete in a race. The first horse to finish wins a blue ribbon, the second wins a red ribbon, and the third wins a yellow ribbon. In how many ways can the ribbons be awarded?

> ☐

Here's How to Crack It

The end of the problem states *in how many ways*, which means this is an arrangement question. There are 3 ribbons to give away, so draw 3 slots on your scratch paper. For that blue ribbon, you could give it to whichever of those 8 horses comes in first, which means you've got 8 options for our first slot. Once you've given one of the horses a blue ribbon, there are only 7 horses left to win the red ribbon, so put a 7 in the second slot. Now there are 6 horses left to win the yellow ribbon, so put 6 in the third slot. You now have $8 \times 7 \times 6 = 336$ different ways of awarding those ribbons.

———————————◯———————————

If a problem contains restrictions on what you can choose at certain points, start with those restricted positions first, and then deal with everything else. It's as though you were seating guests around a table. If you knew that two people just really, really, hated each other, then the first thing you'd do is make sure they sat on opposite ends of the table. Once that's taken care of, you'd then place the rest of your friends in the remaining seats.

Boone is making a playlist of 5 songs, but only 2 are suitable to be last. How many different playlists could Boone make?

- ○   24
- ○   48
- ○   60
- ○   120
- ○   3,125

Here's How to Crack It

The problem asks *how many different lists*, so this is another arrangement question. There are 5 songs you need to put in order, so draw 5 slots on your scratch paper. Here, however, you're limited into what can go in the last spot in the list: It's got to be one of 2 possible songs. So start by putting 2 in the last slot.

$$\underline{}\ \ \underline{}\ \ \underline{}\ \ \underline{}\ \ \underline{2}$$

Now you can deal with the other slots. Since you have no other restrictions, continue by going back to the first slot. Since you put one of the songs in that last spot, you have only 4 songs left to put in the first slot:

$$\underline{4}\ \ \underline{}\ \ \underline{}\ \ \underline{}\ \ \underline{2}$$

The second slot therefore has only 3 songs possible, because you've already placed songs in the first and last slots. Continuing to fill out the slots, you get

$$\underline{4}\ \ \underline{3}\ \ \underline{2}\ \ \underline{1}\ \ \underline{2}$$

Multiplying $4 \times 3 \times 2 \times 1 \times 2$ gives you 48, (B).

The questions we've done so far are all *arrangement* questions, because the order in which our elements are placed matters. Putting our Chico picture before our Harpo picture would be different from putting Harpo before Chico. Switching the first and second place ribbons of two of the horses would mean a different outcome of the race. Switching the middle songs of Boone's playlist would mean a different playlist than we had originally. Arrangement questions are questions in which order matters.

What about when order doesn't matter? Those are called combination questions, and they often contain words such as "groups," "teams," or (obviously), "combinations." If you had to choose two books to loan, at the same time, to a friend, it wouldn't matter if you loaned your friend *Pale Fire* and *The Tin Drum* as opposed to loaning her *The Tin Drum* and *Pale Fire*. Either way, she's borrowing the same two books.

Since order doesn't matter on combination questions, we're going to add one extra step at the end. We need to get rid of the repeat groupings, so we'll divide our answer by the factorial of our number of slots. An easier way to think of it is that we'll count down to 1 underneath our slots.

A group of 4 is to be chosen from among 9 total employees.

Quantity A	Quantity B
The total number of different groups that could be chosen	120

- ○ Quantity A is greater.
- ○ Quantity B is greater.
- ○ The two quantities are equal.
- ○ The relationship cannot be determined from the information given.

Here's How to Crack It
Since there is a group of 4, draw 4 slots on your paper. You could choose one of the 9 people for the first slot, leaving 8 for the second slot, 7 for the third, and 6 for the fourth, giving you $\underline{9} \times \underline{8} \times \underline{7} \times \underline{6}$. However, you're choosing *groups* of people, which means that the order you choose each group doesn't matter. As long as it's got the same people in it, who cares in what order those people were chosen?

The last step, therefore, is to divide by 4!. You can do this by counting down from 4 underneath each slot, making each number a fraction. You now have $\frac{9}{4} \times \frac{8}{3} \times \frac{7}{2} \times \frac{6}{1}$, which you can simplify to $\frac{3}{1} \times \frac{2}{1} \times \frac{7}{1} \times \frac{3}{1} = 126$. Since Quantity A is larger than Quantity B, the answer is (A).

By the way, did you notice how the denominator of the fraction canceled out completely? That will always happen with combinations. Think of it this way: There will never be a fractional number of ways to select groups of people. If the denominators of the fractions don't all cancel out to 1, you may have either made an arithmetic mistake, or missed a chance to cancel out.

To review, if order matters ("arrangements," "schedules," etc.), then it's an arrangement. Draw a slot for each time you need to make a choice, and then fill in each slot with the total number of options for each choice.

If order doesn't matter ("groups," "pairs," "teams," etc.), then it's a combination. Start the problem as you would an arrangement problem, but then divide by the factorial of the number of slots you have.

Arrangements and Combinations Quick Quiz

Question 1 of 5

At a certain ice cream shop, a sundae contains two different scoops of ice cream. If the shop sells 20 varieties of ice cream, how many different sundaes are possible?

○   40

○   190

○   200

○   380

○   400

A delivery driver must make 8 stops over the course of the night.

Quantity A	**Quantity B**
The number of different routes connecting all 8 stops	40,320

- ○ Quantity A is greater.
- ○ Quantity B is greater.
- ○ The two quantities are equal.
- ○ The relationship cannot be determined from the information given.

Question 3 of 5

A website requires a password made up of 2 one-digit numbers followed by 3 of the 26 letters. How many different passwords are possible if repetition of numbers and letters is allowed?

- ○   98
- ○   17,576
- ○ 117,000
- ○ 1,404,000
- ○ 1,757,600

Question 4 of 5

A chef has lamb, carrots, potatoes, celery, and peppers. From these, she chooses three different ingredients for a stew. She will serve the stew with bread, salad, or dumplings. How many different meals could the chef serve?

> [   ]

Ten runners compete in a race. The first 6 to finish receive a $100 prize. In addition, the first 3 to finish receive medals: gold for first, silver for second, and bronze for third.

Quantity A	**Quantity B**
The number of ways of distributing the $100 prizes	The number of ways of distributing the three medals

○ Quantity A is greater.

○ Quantity B is greater.

○ The two quantities are equal.

○ The relationship cannot be determined from the information given.

Explanations for Arrangements and Combinations Quick Quiz

1. Since each sundae contains two scoops of ice cream, draw two slots on your scratch paper: __ __. There are a total of 20 different flavors, so you have 20 options for the first slot: <u>20</u> __ . The problem states that the sundae must have two different types of ice cream, so you can't have the same flavor in the second spot as in the first. Therefore, there are only 19 different options left for the second choice: <u>20</u> <u>19</u>. Before you multiply, ask yourself if order matters. Would a sundae with a scoop of chocolate and a scoop of vanilla be different than a sundae with a scoop of vanilla and a scoop of chocolate? Nope. Order doesn't matter, so this is a combination. Therefore, divide by a factorial of 2 underneath the slots to get $\frac{20}{2} \times \frac{19}{1} = \frac{10}{1} \times \frac{19}{1} = 190$, (B).

2. As the driver decides his route, he's going to have 8 choices to make: Which stop to make first, which to make second, and so on. Draw 8 slots on your scratch paper: __ __ __ __ __ __ __ __. For his first stop, he has 8 options of where to stop, so put an 8 in the first slot. Once he's made that stop, he has only 7 options left for the second stop, so put 7 in the second slot. Continuing to fill in the slots, you have <u>8</u> <u>7</u> <u>6</u> <u>5</u> <u>4</u> <u>3</u> <u>2</u> <u>1</u>. Does order matter? Definitely. If the driver stops at House A before House B, that's a different route than if he stops at House B before House A. This an arrangement. Since order matters,

you can multiply together $\underline{8} \times \underline{7} \times \underline{6} \times \underline{5} \times \underline{4} \times \underline{3} \times \underline{2} \times \underline{1}$, using the calculator and scratch paper, giving you 40,320. Since the quantities are equal, the answer is (C).

3. The password has 5 total numbers or letters, so you'll have to make 5 choices. Draw 5 slots on your scratch paper: __ __ __ __ __. The first thing you'll have to choose is a one-digit number. Since there are 10 one-digit numbers, from 0 to 9, you have 10 options for the first slot. You also need to place a one-digit number in the second spot. However, since the problem states that repetition is allowed, you have 10 options for the second slot as well. In other words, if you choose 4 as the first character of the password, you're allowed to choose any one-digit number, including 4, as the second character. So far, you've got $\underline{10}$ $\underline{10}$ __ __ __. Now you get into the alphabet. The first letter could be any of the 26 letters, so put 26 in the third slot. The second letter could also be any of the 26 letters, since repetition is allowed, so put 26 in the fourth slot. The last character of the password also needs to be a letter, with repetition allowed, so put 26 in the last spot. The slots are now $\underline{10}$ $\underline{10}$ $\underline{26}$ $\underline{26}$ $\underline{26}$. Does order matter? Having 12ABC as a password is different than having 21CBA, so order definitely matters. Multiply together the numbers in the slots: $\underline{10} \times \underline{10} \times \underline{26} \times \underline{26} \times \underline{26} = 1{,}757{,}600$, (E).

4. This is a slightly more difficult problem, because you've got two overall decisions to make: which stew to serve and with what to serve it. Just choosing the stew itself will take some math. The chef has 3 options of what to put in the stew, so you have 3 slots: __ __ __. There are 5 ingredients, so you have 5 options for the first slot. Since you must use 3 *different* ingredients, you have only 4 options left for the second slot, 3 options for the third slot, and the slots are $\underline{5}$ $\underline{4}$ $\underline{3}$. Does order matter? Putting lamb, celery, and potatoes in the stew is the same as putting potatoes, celery, and lamb, so order doesn't matter, so this portion of the problem is a combination. Therefore, you have to divide by the factorial of 3 underneath the slots to get $\frac{5}{3} \times \frac{4}{2} \times \frac{3}{1} = \frac{5}{1} \times \frac{2}{1} \times \frac{1}{1} = 10$ different stews. Now you have to decide the different meals. You'll have to choose a stew and a side, so you have two slots: __ __. For our first slot, you have the option of any of those 10 delicious stews you calculated earlier. For the second slot, you can choose 1 of those 3 sides. The slots are $\underline{10}$ $\underline{3}$. Does order matter? Definitely, because you've got two different types of items here: You can't serve dumplings as a stew, and you can't serve a stew in place of bread. $\underline{10} \times \underline{3} = 30$ different meals.

5. Focus on Quantity A first. You're giving away 6 prizes, so you have 6 slots: __ __ __ __ __ __. For the first slot, you can give the prize to any of the 10 runners in the race. Once you've given away that prize, you only have 9 runners left who can receive a prize, and so on, giving you <u>10</u> <u>9</u> <u>8</u> <u>7</u> <u>6</u> <u>5</u>. Does order matter? Well, if I come in first and get $100, is that any different than coming in sixth and getting $100? No, since I'm getting $100 either way. Since order doesn't matter, this is a combination question, and you'll have to divide by the factorial of 6 underneath the slots: $\frac{10}{6} \times \frac{9}{5} \times \frac{8}{4} \times \frac{7}{3} \times \frac{6}{2} \times \frac{5}{1}$. Before you multiply, see which denominators cancel out with which numerators, and you have $\frac{2}{1} \times \frac{3}{1} \times \frac{1}{1} \times \frac{7}{1} \times \frac{1}{1} \times \frac{5}{1} = 210$ different ways of handing out the six $100 prizes.

Now work on Quantity B. You have 3 medals to give away, so you've got 3 slots: __ __ __. The gold medal could go to any of the 10 runners, so put 10 in the first slot. The silver medal can go to any of the remaining 9 runners, and the bronze can go to any of the remaining 8 runners, so the slots are <u>10</u> <u>9</u> <u>8</u>. Does order matter? If two runners, Dave and Rob, compete and Dave wins the gold medal and Rob wins the bronze, is that the same as Rob winning the gold and Dave winning the bronze? Nope, so order matters. This is an arrangement and you have to multiply together the slots: <u>10</u> × <u>9</u> × <u>8</u> = 720. Quantity B is larger than Quantity A, so the answer is (B).

Congratulations! You've made it through the most arcane topics that the GRE tests. If you can handle yourself here, you're in great shape for the quantitative section. Though these topics are tested infrequently, knowing this stuff could mean the difference between a good score and a great one.

Be sure to keep practicing; you're almost ready to take the test and get on with your life!

For a comprehensive review of every section of the GRE, plus 6 full-length practice tests, video tutorials, and more, check out *Cracking the GRE Premium*.

The Rest of the Story Drill

All but 4 of the counselors on staff at a certain summer camp have sailing certification, first aid certification, or both. Twice as many counselors have neither certification as have both certifications, and 7 counselors have sailing certification. If there are a total of 22 counselors on staff, then how many of the counselors have first aid certification?

What is the value of $\dfrac{8!}{10!}$?

○ $\dfrac{4!}{5!}$

○ $\dfrac{1}{2!}$

○ $9!$

○ $\dfrac{1}{5(6!)}$

○ $\dfrac{1}{15(3!)}$

If set $X = \{12, 16, 20\}$, then which of the following sets has a standard deviation greater than that of set X ?

○ {2, 4, 6}

○ {4, 5, 6}

○ {13, 16, 19}

○ {20, 32, 44}

○ {95, 99, 103}

Ryan's bakery has 212 cakes to sell. 131 cakes are chocolate and the rest are vanilla, while 104 cakes have mocha frosting, and the rest have coconut frosting. If 37 of the chocolate cakes have mocha frosting, how many of the vanilla cakes have coconut frosting?

○   14

○   67

○   81

○   104

○   108

If a value for the integer x is randomly selected and $-10 < x < 10$, what is the probability that x is even?

○ $\dfrac{1}{19}$

○ $\dfrac{1}{4}$

○ $\dfrac{1}{2}$

○ $\dfrac{9}{19}$

○ $\dfrac{11}{21}$

Which of the following is the least value of x for which $\dfrac{x!}{6!}$ is an integer greater than 1 ?

○ 2

○ 3

○ 6

○ 7

○ 12

The purchaser of a certain car must choose 2 of 5 special options and 5 of 6 interior features. How many different combinations of options and features are available to the purchaser?

○ 10

○ 16

○ 18

○ 30

○ 60

Laura has decided to display 5 of her glass animal figurines on a shelf. If she has 6 circus animals and 5 farm animals from which to choose, and she wants a farm animal in the middle of the display, then how many arrangements of the figurines are possible?

○ 30

○ 150

○ 3,024

○ 25,200

○ 30,240

Two six-sided dice with sides numbered 1 through 6 are rolled. If the two resulting numbers are multiplied, what is the probability that their product will be even?

○ $\dfrac{1}{12}$

○ $\dfrac{1}{4}$

○ $\dfrac{1}{2}$

○ $\dfrac{3}{4}$

○ $\dfrac{11}{12}$

Sandy is designing an Internet banner advertisement and has decided to use one background, one font, two different accent images, and four different colors. If Sandy has 5 backgrounds, 4 fonts, 6 accent images, and 12 colors from which to choose, then how many different banners can she make?

The Outdoor Adventure Camp offers 1-week sessions. During the first week, 44 campers go fishing, 33 go orienteering, and 37 do neither activity. The same number of campers goes orienteering in week 2 as in week 1, and 15 campers in week 2 do both activities. If 49 of the 120 campers who attend week 2 do neither activity, and twice as many campers attend week 1 as go fishing in week 2, then how many total campers attended these 2 weeks?

○ 196

○ 226

○ 234

○ 360

○ 662

During this year's fundraiser, students who sell at least 75 subscriptions will win a prize. The fourth-grade students sold an average of 47 magazine subscriptions per student, and the sales have a standard deviation of 14. If the sales of subscriptions are normally distributed, then what percent of the fourth-grade students will receive a prize?

○ 0.02

○ 0.25

○ 2

○ 25

○ It cannot be determined from the information given

A college admissions committee must select candidates for a certain program from among high school applicants and transfer applicants. The committee has already chosen 132 female candidates in a 3 to 1 ratio of high school students to transfer students, and will maintain this ratio in the selection of male candidates. If the final class size must be between 325 and 350 students, then which of the following is an acceptable number of male high school applicants for the committee to choose?

Indicate all such values.

☐ 99

☐ 144

☐ 156

☐ 162

☐ 168

☐ 180

Robin and Terry want to invite 5 of their friends to their wedding. Robin has 7 friends, Terry has 6, and Robin and Terry have no friends in common. If at least 1 of Robin's friends and at least 1 of Terry's friends must be invited, how many different groups of friends could Robin and Terry invite to their wedding?

○ 462

○ 924

○ 1,260

○ 2,520

○ 151,200

Tony's political science final exam consists exclusively of 8 true/false questions. If Tony guesses on every question, what is the probability that he gets exactly 7 questions right?

○ $\dfrac{1}{32}$

○ $\dfrac{1}{16}$

○ $\dfrac{1}{8}$

○ $\dfrac{7}{8}$

○ $\dfrac{31}{32}$

EXPLANATIONS FOR THE REST OF THE STORY DRILL

1. **13**

   First, write down the group formula, *Total = Group$_1$ + Group$_2$ + Neither – Both,* and fill in what you know. If sailing certification is *Group$_1$* and first aid certification is *Group$_2$*, then 22 = 7 + *Group$_2$* + 4 – 2. So, 22 = *Group$_2$* + 9, and you can solve for *Group$_2$* = 13.

2. **E**

   $8! = 8 \times 7 \times 6 \times 5 \times 4 \times 3 \times 2 \times 1$, and $10! = 10 \times 9 \times 8 \times 7 \times 6 \times 5 \times 4 \times 3 \times 2 \times 1$. When dividing $\dfrac{8!}{10!}$, everything but 10×9 in the denominator cancels out, and you have $\dfrac{1}{10 \times 9} = \dfrac{1}{90}$. For (A), $4 \times 3 \times 2 \times 1$ cancels out of the top and bottom, leaving $\dfrac{1}{5}$. Choice (B) is $\dfrac{1}{2 \times 1} = \dfrac{1}{2}$. Estimate that (C) is greater than 1, and you need an answer less than 1. Choice (D) is $\dfrac{1}{5 \times 6 \times 5 \times 4 \times 3 \times 2 \times 1}$. Estimate that the denominator is greater than 90. Choice (E) is $\dfrac{1}{15 \times 3 \times 2 \times 1} = \dfrac{1}{90}$.

3. **D**

   Don't calculate anything on this one. Instead, just remember that standard deviation is a measure of how much numbers in a set vary, or *deviate*, from the average, or *standard*. Since all of the sets contain three equally spaced numbers, the middle number in each case is the average. The other two numbers in the correct answer, (D), differ most from their average.

4. **A**

   Take this problem one step at a time, using a grid layout. 131 cakes are chocolate, so 81 must be vanilla. 104 have mocha frosting, so 108 have coconut frosting. 37 chocolate cakes have mocha frosting, so there are 94 chocolate cakes with coconut frosting, leaving 14 vanilla cakes with coconut frosting.

5. **D**

   There are 19 integers in the range between –10 and 10. Of those, 9 are even. The probability of selecting an even number is $\dfrac{9}{19}$.

6. **D**

   It's an algebra question with numbers for answer choices, so set up your scratch paper to Plug In the Answers. Start with (C): If $x = 6$, then $\dfrac{6!}{6!} = \dfrac{6 \times 5 \times 4 \times 3 \times 2 \times 1}{6 \times 5 \times 4 \times 3 \times 2 \times 1} = 1$; (C) is too small, so eliminate (A), (B), and (C). Now do the same thing for $x = 7$; all the numbers will cancel out of the denominator, and you'll be left with 7 in the numerator, so the whole expression equals 7. Choice (D) is correct. Choice (E) yields an integer as well, but isn't the *least value* among the choices to do so.

7. **E**

The purchaser has 5 options to choose from for his first choice of special options and 4 left to choose from for his second choice. 5 × 4 = 20, but because the order of choice doesn't matter, divide that 20 by the factorial of 2 to get 10 special option groupings. Do the same thing for the interior features: 6 × 5 × 4 × 3 × 2 = 720. Divide 720 by (5 × 4 × 3 × 2 × 1) because the order of choice doesn't matter. Multiplying the 10 special options by the 6 interior features yields 60 possible option groupings.

8. **D**

There are 5 spaces to fill with a restriction on the middle space, so start with the restricted space. The middle space must be a farm animal, and there are 5 potential figurines for that spot, so 5 goes in that space. The remaining spaces are unrestricted, so there are 10 figurines (6 circus and 4 remaining farm animals) left from which to choose. Slot your first of four remaining spaces with 10, then 9, 8, 7 for the remaining spaces as each one fills. 10 × 9 × 5 × 8 × 7 = 25,200, making (D) the best answer. Choice (E) is a trap answer if you don't account for the restricted space.

9. **D**

The only outcome that would not result in an even product is two odd numbers, because even × (even or odd) = even. Subtracting the probability of two odd rolls from 1 will give the probability that the product is even because P(odd product) + P(even product) = 1. The probability that a roll will be odd is $\frac{3}{6}$, or $\frac{1}{2}$. The probability that both will be odd is $\frac{1}{2} \times \frac{1}{2} = \frac{1}{4}$. The probability that the product will be even is $1 - \frac{1}{4} = \frac{3}{4}$.

10. **148,500**

This is a tricky combination question because you have to treat each category as its own combination, and then multiply the results. Find the number of ways you can choose 1 out of 5 backgrounds, 1 out of 4 fonts, 2 out of 6 images, and 4 out of 12 colors, and then multiply those results together. So, $\frac{5}{1} \times \frac{4}{1} \times \left(\frac{6}{2} \times \frac{5}{1} \right) \times \left(\frac{12}{4} \times \frac{11}{3} \times \frac{10}{2} \times \frac{9}{1} \right) = 148,500$.

11. **B**

The question mentions *neither* and *both*, so be sure to write out the group formula, *Total* = *Group₁* + *Group₂* + *Neither* − *Both*, for each week. Let fishing be *Group₁* and orienteering be *Group₂*, and fill in what you know: for week 1, you have *Total* = 44 + 33 + 37 − *Both*; for week 2, you have 120 = *Group₁* + 33 + 49 − 15. Solve for *Group₁* in the latter equation, and 53 people went fishing in week 2. Twice that many, or 106, attended week 1 overall, and over the 2 weeks the camp was attended by a total of 106 + 120 = 226 people.

12. **C**

When you see the words *standard deviation* or *normally distributed*, draw your bell curve and fill in the percentages: 34, 14, and 2. The average of 47 and a standard deviation of 14 means 75 is 2 standard deviations above the mean, so 2% of the students will receive a prize.

13. **C and D**

Since you have two traits (female/male and high school/transfer), use the group chart to organize your information. First, find the acceptable range of the total number of male applicants to be 193–218: 325 total minimum – 132 female = 193, and 350 total maximum – 132 female = 218. Since the question asks for the number of male high school applicants, plug the choices into your chart to solve for the number of male transfer students using the ratio. Then solve for the total number of male applicants to check if it is within the 193–218 range. In (C), the number of male high school applicants is 156, divided by 3 since the male applicants are in a 3 to 1 ratio, and you get 52 male transfer applicants. 156 + 52 = 208 total male applicants, which is within the acceptable range. In (D), the number of male high school applicants in now 162. Divide 162 by 3 to get 54 for the number of male transfer applicants. 162 + 54 = 216, which is also within the acceptable range. Choices (B), (E), and (F) are all either too big or too small. Choice (A) is a trap answer in that it is the number of female applicants, and (G) is also incorrect since it represents the lower range of the total number of male applicants.

14. **C**

In this question, the order in which the friends are invited does not matter, so you're dealing with a combination. With a total of 13 friends between them and 5 slots to fill, Robin and Terry could invite $13 \times 12 \times 11 \times 10 \times 9$ divided by the factorial of 5 = 1,287 groups of 5 friends to their wedding. There are $7 \times 6 \times 5 \times 4 \times 3$ divided by the factorial of 5 = 21 groups that consist of only Robin's friends, and $6 \times 5 \times 4 \times 3 \times 2$ divided by the factorial of 5 = 6 groups that consist of only Terry's friends. Subtract these two numbers from 1,287, and find that there are 1,260 possible groups that contain at least one of Robin's friends and at least one of Terry's. Therefore, (C) is the correct answer.

15. **A**

To find the probability of exactly seven correct choices, think about all of the possible combinations of eight answers with one wrong (W) and seven right (R) choices. For example, Tony could get WRRRRRRR, RWRRRRRR, and so on. There are 8 different arrangements of one wrong and seven correct answers. The probability of choosing a correct answer for one question is $\frac{1}{2}$, and the probability of choosing a wrong answer is the same. Thus, the total number of possible outcomes is $\left(\frac{1}{2}\right)^8$. The probability of seven correct is the number of outcomes with seven correct divided by the total number of outcomes. The probability of exactly seven correct: $8 \times \frac{1}{2^8} = \frac{1}{32}$.

Chapter 10
Sample Section 1

Quantity A	**Quantity B**
$\dfrac{9}{10} - \dfrac{8}{9}$	$\dfrac{8}{9} - \dfrac{9}{10}$

○ Quantity A is greater.

○ Quantity B is greater.

○ The two quantities are equal.

○ The relationship cannot be determined from the information given.

Quantity A	**Quantity B**
$r + t + v$	$s + u + w$

○ Quantity A is greater.

○ Quantity B is greater.

○ The two quantities are equal.

○ The relationship cannot be determined from the information given.

$$x > 0$$
$$\frac{2x}{3} < 7$$

Quantity A	**Quantity B**
x^2	100

○ Quantity A is greater.

○ Quantity B is greater.

○ The two quantities are equal.

○ The relationship cannot be determined from the information given.

k is an integer such that $9(3)^3 + 4 = k$

Quantity A	**Quantity B**
The average of the prime factors of k	16

○ Quantity A is greater.

○ Quantity B is greater.

○ The two quantities are equal.

○ The relationship cannot be determined from the information given.

A bakery can purchase flour at $1.89 per pound or at a bulk rate of 50 pounds for $90.00.

Quantity A	**Quantity B**
The amount saved per pound by purchasing 50 pounds of flour at the bulk rate	$0.09

○ Quantity A is greater.

○ Quantity B is greater.

○ The two quantities are equal.

○ The relationship cannot be determined from the information given.

$$x = ((24 \div 6) + 2) \times 5$$
$$y = (24 \div (6 + 2)) \times 5$$

Quantity A	Quantity B
$x - y$	$y - x$

○ Quantity A is greater.

○ Quantity B is greater.

○ The two quantities are equal.

○ The relationship cannot be determined from the information given.

$$32 = |k|$$
$$31 = |k + 1|$$

Quantity A	Quantity B
k	32

○ Quantity A is greater.

○ Quantity B is greater.

○ The two quantities are equal.

○ The relationship cannot be determined from the information given.

Alice weighs a kilograms, and Bob weighs b kilograms less than Alice.

$$ab \neq 0$$

Quantity A	Quantity B
The sum of Alice's weight and Bob's weight	$2a$ kilograms

○ Quantity A is greater.

○ Quantity B is greater.

○ The two quantities are equal.

○ The relationship cannot be determined from the information given.

$$0 < xy$$

Quantity A	Quantity B
$\dfrac{5}{2x} - \dfrac{2}{2y}$	$\dfrac{5y - 2x}{2x - 2y}$

○ Quantity A is greater.

○ Quantity B is greater.

○ The two quantities are equal.

○ The relationship cannot be determined from the information given.

If $x^* = x^2 + 4$, which of the following is equivalent to 2^* ?

○ $(-2)^*$

○ 0^*

○ 4^*

○ 6^*

○ 8^*

Which of the following is greater than $\dfrac{2}{3}$ and less than $\dfrac{5}{6}$?

Indicate <u>all</u> such values.

☐ $\dfrac{11}{18}$

☐ $\dfrac{13}{18}$

☐ $\dfrac{3}{4}$

☐ $\dfrac{7}{9}$

☐ $\dfrac{8}{9}$

A manufacturer is designing two rectangular game boards. The width of the smaller board is one-half the width of the larger board, and the length of the smaller board is one-sixth the length of the larger board. If the smaller board has area N, then what is the difference between the areas of the game boards, in terms of N ?

- $\quad 3N$
- $\quad 9N$
- $\quad 11N$
- $\quad 12N$
- $\quad 18N$

If one manual weighs 400 grams, how many kilograms does a box of 48 manuals weigh? (1 kilogram = 1,000 grams)

- $\quad 0.192$
- $\quad 1.92$
- $\quad 19.2$
- $\quad 192$
- $\quad 1,920$

What is the sum of the distinct positive even factors of 12 ?

[   ]

A computer store has fixed monthly operating costs of 5,000 dollars. The store buys each computer for 600 dollars and sells each computer for 900 dollars. What is the least number of computers the store must sell each month to cover the fixed operating costs?

- $\quad 14$
- $\quad 15$
- $\quad 16$
- $\quad 17$
- $\quad 18$

If x is equal to 49.5 percent of $\dfrac{11}{23}$ of 0.996, then

- $0.20 < x < 0.25$
- $0.25 < x < 0.30$
- $0.30 < x < 0.35$
- $0.35 < x < 0.40$
- $0.40 < x < 0.45$

Set $A = \{3, 1, 7, 5, 11, x\}$

If the median of Set A above is one less than the mode of Set A, which of the following is a possible value of x ?

- 3
- 5
- 6
- 7
- 9

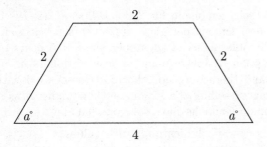

What is the area of the quadrilateral shown above?

○ $2\sqrt{3}$

○ $3\sqrt{3}$

○ 6

○ $6\sqrt{3}$

○ 8

Anne's wage is $10 per hour more than Mary's wage. Andy's wage is $6 per hour more than Mark's wage. Mary's wage is $2 per hour more than Mark's wage.

Quantity A	**Quantity B**
Anne's wage	Andy's wage

○ Quantity A is greater.

○ Quantity B is greater.

○ The two quantities are equal.

○ The relationship cannot be determined from the information given.

M is the sum of three consecutive odd integers, the least of which is t. In terms of M, which of the following is the sum of three consecutive odd integers, the greatest of which is t ?

○ $M + 12$

○ $M + 6$

○ $M - 6$

○ $M - 12$

○ $\dfrac{M}{2}$

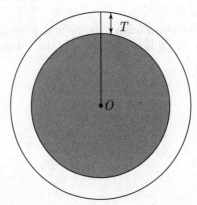

The figure above shows a circular garden plot with center O surrounded by a circular sidewalk, also with center O. If the area covered by the garden and sidewalk together is 169π and of the garden alone is 144π, what is the value of T ?

○   1

○   2

○   3

○   5

○   12.5

If the average (arithmetic mean) of a and b is 6, and $a^2 - b^2 = 2$, what is the value of $a - b$?

○ $\dfrac{1}{6}$

○ $\dfrac{1}{3}$

○ $\dfrac{1}{2}$

○ 2

○ 3

If the sum of two numbers is 19 and their product is 88, what is the difference between the numbers?

○ 2

○ 3

○ 4

○ 5

○ 6

If l is not equal to -3 or -4, then $\dfrac{l}{l+4} + \dfrac{3}{l+3} =$

○ 1

○ $\dfrac{7}{l+4}$

○ $\dfrac{l+3}{2l+7}$

○ $\dfrac{3l}{(l+4)(l+3)}$

○ $\dfrac{l^2 + 6l + 12}{(l+4)(l+3)}$

Pierre sells lemonade for 2 dollars per glass. His costs include 5 lemons per glass at 25 cents per lemon, and 3 tablespoons of sugar per glass at 5 cents per tablespoon. If Pierre made at least 5 dollars in one day, and there were no other costs associated with making or selling the lemonade, how many glasses of lemonade could he have sold on that day?

Indicate all such values.

☐ 6

☐ 7

☐ 8

☐ 9

☐ 10

☐ 11

Aquarium A holds 150 gallons more seawater than does Aquarium B, and both aquariums are currently filled to capacity. If 20 gallons are removed from each aquarium, then Aquarium A would hold four times as much seawater as Aquarium B holds. What is the combined total number of gallons of seawater that can be held in both aquariums?

○ 290

○ 250

○ 220

○ 200

○ 70

Chapter 11
Sample Section 1:
Answers and
Explanations

1. **A**

   Use the Bowtie to find the value of each quantity. Quantity A = $\frac{81-80}{90} = \frac{1}{90}$. Quantity B = $\frac{80-81}{90} = -\frac{1}{90}$. Quantity A is greater than Quantity B.

2. **C**

   When two lines intersect, the big angles and the small angles are equal, so $s = v$, $r = u$, and $t = w$. Therefore, the quantities are equal. To prove it, Plug In. Let $u = 50$, $v = 100$, and $w = 30$. Because the angles are all small angles, $r = 100$, $s = 50$, and $t = 30$. So, both $r + t + v$ and $s + u + w$ total 180.

3. **D**

   First, find the value of x. Multiply both sides by 3 to get $2x < 21$. Divide both sides by 2 to find that $x < 10.5$ as well as being greater than 0. If $x = 2$, then Quantity B is greater because $2^2 = 4$. Eliminate (A) and (C). If $x = 10$, then the two quantities are equal. Eliminate (B), and select (D) because different numbers have given different answers.

4. **C**

   Solve for k: $9(3)^3 + 4 = 9(27) + 4 = 243 + 4 = 247$. So, $k = 247$. Use trial and error to find the prime factors of 247. They are 13 and 19. The average of 13 and 19 is 16, so the quantities are equal.

5. **C**

   First, divide $90 by 50 to find the bulk rate for a single pound of flour: $\frac{\$90}{50} = \$1.80$. The amount saved per pound is $.09. The quantities are equal.

6. **A**

   Remember PEMDAS. $x = ((4) + 2) \times 5 = 6 \times 5 = 30$; $y = (24 \div (8)) \times 5 = 3 \times 5 = 15$. Quantity A = 15, and Quantity B = –15.

7. **B**

   The solutions to the equation $32 = |k|$ are 32 and –32. Of those, only –32 works in the equation $31 = |k + 1|$. Quantity A has the value of –32, so Quantity B is greater.

8. **B**

   Plug In. First, try $a = 100$ and $b = 2$: Alice weighs 100 kilograms, Bob weighs 98 kilograms, and the sum of their weights is 198 kilograms. Quantity B is 2×100, or 200. Quantity B is greater, so eliminate (A) and (C). Now, try a second set of numbers: If $a = 50$ and $b = 10$, then Quantity A is 90 and Quantity B is 100. Quantity B is, again, greater—as it will be with any set of numbers that meets the restriction ($ab \neq 0$).

9. **D**

   Plug In for x and y. Since xy must be positive, either both variables are positive, or both are negative. First, let $x = 5$ and $y = 6$: Quantity A is $\frac{1}{3}$, and Quantity B is –10. Quantity A is greater, so eliminate (B) and

(C). Now let $x = -\dfrac{1}{10}$ and $y = -\dfrac{1}{2}$. Quantity A is –23, and Quantity B is $-\dfrac{23}{8}$. Quantity B is now greater, so eliminate (A), and you're left with (D) because different numbers gave different answers.

10. **A**

The weird little symbol (*) gives you a set of directions. $2^* = (2)^2 + 4 = 4 + 4 = 8$. Find the answer that also equals 8. $(-2)^* = (-2)^2 + 4 = 4 + 4 = 8$.

11. **B, C, and D**

Finding common denominators allows you to compare the values of fractions easily. Because two answer choices are expressed in eighteenths (and two in easily convertible ninths) start there: $\dfrac{2}{3} = \dfrac{12}{18}$, and $\dfrac{5}{6} = \dfrac{15}{18}$. Eliminate (A), and select (B). Choice (D) converts to $\dfrac{14}{18}$, so it's correct; (E), though, converts to $\dfrac{16}{18}$ and can be eliminated. The answers are listed in ascending order, and so (C), falling between correct answers (B) and (D), must be correct as well.

12. **C**

Plug In. If the width of the smaller board is 3, then the width of the larger board must be 6. If the length of the smaller board is 2, then the length of the larger board must be 12. The area of the smaller board is $3 \times 2 = 6$. Therefore, $N = 6$. The area of the larger board is $12 \times 6 = 72$. The question asks for the difference between the areas: $72 - 6 = 66$. The last step is to check which answer choice equals 66 when $N = 6$. Only (C) works.

13. **C**

Since the answer choices are far apart, you can estimate. If one manual weighs 400 grams, then 48 manuals weigh 48×400, or about 20,000 grams. To convert grams to kilograms, divide by 1,000: $20,000 \div 1,000 = 20$. Look for an answer a little less than 20. Only (C) is close.

14. **24**

Start by listing the factors of 12 in pairs: 1 and 12, 2 and 6, and 3 and 4. Because the question asks for the sum of the distinct positive even factors, cross off 1 and 3. Now, add up what's left: $2 + 4 + 6 + 12 = 24$.

15. **D**

The store makes a profit of $300 for each computer sold. Plug In the Answers, starting with (C). 16 computers multiplied by $300 yields a profit of $4,800, not enough to cover costs. You need to sell more computers, so eliminate (A), (B), and (C). Try (D). 17 computers multiplied by $300 yields a profit of $5,100, just enough to cover costs.

16. **A**

Estimate. If x is less than 50% of a fraction that is less than $\frac{1}{2}$ of a number that is less than 1, then x must be less than $\frac{1}{4}$ ($\frac{1}{2} \times \frac{1}{2} \times 1 = \frac{1}{4}$). Therefore, (A) is correct.

17. **D**

Each number in the set occurs only once, and the mode is the most frequently occurring number. To create a mode, x must be the same as one of the other numbers in the set. Eliminate (C) and (E). Plug In the Answers. For (B), the mode is 5. The median of {1, 3, 5, 5, 7, 11} is 5. The median is equal to the mode. You need a larger number for x. For (D), the mode is 7 and the median of {1, 3, 5, 7, 7, 11} is $\frac{(5+7)}{2} = 6$. The mode is now one less than the median. Note that (C) is equal to the median and would be a trap answer if you didn't read the question carefully enough.

18. **B**

Redraw this figure by adding two descending lines from the upper corners of the figure perpendicular to the base below so that you have a rectangle and two right triangles. Each triangle has a base of 1 and a hypotenuse of 2. Use the Pythagorean Theorem or the ratio for 30 : 60 : 90 triangles ($x : x\sqrt{3} : 2x$) to find the height is $\sqrt{3}$. The area of each triangle is $\frac{1}{2}(1)\left(\sqrt{3}\right)$. The area of the rectangle is $(2)\left(\sqrt{3}\right)$. The sum of the rectangle and two triangles is $2\sqrt{3} + 2\left(\frac{1}{2}\sqrt{3}\right) = 2\sqrt{3} + \sqrt{3} = 3\sqrt{3}$.

19. **A**

If Mary's wage is $2 more than Mark's, and Andy's wage is $6 more than Mark's, then Andy's wage is $4 more than Mary's. Anne's wage is $10 more than Mary's, so Anne's wage is $6 more than Andy's. Quantity A is greater than Quantity B.

20. **D**

Plug In, and let $t = 5$. $M = 5 + 7 + 9 = 21$—the sum of the three consecutive odd integers, of which t is the smallest. For the second part of the problem, t is the greatest integer in the series. The sum of the new series is $5 + 3 + 1 = 9$. Plug $M = 21$ into the answers, and (D) matches the target of 9.

21. **A**

The bigger circle that includes the garden and the sidewalk has an area of 169π. The radius of the large circle with the garden and sidewalk is 13. The garden plot has an area 144π, so the radius of the small circle is 12. Since the circles share a center, the width of the sidewalk, T, is the difference between the radii, or $13 - 12 = 1$. Therefore, (A) is correct.

22. **A**

Factor the quadratic expression: $a^2 - b^2$ becomes $(a + b)(a - b)$. The average of two numbers is 6, so their sum, $(a + b)$, is $2 \times 6 = 12$. Substitute the value to get: $12(a - b) = 2$. Thus, $a - b = \dfrac{1}{6}$.

23. **B**

Plug in numbers that have a sum of 19, and check to see if their product is 88. For example, the sum of 9 and 10 is 19, but their product is 90. Therefore, 9 and 10 can't be the two numbers. Try another pair, such as 8 and 11. Their sum is 19, and their product is 88. These numbers match the information given in the problem, and their difference is 3.

24. **E**

Plug In. If $l = 2$, then $\dfrac{l}{l+4} + \dfrac{3}{l+3} = \dfrac{2}{6} + \dfrac{3}{5} = \dfrac{10+18}{30} = \dfrac{28}{30} = \dfrac{14}{15}$. The target is $\dfrac{14}{15}$. Plug 2 for l into the answer choices. Choice (E) is the only answer choice that matches the target.

25. **D, E, and F**

First, figure out Pierre's per-glass profit. His per-glass revenue is $2; his per-glass costs are 25 cents × 5 lemons per glass = 125 cents per glass for lemons, and 5 cents × 3 tablespoons of sugar per glass = 15 cents per glass for sugar, for a total of 140 cents per glass. Pierre's profit on each glass is 60 cents. At a profit of 60 cents per glass, Pierre must sell at least 9 glasses of lemonade to make 5 dollars. Each answer choice greater than or equal to 9 is correct.

26. **A**

Plug In the Answers, starting with (C). If the combined total was 220 and A is 150 more than B, then A is 75 more than half of 220, and B is 75 less than half of 220. So, A is 185 and B is 35. Remove 20 from each to get A is 165 and B is 15. Is 165 four times 15? No, so (C) is not correct. It's hard to tell whether (C) was too large or too small, so just pick a direction. For (A), if the combined total was 290, and A is 150 more than B, then A is 75 more than half of 290, and B is 75 less than half of 290. So, A is 220 and B is 70. Remove 20 from each to get A is 200 and B is 50. Is 200 four times 50? Yes, so (A) is correct.

Chapter 12
Sample Section 2

The average (arithmetic mean) of a, $2a$, and 9 is 7.

Quantity A	**Quantity B**
5	a

○ Quantity A is greater.

○ Quantity B is greater.

○ The two quantities are equal.

○ The relationship cannot be determined from the information given.

$$12 > 3x - 9y$$

Quantity A	**Quantity B**
6	$x - 3y$

○ Quantity A is greater.

○ Quantity B is greater.

○ The two quantities are equal.

○ The relationship cannot be determined from the information given.

Quantity A	**Quantity B**
r	s

○ Quantity A is greater.

○ Quantity B is greater.

○ The two quantities are equal.

○ The relationship cannot be determined from the information given.

$$\begin{array}{r} 145.3 \\ -AB.A \\ \hline 66.6 \end{array}$$

In the correctly calculated subtraction problem shown above, A and B represent digits from 0 to 9, inclusive.

Quantity A	**Quantity B**
15	$A + B$

○ Quantity A is greater.

○ Quantity B is greater.

○ The two quantities are equal.

○ The relationship cannot be determined from the information given.

For all integers a and b, $a \# b = -|a + b|$.

Quantity A	**Quantity B**
$(-10) \# 7$	$7 - 10$

○ Quantity A is greater.

○ Quantity B is greater.

○ The two quantities are equal.

○ The relationship cannot be determined from the information given.

Company X sold 300 products this year. It sold twice as many of Product A as it did of Product C, and half of the products sold were Product B. Company X sold no products other than A, B, and C.

Quantity A	**Quantity B**
The number of Product A sold	100

○ Quantity A is greater.

○ Quantity B is greater.

○ The two quantities are equal.

○ The relationship cannot be determined from the information given.

$$z \neq 0$$

Quantity A	**Quantity B**
$\dfrac{99z}{100}$	$\dfrac{100}{99z}$

○ Quantity A is greater.

○ Quantity B is greater.

○ The two quantities are equal.

○ The relationship cannot be determined from the information given.

In a garden, there are only red, yellow, and blue flowers. One–third of the flowers are red, and 40 percent are blue. One flower is chosen at random.

Quantity A	**Quantity B**
The probability that the flower chosen is not red	The probability the flower chosen is not yellow

○ Quantity A is greater.

○ Quantity B is greater.

○ The two quantities are equal.

○ The relationship cannot be determined from the information given.

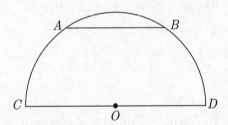

In the semicircle with center O shown above, the length of arc AC is equal to the length of arc BD, and the length of arc AB is less than the length of arc BD.

Quantity A	**Quantity B**
$\dfrac{\text{the length of chord } AB}{\text{the length of chord } CD}$	$\dfrac{1}{2}$

○ Quantity A is greater.

○ Quantity B is greater.

○ The two quantities are equal.

○ The relationship cannot be determined from the information given.

What is the value of $(4 + a)(4 - b)$ when $a = 4$ and $b = -4$?

○ −64

○ −16

○ 0

○ 16

○ 64

If the average (arithmetic mean) of two numbers is 35 and one of the numbers is k, then what is the other number, in terms of k ?

○ $35 + k$

○ $35 - k$

○ $35 - 2k$

○ $70 - k$

○ $70 - 2k$

Alejandro calculated 25 percent of x instead of a 25 percent increase in x. Which of the following operations could Alejandro perform on his answer to produce the correct solution?

Indicate <u>all</u> such values.

☐ Add x

☐ Multiply by x

☐ Divide by 0.25

☐ Multiply by 5

If the ratio of $x : y$ is $6 : 7$, and x is equal to 15, then the value of y is

○ 7

○ 13.5

○ 17

○ 17.5

○ 20

If $x \neq 0$, what is the value of b when $x = a(b + c)$?

○ $c - \dfrac{a}{x}$

○ $\dfrac{x}{a} - c$

○ $ax - c$

○ $ax + c$

○ $x - ac$

$$\frac{3^6 + 3^4 + 3^2}{3^2 + 3^4 + 3^6}$$

☐

If $k = 6 \times 17$, then which of the following is a multiple of k ?

○ 68

○ 78

○ 85

○ 136

○ 204

The ratio of the degree measures of the angles of a triangle is $2 : 3 : 4$. Which of the following is the sum of the degree measures of the smallest and largest angles?

○ $40°$

○ $80°$

○ $100°$

○ $120°$

○ $140°$

The price of a slice of pizza is $(8a + b)$ cents, the price of a soda is $(8b + a)$ cents, and the sum of the two prices is $1.35.

Quantity A	**Quantity B**
a	b

○ Quantity A is greater.

○ Quantity B is greater.

○ The two quantities are equal.

○ The relationship cannot be determined from the information given.

If $y = \sqrt{0.36x^8}$, then $y =$

○ $0.06x^2$

○ $0.06x^4$

○ $0.06x^5$

○ $0.6x^2$

○ $0.6x^4$

If $x^2 + 2xy + y^2 = 25$, then $(x + y)^3$ could be

○ 5

○ 15

○ 50

○ 75

○ 125

A grain elevator moves 200 pounds of grain every 15 minutes. If the elevator starts moving grain at noon, and stops some time from 3:00 P.M. to 4:00 P.M., which of the following could be the weight, in pounds, of the grain moved by the elevator?

Indicate all such values.

☐ 800

☐ 2,400

☐ 2,732

☐ 3,000

☐ 3,200

☐ 3,600

If $a = (0.404)^3$, $b = \sqrt[3]{0.404}$, and $c = 0.404$, then which of the following is true?

○ $a > b > c$

○ $b > a > c$

○ $a > c > b$

○ $c > a > b$

○ $b > c > a$

At least 15 percent of the students registered for Professor Tyler's course dropped out before the end of the course. The drop-out rate for Professor Quin's course was 20 percent greater than that for Professor Tyler's course. If 120 students remained on the last day of Professor Quin's class, which of the following could be the number of students who signed up for Professor Quin's class?

Indicate <u>all</u> such values.

☐ 42

☐ 135

☐ 142

☐ 146

☐ 147

☐ 162

☐ 184

☐ 185

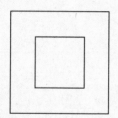

In the figure above, if the area of the larger square region is twice the area of the smaller square region, and if a diagonal of the smaller square has a length of 1 foot, then a side of the larger square is how many feet longer than a side of the smaller square?

○ $\dfrac{2 - \sqrt{2}}{2}$

○ $\sqrt{2} - 1$

○ 1

○ $\sqrt{2}$

○ 2

If $5a - 3b = -9$ and $3a + b = 31$, then $a + b =$

○ −7

○ −3

○ 6

○ 13

○ 19

Claire estimates her chances of being admitted to her top five schools as follows: 80 percent for Debs U, 70 percent for Powderly State, 50 percent for Randolph A&M, 20 percent for Reuther, and 10 percent for Chavez Poly. If Claire's estimates are correct, her chance of being admitted to at least one of her top five schools is between

○ 75% and 79.99%

○ 80% and 84.99%

○ 85% and 89.99%

○ 90% and 94.99%

○ 95% and 99.99%

Chapter 13
Sample Section 2:
Answers and
Explanations

1. **A**

   If the average of 3 things is 7, the total is $(3 \times 7) = 21$. $21 = a + 2a + 9 = 3a + 9$, and $a = 4$. Therefore, Quantity A is greater.

2. **A**

   Divide both sides of the inequality by 3 to get $4 > x - 3y$. Quantity B must be less than 4, and, thus, less than Quantity A.

3. **B**

   Follow the dotted lines. r corresponds to the x-coordinate, –5, and s corresponds to the y-coordinate, –3.5. Quantity B is greater than Quantity A.

4. **C**

   Try rearranging the problem. If $\dfrac{\begin{array}{r}145.3\\-AB.A\end{array}}{66.6}$, then $\dfrac{\begin{array}{r}145.3\\-66.6\end{array}}{AB.A}$. Hence, $AB.A = 78.7$, and $A + B = 15$. The quantities are equal.

5. **C**

   For Quantity A, substitute the numbers provided in the question for the variables in the function: $-|-10 + 7| = -|-3| = -3$. Quantity B is –3. The quantities are equal.

6. **C**

   The company sold $300 \div 2 = 150$ of Product B. The remainder, $A + C = 150$. Since Quantity B is a number, try plugging it in to the problem for Product A. If $A = 100$, then $C = 50$; the quantities are equal.

7. **D**

   Plug in 1 for z. Quantity A is $\dfrac{99 \times 1}{100} = \dfrac{99}{100}$, and Quantity B is $\dfrac{100}{99 \times 1} = \dfrac{100}{99}$. Quantity B is greater, so eliminate (A) and (C). Plug in –1 for z. Quantity A is $\dfrac{99 \times -1}{100} = -\dfrac{99}{100}$, and Quantity B is $\dfrac{100}{99 \times -1} = -\dfrac{100}{99}$. Quantity A is closer to 0, and, thus, is greater. Eliminate (B), and select (D) since different numbers gave different answers.

8. **B**

   The probability that the flower is red is $\dfrac{1}{3}$, so the probability that it is not red is $1 - \dfrac{1}{3} = \dfrac{2}{3}$. Quantity A is $\dfrac{2}{3}$. The probability that the flower is not yellow equals the probability that it is red + the probability that it is blue. $\dfrac{1}{3} + 40\% = \dfrac{1}{3} + \dfrac{2}{5} = \dfrac{11}{15}$. Quantity B is $\dfrac{11}{15}$ and is greater.

9. **B**

Start by assuming that arc AB is equal to arc BD even though the problem states that they cannot be equal. It's often helpful to evaluate a limiting case when solving a math question. That's particularly true with Quantitative Comparison questions. Because arc BD is equal to arc AC, all three arcs are equal: $AB = AC = BD$. Next, draw lines AO and BO. These lines, which are radii of the semicircle, create three central angles: AOC, AOB, and BOD. Because $AB = AB = BD$, the three central angles have equal degree measures: $AOC = AOB = BOD = 60°$. Consider triangle AOB, which was created by drawing the two radii. This triangle is an equilateral triangle because $OA = OB$ and hence, the remaining 120° must be split equally between angles OAB and OBA. Because triangle AOB is equilateral, $OA = OB = AB = r$, where r is the radius of the semicircle. Then, because CD is the diameter of the semicircle, $CD = 2r$. So, Quantity A is $\frac{r}{2r} = \frac{1}{2}$. Now, consider the restriction stipulated in the problem that $AB < BD$. For that to be true, the degree measure of central angle $AOB < 60$. When $AOB < 60$, the length of $AB < r$. For example, AB could be $\frac{1}{2}r$. Then, Quantity A is $\frac{\left(\left(\frac{1}{2}\right)r\right)}{2r} = \frac{1}{4}$. Quantity B is greater whenever $AB < BD$. The correct answer is (B).

10. **E**

You are given a value for each of the variables. If you put these values directly into $(4 + a)(4 - b)$, you get $(4 + 4)(4 - (-4)) = (8)(4 + 4) = (8)(8) = 64$.

11. **D**

If the average of 2 numbers is 35, the total is $(2 \times 35) = 70$. Plug In for k, and let $k = 20$. You get $70 - 20 = 50$, the other number and the target answer. Go to the answer choices and Plug In 20 for k. Only (D) matches your target of 50.

12. **A and D**

If x is 100, then Alejandro found 25% of 100 = 25 instead of increasing 100 by 25 to 125. The question asks what Alejandro could do to turn 25 into 125. If he adds x, this will work because 25 + 100 = 125, or in math terms $0.25x + 1x = 1.25x$. Multiplying by x will not work because 25 × 100 = 2,500, not 125. Dividing by 0.25 will not work because 25 ÷ 0.25 = 100, not 125. Multiplying by 5 works because 25 × 5 = 125.

13. **D**

Use the Ratio Box. Fill in that the ratio of x to y is 6 to 7. Fill in that the actual value of x is 15. The multiplier is $\frac{15}{6} = \frac{5}{2}$. Use this multiplier to find y: $7 \times \frac{5}{2} = \frac{35}{2} = 17.5$.

14. **B**

Plug In. If $b = 2$, $c = 3$, and $a = 4$, then $x = 20$. The question asks for the value of b, so the target answer is 2. Plug $c = 3$, $a = 4$, and $x = 20$ into all the answers to find the answer that yields 2. Choice (A) yields a fraction, not 2. Choice (B) yields $\frac{20}{4} - 3 = 2$, so keep this answer. Estimate that (C) and (D) are larger than 2. Choice (E) yields 8, not 2. Choice (B) is the only choice that yields the target answer.

15. **1**

Notice that the exact same numbers appear in the numerator and denominator of the fraction. Since it doesn't matter in what order you add quantities, the numerator and denominator of the fraction are the same. You don't even have to add it up. The answer is 1 because a nonzero number divided by itself is 1.

16. **E**

You could multiply 6 by 17 and start dividing the answer choices by the result, but there's an easier way. Because 6 = 3 × 2, the correct answer must be a multiple of 2. Eliminate (C) because it's odd. Next, the correct answer is a multiple of 3. To check to see which numbers are multiples of 3, add their digits, and check to see if the sum is a multiple of 3. For example, (A) is 6 + 8 = 14, which is not a multiple of 3. Eliminate (A). You can also eliminate (D) this way. Try dividing (B) by 17. Since you don't get an integer, that leaves only (E).

17. **D**

There are 180° in a triangle, so you know that $2x + 3x + 4x = 180$. Solve for x: $9x = 180$, and $x = 20$. The smallest angle is 40°, the middle angle is 60°, and the largest angle is 80°. The sum of the smallest and largest angles is 120, or (D).

18. **D**

You know only the sum of the two prices: $(8a + b) + (8b + a) = 135$ cents, or $9a + 9b = 135$. You could simplify this by dividing by 9 to get $a + b = 15$. However, you cannot determine the values of a and b individually, nor their values relative to each other. For example, try $a = 5$ and $b = 10$, and then try $a = 10$ and $b = 5$. Different outcomes are possible, so the answer is (D).

19. E

Work with numerical portion of the square root first $\sqrt{0.36} = \dfrac{\sqrt{36}}{\sqrt{100}} = \dfrac{6}{10} = 0.6$. Eliminate (A), (B), and (C). Next, work with the variable. If you are struggling with exponent rules, you can expand it out: $\sqrt{x^8} = \left(\sqrt{\overbrace{x \times x \times x \times x \times x \times x \times x \times x}^{8}}\right)^{\frac{1}{2}} = x^4$. So $y = 0.6\, x^4$.

20. E

Notice that $x^2 + 2xy + y^2 = 25$ is a quadratic equation. The question asks for $(x + y)^3$. The first step is to factor $x^2 + 2xy + y^2 = 25$. It becomes $(x + y)(x + y) = 25$. Therefore, $(x + y) = \pm 5$. Since you know that $(x + y)$ could be 5 or -5, you know $(x + y)^3$ could be 125 or -125. The correct answer is (E).

21. B, C, D, and E

Since the elevator moves 200 pounds of grain every 15 minutes, it moves 800 pounds every hour. Starting at noon and stopping at 3:00, the elevator moves $3 \times 800 = 2{,}400$ pounds of grain. Eliminate (A). At the opposite extreme, starting at noon and stopping at 4:00, the elevator moves $4 \times 800 = 3{,}200$ pounds. Eliminate (F). The upper and lower bounds having been established, any answer choices that fall on or between them—that is, (B), (C), (D), and (E)—are correct.

22. E

Remember that a fraction or decimal between 0 and 1 gets smaller when you cube it. So, $c > a$. Conversely, it gets bigger when you take the cube root, so $b > c$. Therefore, $b > c > a$.

23. E, F, G, and H

If students are dropping out of the course, then there had to have been more than 120 students originally. Eliminate (A). Next, find Professor Quin's drop-out rate: 20% (or $\dfrac{1}{5}$) of 15 is 3, so Professor Quin's rate is 3 greater than 15%, or 18%. If 18% of the students dropped out over the length of the course, then 82% remained on the last day. 82% of x is 120: $\dfrac{82}{100} \times x = 120$. The value of x is 146.34; because you can't have .34 of a person, the total must have been 147. The rate is at least 18%, so there could have been more students originally; hence, any answer choices that are greater than 147 can be correct as well.

24. A

First, find a side of the smaller square. $x^2 + x^2 = 1$. Thus, $2x^2 = 1$ so $x^2 = \dfrac{1}{2}$ and $x = \dfrac{\sqrt{2}}{2}$. Alternatively, you can apply the ratio for the sides of an isosceles right triangle ($x : x : x\sqrt{2}$) to solve for the length of a side. The area of this square is $\left(\dfrac{\sqrt{2}}{2}\right)^2$ or $\dfrac{1}{2}$. Therefore, the area of the larger square must be 1. The formula for the area of a square is $a = s^2$. Since $s^2 = 1$, that means $s = 1$. The difference between the larger and smaller sides is $1 - \dfrac{\sqrt{2}}{2} = \dfrac{2 - \sqrt{2}}{2}$.

25. **E**

Multiply both sides of the second equation by 3 to get $9a + 3b = 93$. Add the first and second equations:

$$5a - 3b = -9$$
$$+\ \underline{9a + 3b = 93}$$
$$14a\qquad = 84$$

Solve to find that $a = 6$. Plug $a = 6$ back into $5a - 3b = -9$ to find the value of b: $5(6) - 3b = -9$, or $30 - 3b = -9$, and $b = 13$. The question asks for $a + b$, which is $6 + 13 = 19$.

26. **E**

To figure out the probability of being accepted to at least one university, use the following formula: P(at least one) = 1 − P(none). The chance that Claire gets into none of her top five schools is $0.2 \times 0.3 \times 0.5 \times 0.8 \times 0.9$, which is about 2%. Therefore, her chance of getting into at least one of her top five schools is about 98%.

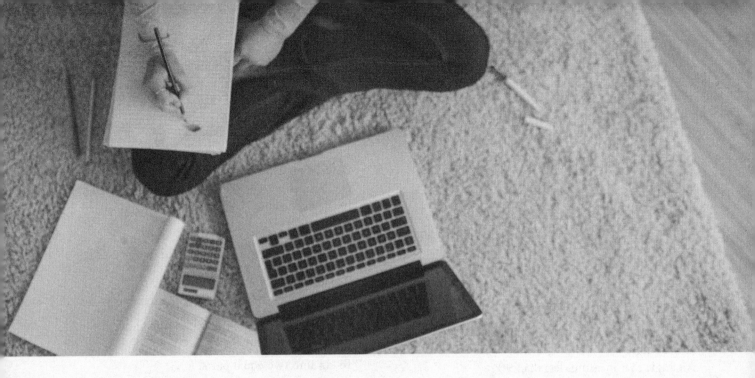

Chapter 14
Glossary of Math Terms

Here is a list of mathematical terms that every GRE student should know well. Terms in *italics* have been cross-referenced from other definitions within this list.

A

Absolute Value
The absolute value of a number is defined as the distance of that number from zero. For the GRE, the important parts of absolute value are that the absolute value of a positive number is positive, the absolute value of a negative number is positive, and if a variable has an absolute value sign around it, then that variable has two solutions: If $|x| = 5$ then $x = 5$ or -5.

Acute Angle
An angle that measures less than 90°.

All That Apply
A GRE question format that has square answer boxes. You must select every answer choice (out of anywhere between 3 and 8 answer choices) that applies. There is no partial credit; if any correct answer choices are not selected, or any incorrect answer choices are selected, the entire response is considered incorrect.

Arc
Any measurement around the circumference of a circle.

Area
The amount of space within a two-dimensional figure.

The important formulas for area are as follows: Triangle Area = $\frac{1}{2}bh$; Parallelogram or Rectangle Area = bh; Square Area = s^2; and Circle Area = πr^2.

Arrangement
A possible arrangement of a certain number of terms when the order in which those items are selected does matter. (See also *Combination*.)

B

Ballparking
Approximating what the right answer might be and eliminating all impossible answer choices.

Base (of an exponent)
The bottom, larger number in an exponential expression. In the expression 3^4, the base is 3.

Base (of a triangle)
The bottom side of a triangle; used to find a triangle's area.

Binomial
An algebraic expression that contains two terms, such as $(x + 2)$.

Bisect
To cut into two equal parts.

C

Chord
A line segment that connects two points on a circle's *circumference*. The longest possible chord, the *diameter*, goes through the center of the circle.

Circumference
The *perimeter* of a circle; $C = 2\pi r$.

Coefficient
A number that appears next to a *variable* and should be multiplied by that variable. In the expression $5a$, which is shorthand for "$5 \times a$," the coefficient is 5.

Combination
A possible arrangement of a certain number of terms when the order in which those items are selected does not matter. (See also *Arrangement*.)

Concentric
Having the same center. (Most often used in terms of circles.)

Constant
Any number that is not a *variable*.

D

Denominator
The bottom number in a fraction. If a denominator equals zero, the fraction is undefined.

Diameter

A line segment that connects two points on a circle's *circumference* and goes through the center. The diameter is the circle's largest *chord*, and it is twice as long as the *radius*.

Difference

The result of subtraction. The difference of 5 and 3 is 2.

Distributive Property

A mathematical property whereby any number multiplied by a *sum* or *difference* of two or more numbers must be multiplied by all the numbers therein. The expression $3(2x + 5)$ can be rewritten, or distributed, to $(3 \times 2x) + (3 \times 5)$, or $6x + 15$.

Divisible

A number a is divisible by another number b if b divides into a evenly, with no remainder. In other words, $\frac{a}{b}$ is an *integer*.

Divisor

A number that can be divided into another number.

E

Equilateral Triangle

A triangle with three sides of the same length and three angles of the same measure (60°).

Exponent

The small number in the upper-right corner of an exponential expression. In the expression 3^4, the exponent is 4. This means the base 3 must be multiplied by itself 4 times $(3 \times 3 \times 3 \times 3)$.

Extra Information

Information in a math problem that doesn't actually help solve the problem. In the GRE, questions rarely have extra information. If you are ever stuck on a GRE problem, reread the question to see if there's any information you haven't used yet.

Even

Divisible by 2.

F

Factor

Any number that can be divided evenly into another number. 3 divides evenly into 12, so 3 is a factor of 12.

Factorial

A process whereby an *integer* is multiplied by each of the positive integers less than itself exactly once. "Eight factorial" is denoted as 8! and can be found by multiplying $8 \times 7 \times 6 \times 5 \times 4 \times 3 \times 2 \times 1$, which equals 40,320.

FOIL

Acronym for First, Outside, Inside, Last that indicates how two *binomials* can be multiplied together.

FROZEN

An acronym to help you remember the weird numbers that can be helpful to Plug In on Must Be or Quant Comp Plug In questions. Try normal, easy numbers first, but then try some of the FROZEN numbers on the remaining answers. FROZEN stands for Fractions, Repeats, One, Zero, Extremes, Negative.

Function

A method of showing a relationship between two or more variables. On the GRE, function questions may involve symbols that are not typically in math questions, and will require following the directions given for that particular function.

I

Improper Fraction

A fraction in which the *numerator* is greater than the *denominator*. These fractions can be converted to mixed fractions.

Integer

Any number that has no fraction or decimal associated with it. Think of integers as the counting numbers on the number line, including 0. Integers can be positive or negative.

Irrational Number

Any number that cannot be denoted as a fraction. Most irrational numbers you'll come in contact with on the GRE will be square roots and π.

Isosceles Triangle

A triangle with two sides of the same length and two angles of the same measure.

L

Like Terms

Any algebraic terms that contain the exact same configuration of variables and therefore can be combined. For example, $3a^2b$ and $6a^2b$ are like terms, so they can be added to make $9a^2b$. The variables in $5xy^3$ and $10x^3y$ are similar but *not* identical, so these are not like terms.

M

MADSPM

A mnemonic device to remember the rules for combining exponents for quantities with the same base: When *Multiplying* terms with the same base, *Add* the exponents. When *Dividing* terms with the same base, *Subtract* the exponents. When raising a term with an exponent to another *Power,* then *Multiply* the exponents.

Mark

A button at the top of the screen during the GRE test. Clicking the Mark button will put a check mark next to that question on the Review screen.

Mean

The average value of a list of numbers.

Median

The middle value in a list of numbers when the numbers are arranged in ascending order. Among an odd number of elements, the median is the middle number; among an even number of elements, the median is the average of the two middle numbers.

Mixed Fraction

A number that contains both an *integer* and a fraction, like $3\frac{1}{5}$.

Mode

The value that occurs most often in a list of numbers.

Multiple

The product of two *integers*.

N

Next

A button at the top of the screen during the GRE test. Clicking on the Next button will move you on to the next question. Simply clicking on an answer alone will not advance you to the next question; you must also hit Next.

Numerator

The top number of a fraction. If the numerator of a fraction equals zero (and the *denominator* does not), the fraction equals zero.

Numeric Entry

A question format on the GRE. Numeric entry questions have an empty box rather than answer choices. Some questions require fractions to be entered: These will have two empty boxes, one on top of another. Fractions don't need to be reduced to lowest terms (e.g., $\frac{1}{2}$, $\frac{16}{32}$, and $\frac{800}{1,600}$ are all considered equivalent), and decimals do not need to be truncated (3.6 is the same as 3.600). Do not round decimals unless explicitly told to do so.

O

Obtuse Angle

An angle that measures between 90° and 180°.

Odd

Not divisible by 2.

P

π (pi)

The result when the *circumference* of a circle is divided by the *diameter* of that same circle. Roughly equal to 3.1415926535897932384626…, but think of it as 3.14.

Parallel Lines

Lines within the same plane that will never intersect. On the coordinate axes, parallel lines have the same slope.

Parallelogram

A quadrilateral with two pairs of parallel sides.

PEMDAS
Acronym for Parentheses, Exponents, Multiply/Divide, Add/Subtract that describes the proper order of operations.

Perimeter
The sum of the lengths of all the sides of a polygon. The perimeter of a circle is called the "circumference."

Perfect Square
A number whose square root is an *integer*. The first five perfect squares are 1, 4, 9, 16, and 25.

Perpendicular
Intersecting at a right angle.

PITA (Plugging In the Answers)
Technique for answering multiple-choice questions without doing any algebra (see Chapter 5).

Plug In
A mathematical technique that changes an algebra problem into an arithmetic problem. Plug In can be used whenever there are variables in the answers or the problem contains an unknown quantity that cannot be directly solved for. For more information see Chapter 5: Turning Algebra into Arithmetic.

Prime Number
Any number whose only factors are itself and 1. The first twenty prime numbers are 2, 3, 5, 7, 11, 13, 17, 19, 23, 29, 31, 37, 41, 43, 47, 53, 59, 61, 67, and 71.

Product
The result of multiplication; the product of 12 and 4 is 12×4, or 48.

Pythagorean Theorem
The formula you can use to find the length of the third side of a right triangle ($a^2 + b^2 = c^2$), where a and b are the lengths of the legs and c is the length of the hypotenuse.

Pythagorean triple
Any set of three integers that works in the Pythagorean Theorem. The four most common Pythagorean triples are 3 : 4 : 5, 5 : 12 : 15, 7 : 24 : 25, and 8 : 15 : 17.

Q

Quadrilateral
A polygon with four sides.

Quantitative Comparison
A question type on the GRE in which two quantities are given and you need to determine which is larger (or if the answer is impossible to determine). Often abbreviated in this book as "Quant Comp."

Quotient
The result of division; the quotient of 12 and 4 is $12 \div 4$, or 3.

R

Radical
Another name for a root; one might refer to $\sqrt{2}$ as "radical 2."

Radicand
The number inside the square root symbol.

Radius
The distance from the center of a circle to any point on the *circumference* of that circle.

Range
The difference between the greatest value and the least value in a set of numbers.

Rational Number
Any number that can be represented as the quotient of two integers.

Reciprocal
The product of any number and its reciprocal is 1: $\frac{2}{5} \times \frac{5}{2} = \frac{10}{10} = 1$. The result when the numerator and denominator are "flipped." The reciprocal of $\frac{2}{5}$ is $\frac{5}{2}$.

Remainder
The result when a number does not divide evenly into another. When 7 is divided by 3, the remainder is 1.

Review
A button at the top of the screen during the GRE test. Clicking on the Review button will show a list of all questions, indicating which questions have been answered, remain unanswered, or have been marked to return to later. Make sure to click on Review before clicking on Exit Section, to make sure you have answered (or at least guessed on) every single question within a section.

Right Angle

An angle that measures 90°.

Right Triangle

A triangle in which one angle measures 90°.

Rhombus

A quadrilateral with four equal sides. (If all four angles are the same measure, then the rhombus is also a square.)

S

Scratch Paper

Your saving grace on the GRE. Your favorite math buddy, more helpful than the calculator, more understanding than the computer screen. All work should be done on the scratch paper provided. In some testing centers, this may be normal paper; in others it may be a series of laminated boards. No matter what, the testing center will always provide scratch paper of some sort and necessary writing utensils. The first step in any GRE problem is to start setting the problem up on the scratch paper. Ask for more during the 10-minute break.

Set

A collection of distinct values.

Square

A quadrilateral with four equal sides and four equal angles (each of which measures 90°).

Square Root $\left(\sqrt{}\right)$

The square root of x is the number that, when squared, results in x. For example, $\sqrt{16} = 4$, because $4^2 = 16$.

Slope

The rate at which a line is rising or falling within a coordinate plane. To find the slope of a line, use the formula $\dfrac{y_2 - y_1}{x_2 - x_1}$, which represents the "rise" over the "run."

Sum

The result of addition; the sum of 12 and 4 is 12 + 4, or 16.

Surface Area

The sum of the areas of each face of a three-dimensional figure.

T

Trapezoid

A quadrilateral with exactly one pair of parallel sides.

Trigger

A word or phrase within a GRE math problem that indicates exactly how you will answer that question. For instance, if a problem contains variables within the answers, then it is a Plug In question.

V

Variable

An element in an algebraic term or equation that is unknown or can vary. Variables are represented as letters.

Y

y-intercept

The point where a line intersects with the y-axis. Represented by b in the equation $y = mx + b$.

Z

Zero

A number that has no value and therefore can't be used as a divisor on the GRE. Zero is not positive or negative, but it is even. It is also the additive identity, because any number plus zero equals that number ($m + 0 = m$).

NOTES

NOTES

NOTES

NOTES

NOTES

NOTES

NOTES

NOTES

NOTES

China (Beijing)
1501 Building A,
Disanji Creative Zone,
No.66 West Section of North 4th Ring Road Beijing
Tel: +86-10-62684481/2/3
Email: tprkor01@chol.com
Website: www.tprbeijing.com

China (Shanghai)
1010 Kaixuan Road
Building B, 5/F
Changning District, Shanghai, China 200052
Sara Beattie, Owner: Email: sbeattie@sarabeattie.com
Tel: +86-21-5108-2798
Fax: +86-21-6386-1039
Website: www.princetonreviewshanghai.com

Hong Kong
5th Floor, Yardley Commercial Building
1-6 Connaught Road West, Sheung Wan, Hong Kong
(MTR Exit C)
Sara Beattie, Owner: Email: sbeattie@sarabeattie.com
Tel: +852-2507-9380
Fax: +852-2827-4630
Website: www.princetonreviewhk.com

India (Mumbai)
Score Plus Academy
Office No.15, Fifth Floor
Manek Mahal 90
Veer Nariman Road
Next to Hotel Ambassador
Churchgate, Mumbai 400020
Maharashtra, India
Ritu Kalwani: Email: director@score-plus.com
Tel: + 91 22 22846801 / 39 / 41
Website: www.score-plus.com

India (New Delhi)
South Extension
K-16, Upper Ground Floor
South Extension Part–1,
New Delhi-110049
Aradhana Mahna: aradhana@manyagroup.com
Monisha Banerjee: monisha@manyagroup.com
Ruchi Tomar: ruchi.tomar@manyagroup.com
Rishi Josan: Rishi.josan@manyagroup.com
Vishal Goswamy: vishal.goswamy@manyagroup.com
Tel: +91-11-64501603/ 4, +91-11-65028379
Website: www.manyagroup.com

Lebanon
463 Bliss Street
AlFarra Building - 2nd floor
Ras Beirut
Beirut, Lebanon
Hassan Coudsi: Email: hassan.coudsi@review.com
Tel: +961-1-367-688
Website: www.princetonreviewlebanon.com

Korea
945-25 Young Shin Building
25 Daechi-Dong, Kangnam-gu
Seoul, Korea 135-280
Yong-Hoon Lee: Email: TPRKor01@chollian.net
In-Woo Kim: Email: iwkim@tpr.co.kr
Tel: + 82-2-554-7762
Fax: +82-2-453-9466
Website: www.tpr.co.kr

Kuwait
ScorePlus Learning Center
Salmiyah Block 3, Street 2 Building 14
Post Box: 559, Zip 1306, Safat, Kuwait
Email: infokuwait@score-plus.com
Tel: +965-25-75-48-02 / 8
Fax: +965-25-75-46-02
Website: www.scorepluseducation.com

Malaysia
Sara Beattie MDC Sdn Bhd
Suites 18E & 18F
18th Floor
Gurney Tower, Persiaran Gurney
Penang, Malaysia
Email: tprkl.my@sarabeattie.com
Sara Beattie, Owner: Email: sbeattie@sarabeattie.com
Tel: +604-2104 333
Fax: +604-2104 330
Website: www.princetonreviewKL.com

Mexico
TPR México
Guanajuato No. 242 Piso 1 Interior 1
Col. Roma Norte
México D.F., C.P.06700
registro@princetonreviewmexico.com
Tel: +52-55-5255-4495
+52-55-5255-4440
+52-55-5255-4442
Website: www.princetonreviewmexico.com

Qatar
Score Plus
Office No: 1A, Al Kuwari (Damas)
Building near Merweb Hotel, Al Saad
Post Box: 2408, Doha, Qatar
Email: infoqatar@score-plus.com
Tel: +974 44 36 8580, +974 526 5032
Fax: +974 44 13 1995
Website: www.scorepluseducation.com

Taiwan
The Princeton Review Taiwan
2F, 169 Zhong Xiao East Road, Section 4
Taipei, Taiwan 10690
Lisa Bartle (Owner): lbartle@princetonreview.com.tw
Tel: +886-2-2751-1293
Fax: +886-2-2776-3201
Website: www.PrincetonReview.com.tw

Thailand
The Princeton Review Thailand
Sathorn Nakorn Tower, 28th floor
100 North Sathorn Road
Bangkok, Thailand 10500
Thavida Bijayendrayodhin (Chairman)
Email: thavida@princetonreviewthailand.com
Mitsara Bijayendrayodhin (Managing Director)
Email: mitsara@princetonreviewthailand.com
Tel: +662-636-6770
Fax: +662-636-6776
Website: www.princetonreviewthailand.com

Turkey
Yeni Sülün Sokak No. 28
Levent, Istanbul, 34330, Turkey
Nuri Ozgur: nuri@tprturkey.com
Rona Ozgur: rona@tprturkey.com
Iren Ozgur: iren@tprturkey.com
Tel: +90-212-324-4747
Fax: +90-212-324-3347
Website: www.tprturkey.com

UAE
Emirates Score Plus
Office No: 506, Fifth Floor
Sultan Business Center
Near Lamcy Plaza, 21 Oud Metha Road
Post Box: 44098, Dubai
United Arab Emirates
Hukumat Kalwani: skoreplus@gmail.com
Ritu Kalwani: director@score-plus.com
Email: info@score-plus.com
Tel: +971-4-334-0004
Fax: +971-4-334-0222
Website: www.princetonreviewuae.com

Our International Partners

The Princeton Review also runs courses with a variety of partners in Africa, Asia, Europe, and South America.

Georgia
LEAF American-Georgian Education Center
www.leaf.ge

Mongolia
English Academy of Mongolia
www.nyescm.org

Nigeria
The Know Place
www.knowplace.com.ng

Panama
Academia Interamericana de Panama
http://aip.edu.pa/

Switzerland
Institut Le Rosey
http://www.rosey.ch/

All other inquiries, please email us at
internationalsupport@review.com